Dr Marion Stell investigates the social and cultural history of sport. She is the author of a number of popular books, including the groundbreaking *Half the Race: A History of Australian Women in Sport*; *Pam Burridge*, a biography of the world champion surfer; *Girls in Sport: Swimming;* and *Girls in Sport: Soccer.* She was also co-author of *Women in Boots: Football and Feminism in the 1970s*. She was the foundation curator of the permanent exhibition *Sportex* at the Australian Institute of Sport, and the *Eternity* and *Women with Attitude* exhibitions at the National Museum. She has been an appointed member of Football Australia's Panel of Historians since 2012 and a keynote speaker at Australian and international conferences on the cultural history of sport. She is currently an Honorary Senior Research Fellow, School of Human Movement and Nutrition Sciences at The University of Queensland, and in the Centre for Heritage and Culture at the University of Southern Queensland in Toowoomba.

The Bodyline Fix

How women saved cricket

MARION STELL

First published 2022 by University of Queensland Press
PO Box 6042, St Lucia, Queensland 4067 Australia

University of Queensland Press (UQP) acknowledges the Traditional Owners
and their custodianship of the lands on which UQP operates. We pay our respects
to their Ancestors and their descendants, who continue cultural and spiritual
connections to Country. We recognise their valuable contributions to Australian
and global society.

uqp.com.au
reception@uqp.com.au

Images on pages vi, 118, 228, 258, 274 and front cover courtesy National Library
of Australia. Image on page 254 courtesy of Australian Women's Cricket Council.
All other images courtesy of National Museum of Australia.

Cover design by Christabella Designs
Cover photograph courtesy of National Library of Australia.
Author photograph by Liz Speed
Typeset in 11.5/15 pt Bembo Std by Post Pre-press Group, Brisbane
Printed in Australia by McPherson's Printing Group

 **Queensland Government** University of Queensland Press is supported by the
Queensland Government through Arts Queensland.

  University of Queensland Press is assisted by
the Australian Government through the
Australia Council, its arts funding and
advisory body.

A catalogue record for this book is available from the National Library of Australia.

ISBN 978 0 7022 6578 5 (pbk)
ISBN 978 0 7022 6729 1 (epdf)
ISBN 978 0 7022 6730 7 (epub)

University of Queensland Press uses papers that are natural, renewable and
recyclable products made from wood grown in well-managed forests and other
controlled sources. The logging and manufacturing processes conform to the
environmental regulations of the country of origin.

*For my friends at the Australian National University
Women's Cricket Club, 1982–90. She who has never indulged in this
noblest of all pastimes has missed one of the
greatest enjoyments of life.*

Australian batter Fernie Blade sends the ball past the outstretched gloves of English wicketkeeper Betty Snowball, as Joy Partridge begins the chase from first slip during the first Test in Brisbane in 1934.

Contents

Metal-spiked bowling shoes worn by Australian fast bowler Mollie Flaherty who was nicknamed 'The Demon' on the tour of England in 1937 where she topped the bowling averages with 41 wickets at 11.44. Her representative career lasted until 1949. Note the wear on the right foot of the canvas and leather shoe where Flaherty scraped her foot in her delivery stride.

Preface

In the late 1980s, I was part of a small consultancy team tasked with cataloguing several major collections of men's cricket memorabilia, 'cricketana', if you like, recently purchased by the National Museum and accessioned into what is termed 'the national collection' – items of significance to the national story. Like all opportunistic consultants, at the end of the project we recommended further acquisitions to round out the story. It was now 1990, so why not try and locate the women who had represented Australia in the inaugural Test match series against England played in Australia in the summer of 1934–35, the year after the infamous bodyline series ended, together with a return Test series in England in 1937? These women were, by now, aged in their late seventies and eighties. Time was quickly running out. A year prior, I had contributed an entry on Margaret Peden, who had captained the Australian cricket team in 1934, to the *Australian Dictionary of Biography*. She, together with her sister Barbara Peden, also a key member of the team, had already passed away. How many of the women who had played in that series would still be alive? And where were they?

How do you find the members of a team who played cricket for Australia in the 1930s some sixty years down the track? Not a difficult proposition if their names are Bradman, Oldfield or Woodfull. Plenty of leads to follow there. But what if their names were Antonio, Monaghan and Clements, and may have changed over time? Sportswomen, especially those from team sports, easily disappear off the radar. Skilled detective work was required.

My co-consultant, Mary-Lou Johnston, and I started with leads from the various state cricket associations. Our goal was to locate the women and their families to determine if they still held any memorabilia. We soon found that few of these former cricketers had kept in touch with national or state cricket associations; not many were recognised and celebrated at local, state or national events. They had also lost touch with each other. Ruby Monaghan had become Ruby Lee, Lorna Kettels had become Lorna Smith. In an era without the internet or social media, we turned to some trusty yet time-consuming measures – in one instance we telephoned every name in the Wollongong phone book with the surname Lee, asking, 'Are you Ruby Monaghan who played cricket for Australia in 1934?' One eventually answered, 'Yes, I am.' At such moments our perseverance was richly rewarded.

In the end, we assembled more than a dozen donated collections of cricket memorabilia relating to women from the 1930s. While the aim was to identify the surviving material culture, I was keen to collect the women's stories and met up with each woman armed with my tape recorder. These women were an outstanding generation of cricketers – highly skilled and playing matches that attracted thousands of spectators. In 1990, I remember being frustrated that many women had brilliant recall of events while on tour, such as the coronation they attended in London or the food served to them by their billet families, but their recollection of the actual cricket games was less acute.

Time and maturity softened my view and in 2020, I rediscovered the interviews we had recorded thirty years earlier. I realised that by now, all these women had certainly passed away. But I was intrigued to test my memory of what they said. Once I converted the tapes to digital form, I became enthralled by the stories that emerged. Listening to their voices brought the women alive again. I found myself transported back into their lounge rooms, reliving the drama as they unveiled their collections and told their stories afresh. It was a joy to sit with their voices. I listened for the nuances, for the silences, for the interactions between women. I noticed their unwillingness to speak ill of the dead, no matter what injustice had been suffered. I heard the class differences present in their language and voices. These women were humble, often shy, and reticent about their achievements. They were a remarkable group, never bragging, but proud of their successes and skills. There was no criticism of later generations. I came to understand the controversies, their passions and disappointments.

I quickly realised their story was bigger than a handful of cricket games. Each ball, each over, each run scored, the match won or drawn, became less important as I finally understood the true meaning of the first cricket series between women in the bodyline era. I could now view the events through the lens of more recent cricket controversies. Women players had performed a role in restoring harmonious relations with New Zealand following the notorious underarm bowling incident of 1981 and were again placed centre-stage in 2018 when the sandpaper incident in South Africa brought shame to Australian cricket. Their role in the resolution of these incidents harked back to the importance and reliance on cricket played by women in the bodyline era. But more than just an antidote to controversy, these women paved the way for future generations of women and girls.

Not often in sport history do the events of men's and women's sport run parallel, adjacent and intertwined in importance. I could not think of another similar example anywhere in the world. Surprisingly, these women were key players in the bodyline saga. This is their story.

*Wollongong-based batter Ruby Monaghan travelled by train every
weekend to play for the Annandale club and to gain selection in the
New South Wales team in Sydney. At seventeen she was selected to
play for Australia and opened the batting in the first and second Tests
in 1934–35. She remembered, 'I liked to take the first ball, and if
it was on the wicket or not, I would still hit it to the boundary'. She
was a surprise omission from the 1937 Australian touring team.*

Introduction

Cars and Corsets

'The beautiful bodylines of the Chevrolet'
— Advertisement, 8 April 1920

It all started with Don Bradman. Before the summer of 1932–33 the word 'bodyline' was highly aesthetic – artful, creative and sexy, devoid of any menace. It was inventively deployed to refer to the seductive angles of, for instance, a new Chevrolet displayed on a car showroom floor. Utilised in advertising language on the motoring pages of magazines and newspapers, it might also be the 'long perfect bodylines' of the 1923 Overland Light Four, the 'handsome bodyline' of the 1926 Hupmobile Straight Eight, the 'unusual bodyline' of the 1927 British Bean Roadster, or the 'graceful bodylines' of the 1929 Reo Flying Cloud.

Doubting that male customers could fully appreciate the aesthetics on their own when viewing the new Light Six Studebaker, Cayce-Paul Motors in Sydney encouraged them to bring along their 'wife or lady friend so as to get a true aesthetic opinion on beauty of bodyline'. Women, it seems, could appreciate the seductiveness of it. Appropriated in descriptions within the women's pages of magazines and newspapers, an appreciation of bodyline might be found in the latest news from Paris, of the new long-waisted outfits – the dress bodice ending in points back and front 'another aid to apparent length of bodyline'. The new women's fashion in 1923 for the 'svelte' or tall willowy figure featured 'a straight bodyline ... more than ever is the skilful corsetiere necessary; there must be no bulges if you would wear the up-to-the-minute gowns with elegance'.

Cricketer Don Bradman had reason to appreciate the aesthetic bodylines of the Chevrolet. Arriving home from the successful Ashes tour to England in 1930, 'the wonder batsman of the team', which had 'regained the Empire's most coveted cricketing trophy for Australia', was met by the marketing machine of General Motors Australia as soon as his ship, the *Oronsay*, docked in Fremantle. Bradman had made his Test cricket debut in 1928, and on the 1930 tour had proved himself a run-making machine for Australia, much to the delight of the Australian public, always eager to beat the old enemy. The phenomenon known as 'Bradmanitis' was in full swing. Even the recently launched women's magazine, *The Australian Women's Weekly*, called Bradman a 'god at 21'.

Ever alert to the commercial opportunities that cricket offered, Bradman agreed to be presented with a special Chevrolet Sports Roadster, the car known as the Don Bradman Model. It was a limited edition, only six models were to roll off the General Motors production line. One car was for his personal use, with General Motors donating the other five to be raffled in each state capital city – well, not quite each: Brisbane, Sydney, Melbourne, Adelaide and Perth were to receive the prizes; Hobart was left off the Chevrolet map.

The Great Depression, which hit Australia in 1929 after the Wall Street stock market collapse, caused widespread unemployment and drew people to sporting events, creating heroes in unprecedented numbers. Don Bradman, the horse Phar Lap, English pilot Amy Johnson, and billiards maestro Walter Lindrum, among others, captured the public imagination with stories of their triumphs, challenges and victories filling many newspaper columns during a time of high unemployment. Naturally, the lord mayor of each city eagerly sought the promotional opportunities afforded by the

Don Bradman Model and a visit from the man himself. Only Brisbane baulked at the charity raffle opportunity, deciding that a private buyer for the car should be sought on the grounds that unemployment relief in that city should not be funded by gambling. The proceeds from each state were directed to the Unemployed Relief Fund.

Disembarking at Fremantle, Bradman, with General Motors officials in tow, set out on a whistle-stop tour to promote the car and its fundraising capacity. Bradman travelled by train to Adelaide, by General Motors chartered plane to Melbourne, before he was flown by aviator Charlie Ulm to Goulburn, and then driven by professional motor speed-racing driver Norman 'Wizard' Smith by car to his home in Bowral. Finally, he was flown to Sydney to receive his own Chevrolet.

The man in the shiny new Chevrolet was born in Cootamundra, New South Wales, in 1908, before the Bradman family moved to Bowral when he was two years old. With no sports coach at school, and few neighbourhood children to share his growing passion for cricket, the story of young Donald amusing himself in the backyard by hitting a golf ball with a wooden stump against the base of the household water tank is part of Australian folklore. Less well known is the fact that his mother, Emily (formerly Emily Whatman), regularly bowled her left-armers to him each afternoon after school. On her death in 1944, the local Bowral newspaper reported: 'as a girl, Mrs. Bradman was one of the few girls who indulged in cricket, and was noted for accurate bowling'. Emily's brother, George Whatman (Bradman's uncle), was the captain of the Bowral Cricket Club. The family had form.

Donald Bradman went into his first Test match against England in 1928 at twenty years of age, having proved himself a prodigious run scorer in grade and Sheffield Shield cricket, including a 452 not out. He notched up two centuries before the end of the English tour. An automatic selection for Australia's return tour to England in 1930 for the five Test series, he scored

131 in the first Test, 254 in the second, 334 in the third – then the highest score in Test match cricket – and after two more Tests had accumulated 974 runs at an average of 139.14. Australia won the 1930 Ashes series against England 2–1.

Back in Australia, Bradman continued to court his sweetheart Jessie Menzies, 'the pretty little daughter of the local bank manager', and followed her when she moved from Bowral to Sydney where he 'sought her out'. Jessie was a designer glass and metal artist who also worked at the bank. Preferring golf and tennis as her chosen sports, she probably saw no need to bowl to Don in the backyard as his mother had done. Not a cricketer, she may nevertheless have been aware of the snowballing interest women her age had in playing cricket. This had culminated in the formation of the English Women's Cricket Association in 1926, and the equivalent association in Australia in 1931.

Women have had a long history of playing cricket, with some of the earliest records dating from 1745 in England and 1855 in Australia. Indeed, Bradman's mother, Emily Whatman, was part of a strong cohort of women who played the game enthusiastically in Australia, where intercolonial matches had been held since 1891. But it wasn't until the early 1930s that women in both countries rekindled their interest in cricket and started to form associations to promote and regulate local, county and interstate matches. Bradman had possessed a fine cricketing pedigree on his mother's side.

By September 1932, a few months before the visiting English cricket team arrived on Australian shores, the song 'Our Don Bradman' was released, the words of which described him as 'the greatest ever played the game'. As Australians sang along to these words, they looked forward with confidence to the unfolding of the five Test Ashes series to be held over the summer months. Surely, with Don Bradman in the team and the contest held at home in familiar conditions, the Ashes would be Australia's to keep.

But before the summer was over the word bodyline would no longer be associated with the Chevrolet that Bradman drove, or the European-inspired fashions worn by his new wife, Jessie. It resounded with a whole new unexpected meaning; a meaning that possessed the potential to shatter colonial relations at the heart of the British Empire.

Australian cricketers (left to right) Hazel Pritchard, Alice Wegemund and Amy Hudson pose together in front of the viaduct at Hogan Park in Annandale, Sydney in 1933 during a game for the NSW state team. All three toured England in 1937.

Chapter 1
New Cricketers

*'Nobody complained, they were just enjoying and
loving the idea of being able to play cricket.'*
— Kathleen Commins, 1990

In the early 1930s, the streets, alleyways and backyards of Australia were alive with cricket games. Children everywhere tried to emulate the feats they listened to on radio, saw on newsreels, read in newspaper headlines or heard adults discussing at the dinner table. It was a mesmerising, seductive and alluring sport, central to the national psyche. Kids would play in the streets, practising until dusk, with nothing more than a piece of wood, a tennis ball and a few keen neighbours. Increasingly, the games became less informal and more organised and competitive. Teams were formed and games moved to dedicated parks and ovals. Girls and young women were part of this movement, with school, university and factory teams starting up to cater for the new and revived interest in cricket. All that was needed to form a team was a couple of sisters, a cousin, some friends and workmates. Word of mouth, friendship circles, family members and neighbours played a central part in creating pathways for new players.

Like all sports, there was a significant gap between the backyard and occasional player and those deemed good enough to represent their country. The 1930s marked a period when groups of women in Australia, England, India, South Africa,

Holland and New Zealand attained the status of international cricketers. In doing so they were, in essence, participating in rites of passage, long familiar to elite male cricketers. They completed their journey from novice to elite cricketer, a journey that brought a degree of recognition and celebrity.

But first, these young women needed to learn the skills of cricket, find a team and belong to an organised competition. None of these things came easily in the early 1930s. The reality of how women and girls embarked on their cricketing journey owed much to persistence, dedication and single bloody-mindedness. Often, they needed to invent the opportunities themselves.

The cricketers in this era were an unusual mix of upper-, middle- and working-class young women. In New South Wales, sisters Margaret and Barbara Peden were the daughters of Sir John Peden, Professor of Law at the University of Sydney and President of the New South Wales Legislative Council. Coming from such a background, doors opened more readily for the two sisters, and they expected them to. Margaret Peden (born 1905) was three years older than Don Bradman. The Peden sisters were educated at Abbotsleigh School in Sydney, one of the few to offer cricket for women, and both went on to university where they played for the women's university cricket club.

Their friend at university, journalist Kathleen Commins, came from the same social sphere. She described Margaret as 'determined; she was a very good organiser and very capable and she had the full support of her father. Her father was devoted to his two daughters.' Although Kathleen regarded Margaret's younger sister, Barbara, as the better cricketer, Margaret 'was a very good captain, very astute, she knew everything about cricket and loved the game'. She thought of her as a motivator and facilitator:

> She was a very quiet person and never threw her weight
> around, but she could always get people of all kinds and
> types moving and doing things. The name 'Peden' in

this state meant a great deal, and she just went quietly about getting teams formed in all sorts of places. They'd come to her and she'd say, 'Well can't you get a group together?', you know, and she brought the university team together and then when she graduated from university, in about 1928 she finished, she went ahead and formed the Ku-ring-gai Club.

New clubs could not be established without access to land and a cricket pitch. Kathleen Commins recalled that Margaret Peden lived in Chatswood, on the upper North Shore of Sydney, and found some land near Willoughby that had once been a Chinese market garden: 'She saw the Willoughby council and she got it at a very cheap rental.' The women cleared the land to form a pitch with the help from 'fathers and uncles and boyfriends', and together they 'made a respectable pitch, but the outfield – I know I was fielding among the potatoes that were still growing up,' Kathleen recalled.

Teenager and aspiring cricketer Ruby Monaghan remembered the kindness of the Pedens' father at early state-level cricket games:

> Sir John used to come and watch the game – Sir John Peden – and he didn't know my mum, but I'd perhaps run around and take a nice catch or something and he'd have this hard bowler hat on, and he'd lift the hat and say, 'That's my Ruby'. He did too, he was a lovely old fellow, Sir John Peden.

Ruby Monaghan (born 1917) left school at sixteen and never sought employment. Hers was a working-class family living in Coniston, an industrial suburb just north of the Port Kembla steelworks in Wollongong. Ruby described times in Wollongong during the economic Depression of the 1930s as 'bad'; 'we didn't have much going for us'. After leaving school she would spend her days 'riding the pushbike, or go visiting somebody, or running around somewhere'. Cricket had not been offered at school where Ruby played vigoro (a sport with elements of cricket and baseball) and basketball. Out on their pushbikes, Ruby and her friends watched the men play cricket at a local ground and together they decided to form a cricket team: 'We used to go over when the men were playing cricket and bat against them, [against] their bowling – that's how we got to like the fast bowling and that kind of thing.'

Ruby was a good runner, and to keep fit she ran 'round the paddocks, like I was chasing something, climbed a few trees'. Along the Illawarra coastline two cricket associations were formed by women, Ruby remembered: 'Down the far south coast and up the north coast – it was both ends you know – like we used to meet and play the far south coast girls.' They played on concrete wickets that 'weren't real good', with coir matting laid on top – 'that's terrible' – but there was nothing better for male cricketers either. 'We played on some of the wickets that they played on,' she said.

Ruby lived at home and both her parents supported her interest in cricket. There was no coach for her team – 'We just coached ourselves, played cricket among the men and just got better and better.' When Ruby's cricket talent became noticed in the press, cricket commentator Dr Eric Barbour described her as 'a tiny but delightful bat'. Asked how she developed and honed her favourite run-scoring cut shot, the former opening batswoman said, 'it just come naturally'.

A standout in her local team, Ruby played cricket every Sunday – 'Shouldn't be Sunday should it?' she commented – and when the Annandale team from Sydney travelled down to Wollongong, they saw Ruby's potential and immediately invited her to play for them in Sydney. Every Saturday, accompanied by both her parents and often her younger sister, Mona, Ruby boarded the train at Coniston Station. 'I got into the club up there in Sydney – Annandale,' she said. 'Amy Hudson was captain of that, I used to travel up from Wollongong every Saturday and play in the competition then travel back again Saturday night.'

Opening batswoman and useful fast-medium pace bowler, Amy Hudson (born 1916) grew up in the inner-western Sydney suburb of Annandale. Amy played cricket in the street with the local boys and remembered the freedoms she enjoyed:

> In the street where I lived there were about twenty boys and I was the only girl, and I had two brothers. I was allowed to play out in the street. I was allowed to go down the park, play with the boys, but as long as Bobby and Tommy were with me, so I learnt to play cricket down Jubilee Park.

Playing in the streets required accuracy and restraint, especially during the Depression: 'If we hit the ball into a particular lady's place she'd keep the ball, and being the Depression time you wouldn't have too many tennis balls.'

Cricket wasn't the only street game for Amy: 'I used to play football with the boys too – soccer, not the other.' Around about the time she turned fourteen, Amy saw a photograph of the Sans Souci Women's Cricket team in the paper, sparking her interest. She told her mother that she would like to play cricket. Her mother 'went about it in a professional way' and placed an advertisement with the Royal Film Theatre in Johnston Street, Annandale, and within a week she had a team of cricketers made up of women from around Forest Lodge, Annandale and Leichhardt. Describing herself as originally a 'hit and miss batswoman', Amy and the Annandale team played their first season of matches at the Sydney Domain where one of the regular umpires, Mr Simpkins, noticed that Amy was getting 'yorkered' all the time. He approached her with advice. 'Amy, I think you could make a good batswoman if you were more patient,' he told her. She took the advice. 'We sort of loved Mr Simpkins, we thought he was a great old man … so I took notice of him.'

Simpkins was already heavily involved in coaching women in hockey, vigoro and cricket, giving popular lectures on vigoro to women in 1931. But the Annandale team needed practice and grounds closer to home. Amy's mother was aware of some space on the recreational reserve down in Hogan Park, off Nelson Street, that carried the Johnstons Creek Sewage Aqueduct, an imposing concrete structure, now heritage-listed, that was completed in 1897 to carry wastewater to the outfall sewer at Bondi. Heavily involved in charity work and well connected in her local community, Amy's mother convinced Annandale Council to put a concrete pitch down at Hogan Park so the women could play on it on Saturdays. But to the team's dismay, 'as soon as we got the concrete pitch down at Hogan Park the men took it over and we couldn't get on there to practise'.

Amy's mother was not a woman to mess with:

> It was the Depression time and my mum had something to do with giving out the coupons and like, people didn't get money in those days. When the men who took our wicket over and came up to get these coupons, she's threatened them – they wouldn't get them unless they got off our cricket wicket, which they did. As soon as the Annandale girls went down there to play, well they got off it. So, I don't know if that was blackmail or not. But we always got our wicket when we went down there, and they never played on that ground – they went down to Federal Park to play.

With the publicity in the local paper regarding her cricketing prowess, Amy was becoming well known in her local area:

> In Annandale at the time we had a couple of bad boys living in Nelson Street and I went somewhere with some girls from work. Of course, me being me, I didn't know I couldn't get a bus home, but I got one that came along

Parramatta Road, Annandale, and I had to walk right down Nelson Street past some factories. I'm walking down the street this night and I hear these footsteps behind me. But, anyway, to make a long story short, a hand clutched me on the shoulder, and I nearly died. And it was one of these so-called bad boys and he said to me, 'What are you doing out this time of the night, Amy?' I turned round and I said to him, 'Oh, it's only you!' And he said, 'Come on, I'll take you home to your front gate.' Now that was somebody with a bad reputation but somebody that knew me and took me home. So, people knew you, knew me at any rate – once seen, never forgotten!

Amy considered herself a bit of a tomboy. She also enjoyed swimming regularly in Sydney Harbour every Sunday, but never the surf: 'I don't like the surf, I nearly drowned in the surf at Coogee, but we used to go to Nielsen Park where there was shark nets around and you could swim. I liked that.' In her leisure time during the Depression she also went to films two or three times a week – it cost threepence: 'You'd go do messages [errands] for people and they'd give you a penny or halfpenny and if you got a penny or a halfpenny, oh boy, that was something great.'

Kathleen Commins (born 1908) remembered how 'extremely difficult' it was to get to various cricket grounds to play. 'It wasn't very funny to play Sans Souci, to have to get on a train, I think it was to Kogarah, and then a steam tram to some place, and then trail all the way back afterwards. And there were no proper dressing rooms or anything like that.' She recalled playing at Annandale Park against Amy Hudson: 'I remember going down one of those great viaducts.' But the travel was worth it, she said, and 'nobody complained, they were just enjoying and loving the idea of being able to play cricket'.

The photograph in the paper featuring women in the Sans Souci district that inspired Amy to take up cricket no doubt featured the four dominant women from that area: Hazel Pritchard and the three Shevill sisters: Fern Blade (now married) and twins Rene and Essie. One of the most accomplished batswomen in this era, Hazel Pritchard (born 1916), attended cricket clinics for girls run by Ruth Preddey in the Sydney Domain in 1927. Ruth Preddey, herself a cricketer from 1912, founded the NSW Women's Cricket Association in 1927 and the clinics were part of her push to get girls and women involved in the game. Both Hazel and her sister, Edna Pritchard, were surf lifesavers at Brighton-le-Sands in 1931 and played cricket for the Cheerio Club in Sans Souci.

When the interstate cricket series between women was played in Sydney in 1931, featuring teams from New South Wales, Queensland and Victoria, both Pritchard girls were selected for New South Wales. They credited their father: 'Many a backyard practice was held with Dad patiently showing us how to play a straight bat and many other things.' The sisters played cricket, baseball, basketball, tennis and golf, along with their life-saving duties. New South Wales player Patricia Holmes described Hazel Pritchard as 'a very attacking bat; pretty player'. When Ruby Monaghan was asked who she thought was the best cricketer she had ever seen, she immediately named her batting partner: 'I thought Hazel was one of the best cricketers.' English player Betty Archdale concurred: 'Yes, Hazel Pritchard, she was very good, beautiful bat.' Victorian cricketer Nell McLarty recalled that 'when we played we had a lass named Hazel Pritchard and she'd been coached by a man and now when I come to compare it she was absolutely spot on with her technique'. Amy Hudson also described Hazel 'as one of the prettiest bats that we had', and remembered she herself had been coached, somewhat reluctantly, by Fred Griffiths alongside Hazel Pritchard at indoor nets in a building directly opposite Central Station in Sydney:

> That was at Wembley House at Railway Square. Don't ask me how I come to go down there 'cause I couldn't

tell you, but when I used to get down there I used to sometimes think, I suppose this sounds catty, that he was a bit inclined to rather coach somebody that he thought had a lot of promise. Now he coached Hazel Pritchard and she was a really beautiful batswoman. Alicia Walsh used to go down there, but I used to go down there and sit like a shag on a rock in the corner until, like, he'd condescend, 'Oh, you can go get out in the nets now', sort of thing.

Amy Hudson preferred her interaction with the brilliant batsman and popular Balmain boy Archie Jackson:

I used to go down to Murdoch's, they had nets up on the top of Murdoch's building on the corner of Park Street and George Street. I used to go down there and my favourite cricketer, I thought he was the ant's pants, was Archie Jackson. We used to go down there and bowl to him. Oh … he used to coach us a little bit but we used to delight in just bowling to him, you know – it was beaut!

Archie Jackson played only eight Test matches for Australia before he sadly died from tuberculosis at the age of twenty-three in hospital in February 1933, on the day that England regained the Ashes in the fourth Test in the 1932–33 series.

Hazel Pritchard, her sister, Edna, and the three Shevill sisters provided the important critical mass of players for their clubs to survive and flourish in Sydney in the early 1930s. Essie Shevill (born 1908), an embroidery machinist, was the standout player from her family. Cricket commentator Dr Eric Barbour sang the family's praises in 1934:

Outstanding is the Shevill family, of which there were originally four sisters playing in the same team. One of them, Lily, has now retired … Essie Shevill is probably

the best batswoman in New South Wales – correct,
steady and attractive to watch. She also bowls a useful
off-break with a deceptive flight. Rene Shevill is a fine
wicket-keeper and her batting, though not so correct as
Essie's, is effective. Fernie Shevill is now Fernie Blade,
and has a bright three-year-old daughter, who has already
learned to toddle out on the ground and call out, 'Good
shot, mummy!' and also, alas, 'Rotten shot, mummy!'
Fernie is a fast-medium bowler who is very accurate and
can keep going all day. With the bat she hits hard, and
she is a beautiful field, combining with her sister to effect
many 'run-outs'.

Young women in Melbourne also made their own opportunities.
Nell McLarty (born 1912) was from North Fremantle, Western
Australia, but due to family circumstances was raised by an auntie
in Albert Park in Melbourne. 'She was quite old and she had
grown-up daughters and sons and they were married,' she said. At
5 foot 10 inches, Nell was quite tall for her age. She attended Albert
Park Primary School. The house and working-class neighbourhood
was a haven for others who enjoyed cricket: 'I had a cousin, he was
a second cousin really, and we played in the backyard and from
there I got out into the street and played with the boys, and that's
how I learnt to play – in the street with the boys.'

Peggy Antonio (born 1917), the daughter of an Australian
mother and a Chilean-born father who worked as a seaman,
grew up in the working-class suburb of Port Melbourne and
attended Graham Street State School. Both Nell and Peggy
played sport at school, where basketball and rounders were
offered. They were both from tough neighbourhoods, and it was
during a scratch basketball game that their paths crossed for the
first time. Nell recalled:

Peg was down Port Melbourne, and we'd go down
there, and I was always tall and if we won they would

stone us, and they would always say – Peggy was in this,
too, she was looking on. They'd say, 'Get the long girl',
and that was me, and they'd stone us and we'd have to
run like mad.

Peggy didn't get off unscathed: 'I got called into the school
office for that because I threw a stone and broke the spikes on
somebody's bike.'

It wasn't until she was about seventeen or eighteen that Nell
realised girls and women could play cricket. 'I walked over to
Albert Park one day and I saw the girls playing there,' she said.
'I didn't know girls played and I always wanted to play in a
team.' But how does a shy girl get to play in a team? She found
an unlikely advocate in her paperman, Leo, who had seen her
playing cricket in the street and told her cousins that they should
put her in a proper team. Nell recalled, 'they didn't take any
notice', so Leo approached the girls' team at Albert Park on her
behalf. 'He said to one of the captains, "This girl can play cricket.
How about giving her a game?" They wouldn't have a bar of me,
because I was tall and rangy.' It wasn't until a girl called Nancy
dropped out of the Clarendon team, leaving them a player short,
that 'they decided, well, I'd be better than nothing, so they gave
me a game. They asked me if I could bowl and I said, "Well, I'd
only bowled with a tennis ball and I'd never used a hard ball." So
I got a bowl, and it turned out all right. I got 7 for 2.' The tall,
rangy fast bowler was on her way.

Peggy Antonio's transition from playing street cricket with
the boys to an organised team was serendipitous. When she was
twelve or thirteen years old:

> I didn't know anything about girls' teams, or anything
> like that, and my sister happened to meet somebody in
> town and they just got talking, and this particular person
> said how her niece played cricket, and so on, and then
> my sister said, 'Oh, well, I've got a sister who likes to

play cricket but she doesn't know anything about it', so
then it was arranged for me to meet up with this girl.

The girls' team practised on a 'paddock' in Preston, but were
missing some elements of equipment, Peggy recalled: 'They
were using bits of broomsticks as wickets and things like that,
and we just had a practice on the rough ground on Preston
Park.' In time this team became the Collingwood Cricket Club.
'Well, then I just sort of went along with them,' she said. She
remembered the sport was expensive – 'In those days, I think
you were too busy worrying about surviving in the Depression
days without thinking about playing much sport that was likely
to cost money.' Fundraising efforts meant it didn't end up costing
the girls or their families too much. 'The team held threepenny
raffles to get bats and equipment.'

Both Peggy and Nell noted that recruitment to teams was
helped by the press reports of their games. Nell stated: 'If you did
something that was reasonably good, you'd have a paragraph and
a photo and that probably helped people to turn up.' The captain
of Nell's team, Clarendon, was Dot Debnam, sports journalist
for the *Melbourne Sporting Globe*. Peggy and Nell were part of
the five or six teams that played in inner Melbourne in the early
1930s. The summer fixtures were simple – each team played
each other and then progressed to semi-finals and finals. Access
to sporting grounds and cricket pitches, though, was always
an issue. Peggy explained that councils were approached 'or
whoever was controlling the particular pitch at the park, and [we
were] saying can we hire this for such and such a time'. Raffles
and 'house parties' raised the money to pay for the grounds.

Women in the Melbourne competition played on concrete
pitches with malthoid matting laid on top. According to Peggy,
'There was no such thing as turf wickets.' Malthoid was a
relatively new material. It was a bitumenised rubber surface laid
on top of concrete, which was thought to be 'the nearest approach
to a turf surface' that had been found. The wicket was reported

to play accurately, and it could be utilised on both wet and dry days, a feature of importance in Melbourne weather. The surface had wide appeal: to batters 'the material wore well and it was a batsman's paradise'; to bowlers, including prodigious wrist-spin bowler Clarrie Grimmett in the Australian men's team, 'they played true', without the usual kick, and they therefore required you to bowl slower to get the same result off the faster wicket.

Developing leg-spin bowler Peggy Antonio was 'thankful' to play on the malthoid. She started out bowling off breaks while playing with the kids in the street, but inventively tried to mix them up with a few leg breaks: 'We were always trying to do something different to get the other one out.' Just over 5 feet tall, she said, 'fast bowling didn't enter my head'. Looking back on her start in cricket, in 1936 the Melbourne *Herald* described her journey: 'Peggy was a schoolgirl of 13, very shy, and with two long plaits when she made her cricket debut with the Collingwood club. In those days she showed possibilities, but her batting and bowling styles were most unorthodox.' Peggy knew that her 'natural' bowling action exhibited some kinks: 'I had an action that did this sort of thing and that sort of thing, which was obviously all wrong.'

A local friend of her sister's took an interest in her career and offered to be her coach. Eddie Conlon was a retired South Melbourne cricketer who played for South Districts, and he 'got onto it and ironed out everything and improved things. A lot of practice went into it, too,' Peggy said. Conlon adopted a systematic plan for coaching Peggy, which involved 'many hours of serious concentration and patience. His plan allowed for one and a half hours batting and a half-hour bowling practice two nights each week, and for five hours on weekends.' According to the article in *The Herald*, 'He was quick to see the possibility of developing the young girl into a good all-round cricketer, and at once set about to teach her to bowl the leg break.' Peggy had won success as a slow off-spin bowler, so that it was some months before she perfected the leg break. But perfect it, she did.

Her friend Nell McLarty, looking back in 1990, described Peggy as 'the best leg-spin bowler then and now, she was just out of the box. She had that lovely wrist action and flexibility, very loose-limbed sort of person.'

Peggy modestly batted away all compliments: 'I was just very lucky ... there was always somebody ready and willing to tell you things and any information is good when you are learning, so it was just a question of putting them together.' The 1936 Melbourne *Herald* stated: 'A remarkable feature of her bowling is the amount of spin she gets on the ball, considering her small hands and short fingers, and also the fact that she is a woman.' Perhaps Conlon just saw a remarkably talented cricketer. He played the long game to improve Peggy's batting. *The Herald* continued: 'For an entire season she was shown nothing but the two defence strokes, but her perseverance has been rewarded, and she is now recognised as Australia's most perfect stroke maker.' *The Herald* reflected later in 1936, 'If there is any secret to Peggy Antonio's success, I believe that it is her complete faith in Mr Conlon as a coach. This also applies to Mr Conlon in the ability of his young pupil.'

Peggy recalled the long hours of practice every Sunday at Albert Park; *The Herald* put extra spin on the feat: '... this was not an easy task for the young cricketer. Often the temperature has been near the 100 mark when she has batted for hours in Albert Park, while being coached by Mr Conlon.' In our 1990 interview, Peggy modestly turned the attention back to her friend Nell: 'I would say that Nell was more of a natural, perhaps shall we say that I had a little bit of ability that somebody else brought out.'

Nell McLarty was five years older than Peggy when she began her cricketing career and had less time than the schoolgirl to practise – 'I didn't have the chance'. She was working for Henry Bucks, an exclusive Melbourne clothing establishment, as a machinist. The tall fast bowler, who would later become a respected coach, had no coaching herself as a beginner:

I worked on myself. When I started to bowl I discovered that I wasn't getting around on the side, I was bowling too square on. I saw, someone had taken a snap of me and I had read a bit about it and I could see, well, that's not right, so I tried to fix that. In a way, I got round a lot better but I can see, now that I coach, I could have done a lot better.

As well as her bowling and batting, Nell's forte was her sharp reflexes, fielding intimidatingly close to the batter. Due to her work commitments, Nell practised with her Clarendon team every Tuesday and Thursday night – 'but even if I was home in the yard I would be bouncing the ball or throwing it against the shed door or out in the streets playing with the boys'. Peggy elaborated on Nell's close-in fielding:

> Nell was absolutely brilliant at that. That helped her get such a lot of wickets because from the batsman's point of view, including me when I was playing against her, you didn't ever know when that arm was going to project out, that was the finish, you were out. You just couldn't afford to take a chance close in. I think she was the luckiest person out, that she wasn't hit out of the game, really it [her close-in fielding] was suicide.

Nell's brilliance at catching was captured in a press photograph later, proudly displayed in the Henry Bucks store. She was legendary. In 1990, Amy Hudson asked me, 'Did you ever see that photograph of her, that catch and bowl? I was there and I saw it and I couldn't believe it.' Nell attributed her sharp reflexes 'to getting out in the backyard and always throwing the ball and catching it. I'd just go until I couldn't see and, even then, I'd still try. I was very keen, I loved it.'

Unlike cricketers today, neither Nell nor Peggy did additional physical training for cricket other than practice. In the off-season, winter in Australia, Peggy played hockey competitively. She also 'had a go' at baseball, archery and golf, 'but nothing competitive'. The taller Nell played some basketball but there was no other physical training for their cricket. Peggy remarked that 'it was just unthought of'. Even for preliminary warm-ups or exercises for cricket, Nell recalled: 'We wouldn't be game to roll our arm over before we bowled because we'd say people would think we were showing off. We'd just go out there and bowl.'

On occasions, Peggy was joined at practice by her spin-bowling partner at the Clarendon club, Anne Palmer. Anne (born 1915) emigrated to Australia from London with her sporting family. Her father, Billy Palmer, was a former English soccer international who believed in practice and helped Anne acquire her 'quickness of eye.' She recalled: 'I had a basketball and he used to take me down into the yard and he would try and trick me with his feet, and he said it made me quick in the eye to watch a ball. I'd try and take it off him, that sort of thing, and that probably improved the eye coordination.' She grew up interested in cricket: 'I rather liked the idea of Bert Ironmonger because he was a left-hander; I was always most interested in what he did and how he did it. I was taken to the MCG [Melbourne Cricket Ground] to watch some of the Tests in those days, and watched him very avidly. Don Bradman, of course, he was unique.'

Like many other young women at the time, Anne Palmer 'used to play in the back street. There were two boys who played with South Melbourne thirds and at the age of about ten they had us bowling to them while they batted. We did this regularly every night.' As with other women cricketers, serendipity stepped in:

> At one stage one of the boys was friendly with a girl from the Clarendon Cricket Club and they were seeking recruits. She asked the boys if they knew of anybody. I had been fairly effective with my left-arm bowling against these boys, and they discussed it with her. She

came across and saw my parents and they gave permission
for me to play on a Saturday afternoon with Clarendon.

That was in 1932. Just two years later, former hockey international
player turned sports journalist Carlie Hansen, who reported
and wrote on women and sport for Brisbane-based newspapers
(a profession she shared with her sister Pat Hansen, who wrote on
women and sport for the conglomerate Associated Newspapers
Ltd publishers of *The Sun* and *Woman's Budget*) described Anne
Palmer as 'of petite build, a pleasant manner, and wavy black hair'.
The journalist encouraged her to reflect on her career, based on
her natural ability for the game: 'Palmer said that she had never
been coached, except in batting, by Miss Debnan [sic]. Her own
natural left-arm style she developed by hard experience in backyard
cricket with boys, gradually gaining control of her deliveries.'
Anne Palmer later recalled:

> The fact that I was playing at a very early age after school
> against these older boys in the street – and of course they
> wouldn't bowl to us, we had to bowl to them so that they
> got the batting practice – so the idea was to be as skilful as
> you could to get them out, and you certainly couldn't get
> them out with a big fast bowl. They played that all day, so
> you had to try and trick them by doing something with
> the ball, and I think I had a natural off-break anyway.

In fact, Anne remembered she did have some bowling coaching:

> There was a chap named Eddie [Conlon], and he was
> very involved with the Antonios on a Sunday … he had
> nets and he'd go behind the South Melbourne Technical
> College, which was in Albert Park. Peg and I would
> play … he would bat and we would bowl to him, or vice
> versa, and play into the nets. We used to do that fairly
> regularly in the summer months.

Clarendon Club would train twice a week with a game on Saturdays, but she remembered: 'In my early days, of course, up to when I was fourteen, fifteen, I would play in the back street with these boys night after night, you know, so I was really playing a lot, practising.' Anne also played basketball and enjoyed running: 'I was rather fleet of foot, and I did a lot of running in the area. I belonged to a church there and it was quite an active church for young people, and they had basketball teams for girls and boys, and also running.' Cricket was not yet something that was offered for girls at school. 'Each school had school sports every year and you competed against the surrounding schools,' Anne said. 'I went to Middle Park, then subsequently I won a scholarship to a higher school [J.H. Boyd Domestic College for Girls in South Melbourne] and finished there, and mostly it was tennis and basketball.' Soon Anne found herself recognised in the local area:

> I was well known in the Albert Park area, as Peggy was in Port Melbourne. It was nothing to have someone speak to you as you were walking around the South Melbourne market and make some comment. It's amazing the number of people who came to watch our weekly games and got to recognise you, things we didn't anticipate ... then you've got to remember that there was a Depression and that men had little to do as far as sport, perhaps, or doing something on a Saturday or Sunday, so they would gravitate to where the girls were playing and, although there were men playing 200 yards away, they would ignore that and come and watch the girls. We always had a good following of people.

Also at the Clarendon Club was Hilda Hills, who grew up in the Preston area and, after seeing cricket played locally, joined a team. Hilda, her three brothers and a sister all played sport. Because her first team did not yet have a regular wicketkeeper, Hilda got the job and began practising twice a week. Cricket was not offered at her school in Preston – rounders and basketball were the only sports for girls. After leaving school Hilda worked in the clothing manufacturing industry with the company Matear Brothers in Regent Street, North Richmond. The company gave her time off to play cricket and, although she did not receive financial assistance from the firm, they kept her job open. Fortunately, the cricket season corresponded with the slow period in the clothing manufacturing industry, so she received time off without pay. As the team's wicketkeeper she was in a position to assess the bowlers and she considered Peggy Antonio the best cricketer she had ever seen: 'She knew what to do and when to do it.'

Lorna Kettels (born 1912) grew up in the farming district of Tabilk, about 140 kilometres north-east of Melbourne, before moving to Kensington. Describing herself as 'a bit of a tomboy at the time', she was asked to fill in for a cricket team in Kensington that was a girl short. One of the team members, Nellie Rigg, who lived down in the lower part of Kensington, knew the bookmaker Harry Youlden. 'She approached him and he said if we formed a team he would set us up with the matting and the bats and the pads, and that's how we started off in our cricket career'. *Truth* newspaper described Youlden in 1931 as 'one of the biggest men in the Victorian betting arena'; in fact he was one of the top six bookmakers at the time in Victoria. Youlden had married Irene Burns in 1919, who had grown up in Kensington and may also have had a connection to cricket or to some of the women and girls in the team. Their daughter, named Joy, was a champion school athlete at Firbank Girls Grammar, where Harry saw her win races in the Under 16 division before his death in 1935. Whatever the family connection to cricket or sport, the eponymously named Youldens team funded by the philanthropist bookmaker became a fixture in the Melbourne cricket scene for women around Kensington.

According to Lorna, the team was based 'down where the army base is in South Kensington', where a pitch already existed.

'I think we were allowed to have it for nothing. Mr Youlden might have financed it, I don't know, but it was matting over concrete, so you can imagine.' Lorna remembered the coir matting being in two pieces, which the players had to roll out onto the pitch whenever they played and peg it down on the sides.

Lorna had played rounders and basketball at Kensington State School, but cricket was not offered: 'It just wasn't played at all.' She had seen games of vigoro played locally – 'That's a type of cricket, but you had a long, funny-shaped bat that was the nearest I'd ever seen to women's cricket,' she said. The Kettels were not a sporting family – 'I had one sister and a brother and I was the only one who played sport' – but both parents thought it was 'marvellous' when Lorna joined the cricket team. 'Dad used to go with me every Saturday, if and when he had the time off from work he used to watch me play. Mum and my sister never missed the Test matches or interstate matches when they were on, they were always good.'

Lorna travelled by train to play against the other teams in her competition, to Albert Park, to Clifton Hill, to Brunswick, and 'we had to find our own way there'. The standards of the grounds they played on 'were a bit rough at times, bumpy'. With no local newspaper, Youldens relied on contacts to fill the team. Lorna recalled recruitment being 'mainly with girls that I used to go to school with. I got in touch with them.' The team was coached by the local North Melbourne butcher Ernie Spencer. 'He used to live on top of the hill on Kensington Road and we used to play on the flats down below and he was interested. We asked and he decided, yes, and came down to coach us.'

Ernie Spencer was more than just a friendly butcher. In his early forties, he had played for the Victorian men's cricket team against New South Wales in the 1911–12 season. The *Sporting Globe* in 1926 described him as a 'safe and consistent' batsman, he was later passed over for selection and was 'heartbroken, and subsequently lost all ambition for big cricket. As a pennant cricketer, however, he still continued to perform with brilliance.' After the death of his father, he found himself with two butcher shops to run, but the *Sporting Globe* added the advent of 'matting cricket ... where practice was indulged in at a later hour of the day', allowed him to continue cricket and he 'quickly adapted himself to the altered conditions'. Known for hitting the ball hard, Spencer favoured forceful drives off the fast bowlers in front of the wicket 'with excellent timing and powerful strokes', according to the *Sporting Globe*. Lorna and her teammates at Youldens were in good hands, but their commitment was also core to their team's success:

> We used to eat sleep and drink cricket in those days. Sunday morning was a big day, we had practice and then, more often than not, we had a social game with somebody in the afternoon. We used to come down after work at night in the summertime, perhaps Tuesday and Thursday nights after work, if you could get there.

In addition, Lorna put up a string with a ball hanging on the clothesline in her backyard at home to practise batting between the team events. Her dedication paid off.

The selector of the Victorian team, Dot Debnam, described Lorna, now wearing her distinctive round glasses, in the *Argus* as having a 'beautiful batting style and is not afraid to punish loose bowling. She is smart in the field.' Sports journalist Pat Jarrett, writing in *The Herald*, described her thus: 'Lorna Kettels has a beautiful style with the bat and has impressed ... she plays a solid hand and defends her wicket well.' Several years later Jarrett wrote that Lorna was 'the stylist of the team ... Lorna Kettels has better footwork than any player in women's cricket ... She is also versatile in the field and is a fast-medium bowler.'

Throughout the early 1930s the infrastructure and competition around these women in Victoria was rapidly growing. Teams sprang up in districts and suburbs like Collingwood, but were also associated with factories where women worked. Raymonds box factory sponsored a team, as did the sewing outlet Semco at Brighton, who had two or three teams and also owned their own ground. Peggy Antonio commented that 'Semco was a very good match to play in because it was in very picturesque surroundings down at Black Rock. It was a lovely ground … Semco used to supply afternoon tea in the workroom.' To get to Brighton the teams would hire a van with 'a few supporters – we had to get them because we had to pay for the van, which used to be a shilling a head. And that was the only way of getting there then, and you used to be able to sit on the tailboard in those days and there'd be a sing-song going down.'

Factories all around inner Melbourne fielded cricket teams, including the Pelaco Shirt Company. Anne Palmer described the Clarendon Club as 'just a mish-mash of anybody that they could find available to recruit'. Anne also recalled 'at our club matches [there was] quite a large audience, mostly men, would you believe it, and they seemed to enjoy it and they barracked very loudly, and it was quite a good game'.

Nell McLarty attributed the rapid rise in interest to the newspaper publicity that cricket for women was beginning to attract. Peggy named journalists Pat Jarrett and Dot Debnam, and Fred Laby from the *Sporting Globe* as promoting the game with 'marvellous publicity'. She attributed the publicity to it being a 'novelty', but also generated by the crowds at the women's matches, with about three thousand turning up each week to watch local games. Nell recalled, 'they'd come, men would come, and they'd only have a few seats around the ground, and they'd come early, the old people, to get a seat, and they'd barrack! And they'd really barrack!'

Peggy Antonio recalled rival antagonism at the grounds: 'There were actual fights, too, weren't there, Nell? Different men had their different heroines, shall we say. Oh, and there was quite a faction when Collingwood and Clarendon played.' Fast bowler Nell recalled one incident when she came on to bowl 'and one of the men said, "Ah, she must eat raw meat before she comes out to play", and I don't even eat meat!' Peggy recalled,

'Nell had that kind of action, too, where she had a long run and she used to come pounding into the wicket and then let go and she also had a very ferocious look on her face.' Peggy also recalled the prevalence of 'threepenny bets' on the matches.

Victorian Nance Clements (born 1914) was one of the few players who originally learnt their cricket at school. She played at Hampton High Elementary School, Hampton, in a regular cricket competition between the four school houses. Despite this, her transition to grade cricket was not any easier, and it relied on her passing the Brighton Technical School Grounds where she saw other girls playing cricket: 'So I made enquiries.' The sports offered at school were 'hockey, tennis and football, of course for the boys, and basketball. But I wasn't interested in basketball although I played in the house basketball team, and hockey and cricket.' Her parents supported her decision to take up cricket. 'My father and my mother were always interested in what I was doing and my father was interested in sport and they didn't mind at all, as long as I did well in it.' But she thought: 'It might have been a bit tomboyish in those days if you wielded the willow.' Her cricket was played on coir matting – 'cost a lot of money in those days' – with the same facilities as available for men's and boy's grade cricket. She received no coaching: 'I've never been coached at anything, that goes for bowls today, I just picked it up as I went along.' The backyard of her home was the centre of cricket practice for the only child:

> In those days, this house had a shed right down the bottom of the garden, which was roughly about the length of a cricket pitch, might have been a bit more, so I used to put tin in the doorway with one stump and during the fruit season all the plums and all the little apples and anything that fell on the ground I used to collect, put it in the basket, and shy at the wicket. Then it came time to practise with the bat and once again the old clothes line with the stake – what do you call it, in

the middle with a V to keep the wire up? – and a piece of
cloth, one of my mother's stockings, where I used to put
the cricket ball in the bottom just at the right height and
practise straight back. Hit a bit harder it would swing
around you and then you'd hit it anywhere – hit it to
the leg, hit it to mid-on, hit it anywhere – but I used to
practise a lot.

After leaving school, to keep fit, Nance swam and 'played
baseball during the winter to keep trim for cricket – I played for
St Kilda Baseball Club. I used to pitch at baseball, and quite a bit
of tennis on weekends.'

Brisbane also had a number of women's teams in the early 1930s,
and they were sponsored by department stores and manufacturers
where women were employed, such as McWhirters, T.C. Beirne,
T.B. Luke's, Paramounts, Allan and Stark, Alderleys, Alexanders
and Overells, as well as teams from Caledonians, Bluebells,
St Phillips, Holland Park and Ballymores. Among these players,
Kath Smith (born 1916) was educated at St Joan of Arc Convent
and worked as a merchandise forewoman. An all-rounder – a
fast left-arm bowler and a powerful right-hand bat – she was
captain of the Queensland team. Her club side was Bluebells.

Another Queenslander, Joyce Brewer (born 1915) was one
of three sisters – along with Dulcie and Jean – to play cricket
for the Excelsiors team in Brisbane. Joyce took up cricket in
1929 and was also a keen runner. Born near Bundaberg, Joyce
later captained Eastern Suburbs. Together, Joyce and Jean were
renowned for their ability to bowl out the opposition between
them. All three sisters were chosen to play for Queensland
in January 1934 at the cricket carnival in Sydney. Joyce was
acknowledged as a strong opening bat and reliable right-arm
medium-pace bowler, but her inability to secure leave from her
employer prevented her from attending interstate matches.

~

These cricketers were drawn from a cross-section of society, from the well-connected, private school- and university-educated Pedens, strong believers in King and country, to professional women with careers in business, factory workers and the unemployed. These young women went to great lengths in order to excel at the game they loved. Some utilised the backyard and family to put in the hours of practice, others went to training regularly. Some were coached on weekends, while others attended indoor net sessions that were all the fashion. Many balls were bowled and hit and fielded to achieve a level of competence in the game. They immersed themselves in cricket culture, cricket lore, history and tradition in order to be worthy ambassadors for the sport. This included being informed about all the issues in the wider cricket world, not just on their own patch. It meant being part of the British Empire and its long tradition of cricket. As the 1930s unfolded, and they began their cricketing careers, these young women were to find themselves enmeshed in one of the biggest controversies the cricketing world had witnessed.

Studio portrait of middle-order bat and medium-pace bowler Nance Clements who was selected in the Australian team in 1934–35 and toured England in 1937. Saving five shillings a week from her pay for several years, she financed her overseas trip and acted as the team's treasurer. Making the most of her limited chances, she returned a touring batting average over 11.

Chapter 2
The Bodyline Series

'Cricket is a happy, friendly game.'
— Plum Warner, England co-manager, 1932

Australia's close ties to Britain and the Empire were through blood and race, epitomised by NSW politician and English-born Henry Parkes' co-opted phrase delivered to the 1890 Federation Convention: 'The crimson thread of kinship runs through us all.' But the ties of Empire were never that simplistic. By the early 1930s these ties were beginning to be questioned. The impact and causes of the economic Depression and resulting high levels of unemployment and financial hardship were complex. In 1931, the NSW Labor premier, Jack Lang, had proposed a controversial temporary cessation of interest payments on loans from Britain during the Depression. Cracks in the relationship emerged when,in 1932, the British Empire Economic Conference established a preferential three-tiered scale of tariffs, which gave preference to British goods above Empire and foreign producers (the Ottawa Agreement). These Empire sensitivities and complicated relationships were to play out on the cricket field.

Official Test matches between men from Australia and England began in Australia in 1877, preceded by several professional tours of English cricketers sponsored by promoters, and the tour of Aboriginal Australian cricketers to England in 1868. Each Australian Test series or Ashes (the name itself suggested life and death) had been keenly contested and many were not without some kind of controversy, dispute or fuss. Many Australian cricketers had strong family ties to England, and in 1932 it was still possible that there were people alive in Australia who had in fact seen all Test matches played in their home city against England since 1877, a gap of only fifty-five years. Many would have at least heard stories about those Test matches and players passed down by their parents.

Before leaving England for Australia on the 1932–33 cricket tour, the co-manager of the English Marylebone Cricket Club [MCC] team, the panama hat-wearing Pelham 'Plum' Warner (born 1873), a former captain and batsman who played over a hundred times for England between 1899 and 1912, gave an expansive interview to the journalist R.W.E. Wilmot in which he expounded on the role of cricket in Britain's empire building:

> I believe that cricket has been a great factor in Empire building ... It has brought peoples all over the world into closer touch, and has enabled them to understand one another. The very word cricket has become a synonym for all that is true and honest. To say, 'that is not cricket,' implies something underhand, something not in keeping with the best ideals. There is no game which calls forth so many fine attributes, which makes so many demands on its votaries, and, that being so, all who love it as players, or officials, or spectators, must be careful lest anything they do should do it harm. An incautious attitude or gesture in the field, a lack of consideration in the committee-room, and a failure to see the other side's point of view, a hasty judgment by an onlooker, and a misconstruction of an incident, may cause trouble and misunderstanding which could, and should, be avoided. This is the aim of the Marylebone Cricket Club – of which I am a humble, if devoted,

servant in sending teams to all parts of the world to spread the gospel of British fair play as developed in its national sport.

Lofty sentiments regarding the value of cricket within the British Empire had been expressed ever since articles and books about cricket had been published. The game had long and deep origins surpassing sport itself. It meant more to its participants and spectators than just a game. From the 1860s, books on cricket had been published 'in abundance'. The joy to be derived from the sport extended to the pleasure in reading about the art and significance of cricket written by cricketing greats, including W.G. Grace, K.S. Ranjitsinhji and Richard Daft. All three batsmen published highly successful books in the late nineteenth century. Such were their connections to Empire that Prince Ranjitsinhji went so far as to dedicate his *Jubilee Book of Cricket* (1897) to Queen Victoria, claiming perhaps optimistically: 'No doubt her Majesty takes some interest in cricket as one of the pleasures of her people.' Andrew Lang wrote in the preface to Richard Daft's 1893 book *Kings of Cricket*: 'Cricket is a very humanising game. It appeals to the emotions of local patriotism and pride. It is eminently unselfish; the love of it never leaves us and binds all the brethren together, whatever their politics and rank may be.' Richard Daft epitomised this nostalgia conjured by former players when he wrote:

> And now that I have gone through the whole of my career down to the present time and look back to the time I was a young man, I am far from regretting that I have been a cricketer; and he who has never indulged in this noblest of all pastimes, be he prince or peasant, has missed one of the greatest enjoyments of life.

Such sentiments persisted into the twentieth century with Lord Harris in his 1920 history *Lord's and the MCC*, referring to 'the

honourable traditions of the game' with 'the highest encomium
which is to be heard in Parliament, in the Pulpit, on the Platform,
and is constantly in the Press, that anything dishonourable,
mean, or savouring of sharp practice "is not cricket"'. The game
of cricket represented the commonalities of purpose between
members of the British Empire as trading, immigration, defence
and financial partners in a larger world. The trust needed to be
strong from all sides; the crimson thread of kinship could be, in
part, the stitches on the red leather cricket ball.

In his interview for *The Australasian* just prior to the 1932–33
tour, Warner reflected on the need for both sides to uphold these
traditions of cricket, but his words demonstrated that he was not
a naive manager or blind to controversies that might arise:

> In all the long series of Tests we have had what have been
> described as 'incidents', and these are inseparable from
> the game; but never has there been a suspicion of unfair
> play, of one side endeavouring to take undue advantage
> of the other. In all the games that have been played one
> would think that all the possible happenings would have
> been disclosed and discovered, but every now and again
> something occurs which is quite unexpected and is hard
> to explain. Then must all concerned be patient and view
> the position fairly. The responsibility is on us all; and we
> must be conscious of it. This game of cricket is too great,
> too important, to be spoiled by any untoward act, and I
> am keen to see the present tour an object-lesson in fair
> play all round. Cricket is a happy, friendly game.

A happy, friendly game perhaps, but also one that had winners
and losers. Having surrendered the Ashes at home to Australia
in 1930, who could blame the English for seeking to devise a
plan to thwart the prodigious run scoring of Don Bradman,
already acknowledged as cricket's most successful batsman?
The MCC English touring team to Australia was captained by

lawyer Douglas Jardine (born 1900). Before the team's departure for Australia, Jardine held a dinner at the Piccadilly Hotel in London, not with the English co-manager Plum Warner, but with the Nottinghamshire County and former English captain Arthur Carr (born 1893) and Nottinghamshire's two pace bowlers selected for the forthcoming tour: Harold Larwood and Bill Voce. The purpose of the meeting was to discuss how they might end Bradman's run-scoring genius.

Voce (born 1909) was a tall, left-arm, fast-medium, over-the-wicket bowler who had enjoyed success bowling quick-rising deliveries in the 1931 and 1932 seasons that saw him named *Wisden's* Cricketer of the Year. Harold Larwood (born 1904) was a right-arm fast bowler who had made his Test debut for England in 1926. He combined a high degree of accuracy with blistering pace bowling. Together the men discussed what others had noted as a perceived weakness in Bradman's technique against a rising ball in the 1930 Ashes series in England. The tactic that emerged from the dinner meeting drew on antecedents from several cricketing quarters over many years. It combined what was already known as 'leg theory' – where a bowler aimed predominantly at the leg stump with a packed leg-side field in order to try and restrict the batsman's scoring opportunities, a legitimate tactic that was widely used on cricketing fields – with an intention to make the ball rise quickly off the wicket and so inconvenience or indeed threaten the batsman.

The packed, short leg-side field, featuring a semi-circle of five fielders, together with two set in the deep, could opportunistically harvest any deflections. The bowler delivered short balls that flew at the batter, rather than at the stumps. The ball could be impossible to keep down safely. The only alternative to getting out was to get hit. It was leg theory with menace. Larwood later wrote that the tactic was devised to stifle Bradman's genius.

The new theory, that then did not yet have an agreed name, had antecedents in previous matches, including a tour to Australia in 1911–12, and had reputedly also been used in the 1930 Ashes series, after which English managers Warner and Richard Palairet had protested against the use of such tactics. Once in Australia, the English slowly and guilefully unwrapped their tactic against the state sides and an Australian XI in the lead-in games to the first Test. The variations they employed cleverly hid the tactics – sometimes not all the fast bowlers played or not all of them used leg theory, maybe the off-side was packed rather than the leg side, sometimes they bowled short, other times they attacked the stumps.

To be fair, in these matches Australia also coyly omitted some of their own bowlers, including spin bowler Bill O'Reilly, so that their impact would remain hidden as long as possible from the visiting team. The Australian crowds also played their part, jeering and booing the English captain whenever he appeared on the field – a tactic Australian journalists described as friendly 'barracking' and said to be caused by Jardine's supposed slow batting, or perhaps it was the infuriating harlequin cap he wore. It was crowd behaviour journalists travelling with the team for the London *Daily Mail* condemned. On the other hand, Australian journalists thought the English were just too sensitive. Hugh Buggy writing in the *Adelaide News* claimed the barracking was 'satirical not malicious' and, despite the fact that it was necessary to call the police to intervene in Adelaide to stop the abuse, former Australian cricketer (1896–1912) turned cricket official Clem Hill described it as 'nothing to worry about' and 'trivial'. Buggy thought the practice was endemic and was resigned to its presence in Australian crowds – '… barracking cannot be stopped without a machine gun battalion,' he wrote.

But the new bowling tactic was beginning to unsettle and impact not just batsmen but public opinion. The tone of the press reports and newspaper headlines in the lead-up matches began to change from predicting and proclaiming Australia's expected dominance through batsmen such as Don Bradman, Bill Woodfull and Bill Ponsford, to the realisation that England indeed possessed what they were now describing as a 'shock bowling attack'. Newspaper headlines screamed with phrases like 'catapault', 'shock bowlers', 'great pace' and 'mow down'. The fast–leg theory tactic was most clearly demonstrated in a match held at the Melbourne Cricket Ground (MCG) between an Australian XI, featuring Bradman, and the English touring team (in this instance not captained by Jardine), leading up to the 1932–33 Tests. The tour match began on 18 November 1932 when England played four fast bowlers in their side: Larwood, Voce, Bill Bowes ('the be-spectacled giant from Yorkshire'), and G.O. Allen, the Middlesex fast bowler. According to Claude Corbett writing in the *Daily Telegraph*, the four were chosen to play 'with the object of launching an avalanche of speed against Bradman'.

Hugh Buggy later described all four men as England's 'hurricane bowlers'. Buggy reported that the 'irate crowd' of 42,000 spectators 'howled with protest' at Larwood's tactics when he hit captain and opener Woodfull over the heart with a flying ball. Buggy claimed: 'Larwood and Bowes were bumping them more frequently than in previous games.' Although the match was eventually washed out, it was now obvious 'that this was not the customary form of leg theory'.

Describing the events of the final tour match before the first Test against New South Wales at the Sydney Cricket Ground (SCG), Buggy condemned the use of 'leg fliers' on 28 November 1932 and reported: 'English bowlers' shock tactics of bumping the ball on the leg side have aroused a storm of criticism here.' The team masseur reported that 'he had been looking after cricketers for many years, but had never seen so many bruises in one match'. Buggy added: 'The newspapers are being flooded with letters railing at what the writers consider the unfairness of the fearsome leg stump onslaught ... Sydney is gradually working up a form of hysteria about this bowling attack.' In these early days of witnessing the tactics, not all cricket commentators yet shared this outrage and 'hysteria'.

Buggy sought the opinions of three former NSW and Australian cricketers. Tom Garrett, who had played in the 1870s and 1880s, claimed 'the Englishmen's tactics were not cricket and were shocking'. Monty Noble, who played his last Test in 1909, thought it 'would be foolish to disregard the value of his [Voce] methods'. The younger Charlie Macartney, who played his last Test in 1926, said it was 'hardly cricket to hurl short, bumping balls straight at the batsman's body, but some day Australia might have bowlers who would employ the same tactics. It was legitimate cricket.'

Summing up the tour matches on 25 November under the headline. 'Larwood, the Batsman's Menace; Undisguised Bowling at Body Arouses Feeling', Buggy wrote, 'There is wide condemnation of the "bowling-at-the-man" policy'. Both Bradman and Woodfull 'were aware that they were being made targets for the fearsome delivery for which the players' slang term is the "scone" ball. It was undisguised.' Arthur Mailey, a contemporary of Macartney's wrote in the Adelaide *Advertiser* that he was worried by the tactic: 'Bradman's success is more essential to Australia than we care to admit.'

The tactic was fully unleashed against Australia in the first Test in Sydney, which began on 2 December 1932, but Bradman was absent due to a lingering sore throat. That day, an editorial in the Launceston *Examiner* reported that Larwood's bowling subjected a batsman to 'a persistent attack at express speed in a line with his body'. During the Sydney Test, Larwood had success taking five Australian wickets in each innings and Australia lost this first Test resoundingly by ten wickets. Newspaper reporters initially struggled to name what they saw, deploying the phrases 'shock attack', 'human skittles' and 'fast leg theory'. Although Bradman watched the Test match from the stands in Sydney, the former Australian captain Joe Darling called it 'Bradman theory'. Whatever it was, it added new life and controversy to what already promised to be a compelling Ashes series. One historian writing fifty years later summed up and speculated on its naming:

> There are many versions of who first thought of the word 'Bodyline'. Larwood thought it was the Sydney *Sun*'s

Claude Corbett, but Jardine probably was more accurate
in thinking it was Hugh Buggy, then the *Melbourne
Herald* cricket writer. Former Test cricketer Jack Worrall
after the Australian XI-England match spoke of 'half-
pitched slingers on the body line'. Buggy had read an
article by R.W.E. Wilmot, in the opposition Melbourne
Argus, that said England's attack was 'on the line of the
body'. To save money in those days of high telegram
costs Buggy condensed Worrall's words to 'Bodyline',
and overnight the word became infamous.

Such a claim is not readily verifiable, even today. But the word
quickly seeped into the cricket lexicon. Bradman rejoined
his Australian teammates for the start of the second Test in
Melbourne on 30 December 1932. Talk had already begun of
the unsportsmanlike behaviour of the English bowlers. Australia
batted first with Jack Fingleton and Woodfull opening. When
Bradman came in to bat at number four, with the score at 2 for 67,
he fell to Bowes' first ball. But Bradman was still Bradman and
he adapted quickly. In the second innings he used his exceptional
footwork to dodge the fast-rising ball, making himself a moving
target, and scored 103 not out, guiding Australia to a win on
3 January 1933 to level the series 1–1. Ominously, seven of his
teammates failed to reach double figures. By now the crowd at
each day's play realised that the English bowlers were deliberately
trying to hit Bradman and other Australian batsmen. Soon, all
of Australia knew.

A complex set of messages began to swirl around the
series, drawn from a variety of sources and delivered through
different media. Live radio descriptions of the play, introduced
during the 1924 cricket series, brought the scenes to radio
listeners. A cartoon published in *The Mail* depicted a nation
paused and gathered to listen to the cricket coverage on every
available radio. We can speculate that the coverage was both
parochial and sensational, and may have heightened the sense of

menace and perhaps injustice as each short ball was delivered. Newspaper coverage and headlines added to the daily drama and were designed to sell newspapers. Major city newspapers at this time still included morning and afternoon editions that provided both a preview of the day's play and an afternoon summary of events. Such was their viability in the 1930s that newspapers were often updated during the day with different editions carrying the latest news. Speculation mounted. One newspaper even went so far as to repudiate a conspiracy theory that was circulating by reassuring its readers: 'it is clearly established that body-line bowling is not an invention of Australian newspapers.'

Cricketers themselves were freely available to the media to comment extensively after each day's play. With, of course, no television or immediate live newsreel action of the incidents, another visual source was employed to convey the drama. Something of a 'cartoon war' emerged between London's *Daily Mail* with English cartoonist Tom Webster depicting Australian batsmen swathed in cotton wool and Larwood bowling (ahem) underarm. Australian cricketer (1920–26) turned journalist and cartoonist Arthur Mailey fired back in the Adelaide *Advertiser* and other syndicated papers with written articles often accompanied by his cartoons, which depicted a bruised and battered Australian line-up also resorting to wearing armour.

Interestingly, poets added their own take on the growing menace to Australian batsmen. 'Oriel' in the feature 'The Passing Show' in the Melbourne *Argus* adapted a children's counting rhyme after the first Test about 'twelve little cricketers', including the lines 'Six little cricketers, glad to be alive, Saw Larwood skittle Kippax and then there were five' who all eventually 'perished on an Emerald sward to make a British glory'. 'Piripi' wrote in the *Brisbane Courier*'s 'On the Game of Cricket' about 'the lethal game of cricket' that for the batsman, 'though well he knows when the missile goes that Death is in the air', and 'The bowler is got up to kill, and his ball is of hardened steel ... And now and then he skittles the bails, With a well-placed Mills's bomb'.

With few avenues for the public or cricket lovers to express their opinions, other than attending a match, letters began to pour into newspaper offices, many expressing their outrage at the new tactic. But some of these letters picked up on a theme that was emerging from the commentary of past cricketers and other pundits – namely, that Australian batsmen needed to 'toughen up'. Especially when it was noted that Australian batsmen had started to wear chest guards under their shirts and elbow protection in an era where only batting pads, gloves and a box had been the norm. It would be another forty-five years until helmets were an acceptable part of their kit. Journalists and letter writers encouraged the Australian selectors to select and play batsmen, such as Victor Richardson, who they thought could hook and pull their way out of the trap set by the English bowlers. Indeed, it was argued that had Australian batsmen Stan McCabe and Richardson succeeded in batting through a barrage of short pitch deliveries in the second Test, that England may well have abandoned the tactic of their own volition. On the receiving end of the shock bowling attack were Australian batsmen who were starting to be perceived as 'soft'.

The response to the tactics was quick, enthusiastic and varied. By the end of the second Test between the two countries (30 December 1932 to 3 January 1933) the evocative word 'bodyline' had been taken up with relish to describe the new tactics, and was in full usage by journalists, players, poets, cartoonists, the crowds, the public and letter writers.

The bonds of Empire were immediately under threat. William Kelly a former member of the House of Representatives, asked in a letter to *The Sydney Morning Herald* on 7 December 1932: 'Is test cricket desirable if it so blinds fairplay with partisanship as to foment ill-feeling between the people that compose the Empire?' The six-stitch red leather cricket ball in the hand of Larwood, bowled to hit the batsman, gave a nuanced and unwelcome challenge and new meaning to 'the crimson thread of kinship'. What was certain was that bodyline no longer referred to the aesthetic bodylines of the Special Chevrolet Roadster – the Bradman Model – or to women's Paris fashions. Bodyline was no longer a car or a corset.

As tension built in Australia, with the five Test series levelled at 1–1, all eyes and ears turned to Adelaide Oval, the site of the third Test (13–19 January 1933). The ground was packed with spectators. England won the toss and batted first, scoring 341, fewer than the number of mounted police stationed nearby the ground in case of trouble. While the bodyline tactic was not employed by the English team continuously, when it was it had a breathtaking effect. When Australia began their innings midway through the second day, opener Fingleton was out for a duck to Allen with only one run on the scoreboard, and co-opener, Captain Woodfull, was shockingly hit by Larwood over the heart, before being out to Allen. Batting at first drop, Bradman was out to Larwood cheaply. When Bert Oldfield, the Australian wicketkeeper, was hit by Larwood on the skull while trying to hook a delivery, the crowd had seen enough.

Writing in Sydney's *Daily Telegraph*, Claude Corbett captured the reactions of men and women in the crowd:

> The hostility when Oldfield was hit on the head by a ball from Larwood and dropped as if he had been shot after staggering a few yards, was the most intense I have ever heard at a cricket match. Hoots and yells from one section, counting out from another, and cries of dismay from the women's stand made a bedlam of noise. So hostile was the crowd at one stage that more police were rushed to the ground, and others were mustered to stand by. Australian crowds are being worked to such high tension by the leg theory attack that the day may not be too far distant when something more serious than vocal demonstrations will be the culminating scene.

Captain Woodfull had also had enough. It was the second time he had been hit. When the English manager, Plum Warner, made concerned enquiries as to his health following the blow to his heart, Woodfull was in no mood for niceties. The Australian captain was said to have remarked:

> There are two teams out there. One of them is playing cricket and the other is making no effort to play the game. Cricket is too great a game to be spoilt by the tactics your team is adopting. I do not approve of them, and never will. If they are persevered with it may be better that I do not play the game. The matter is in your hands and I have nothing further to say to you.

The comments were reported by several members of the Australian team and others present at the time. They said Warner did not reply and walked out of the dressing room.

The injured Australian wicketkeeper, Bert Oldfield, under assessment from doctors and taking no further part in the game (Richardson temporarily deputised behind the stumps), provided his own eyewitness account to the press:

> The ball which hit me was pitched on a line with the wicket. I lost it and it hit me. Previously I had to dodge Larwood's fliers, and I have no doubt that my knock was indirectly caused by the leg-field tactics. One has to be so careful with a field placed in that way. Larwood's pace is such that a batsman must, in a split second, make up his mind what shot to play or whether to play one or to duck. The ball may swing in to the body, it may come stump high, or it may fly. With all these things to consider, it is a most difficult job to defend without being caught.

The press had commented, the crowds of men and women had voiced their anger, some of the players had spoken, the letter

writers were incensed, the cartoonists were sketching and the
poets were rhyming. Where were the cricket officials?

In the middle of the third Test, even before England had
claimed victory, a meeting was hastily convened at Adelaide
Oval, resulting in an official message from the Australian Board
of Control for International Cricket to the Marylebone Cricket
Club, who were responsible not only for the tour arrangements
but also for the laws of cricket. It was thought that 'Oldfield's
injury finally spurred the members of the board to action'. By
necessity, the message was sent as a telegraph cable. There was
no diplomacy. The English managers on tour were only advised
of the contents of the cable after the fact. The message to their
bosses was short, sharp and to the point:

> Bodyline bowling has assumed such proportions
> as to menace the best interest of the game, making
> the protection of the body by the batsmen the main
> consideration. It is causing intensely bitter feeling
> between the players as well as injury. In our opinion, it is
> unsportsmanlike. Unless it is stopped at once, it is likely
> to upset friendly relations existing between Australia and
> England.

It was less than seventy words, but it shook the cricketing world
to its foundations. There it was, two charges: unsportsmanlike,
and with the potential to damage international relations. Perhaps
they forgot they were talking about cricket, which was, after all,
a game. But it was a game that, according to Warner, 'has been
a great factor in Empire building'. Could it now be a factor in
Empire unravelling? Indeed, it was a cable with the same shock
value as the English bowling attack.

Speculation mounted that the Australian officials had stepped
in to save the Australian players from having to complain
themselves, and thereby 'save them the possible humiliation
of a public protest'. The cricketing world erupted. It seemed

that everyone had a strong opinion; even the Catholic church had a view. Dr James Byrne, the Roman Catholic Bishop of Toowoomba (Irish-born, so perhaps no lover of the English), on his way home from Rome by the *Ormonde* and a spectator at the Adelaide Test, claimed it was little short of a miracle that Woodfull was not killed when struck over the heart by Larwood. Monty Noble, former Australian cricketer (1898–1909) and captain, broadcasting on radio at the Adelaide Test, called out bodyline – although not against the rules, he claimed, 'there is a common ethical code, and a spirit of the game which prevents players from doing something which, by common consent, is taboo'. Arthur Mailey reiterated that if bodyline continued to be practised 'batsmen will be compelled to wear baseball masks and wear heavy padding'. Former first-class cricketer, doctor and cricket commentator Eric Barbour, reviewing the Tests in the *Sydney Mail*, considered that 'perhaps a more serious aspect still is the imminent danger to the good-fellowship and friendly rivalry that has always been associated with cricket'.

The controversy became all-consuming. By 4 February 1933, *Smith's Weekly* claimed: 'All else has been excluded from the daily press to make way for the "body-line" brawl.' Like a royal scandal, it made great copy and it sold newspapers. There was always a new angle to pursue. One historian has since argued that the controversy was welcomed because it produced 'voluminous commentary that strayed from the technicalities and clichés of everyday cricket reporting and instead revealed why the game was important to the societies that played it'. It was in everyone's interests to keep the story rolling. The Sydney *Arrow* reaffirmed that 'Cricket has always stood for the acme of sportsmanship' and described Jardine's actions as the 'very antithesis of traditions our forefathers built for us'. They warned 'Jardine's actions will reverberate against what is undoubtedly the pride and joy of English sport'.

Letters to the editor poured in. Were the Australian batsmen to blame? Were they too slow with their footwork? Were they too 'petted and coddled'? Did their behaviour indicate 'that we squeal when we are hurt or when we think we are going to be'? That Australian batsmen were 'squealing' became a popular refrain in English newspapers. Squealing like what – a pig or perhaps a girl? The Brisbane *Worker* stated: 'Squealing is a favourite description of the Australian attitude. Australians are accused of lack of courage and are advised to use tennis balls instead of cricket balls.' Even without that overlay of gendered meaning, the 'manliness' of the Australian batsmen and indeed of the English bowlers was under question. By using the word 'unsportsmanlike' in their cable the Australian Board of Control had challenged both English sporting traditions and manliness. One letter writer implored 'let the play be fair and manly'. The *Arrow* had already called the English 'a bunch of old women'. Test cricketer Alan Kippax contributed his definition: 'Sportsmanship is not a strictly defined and absolute code. Is it not even an absolute virtue, such as honesty, courage or modesty. It is, in fact, a convention, established by public opinion as a result of experience.'

So where did women actually stand on the bodyline controversy? Did they have a singular view? As groups of young women were now themselves cricketers, where were women in the so-called 'humanising game' as described by Andrew Lang in 1893? We already know that women spectators in the stands at the Adelaide Oval had let out 'cries of dismay' when Woodfull and Oldfield were hit on the body. An Adelaide letter writer, who signed herself 'Lover of Good Sport', and who had most likely been present at Adelaide Oval, wrote: 'As an Australian woman who admires England and all her noble traditions, and one who has been a keen follower of cricket for 30 years, may I say how much we women regret this dragging in the mud of our fine old game. It is its unwritten laws that have helped to make cricket what it is today.' A woman correspondent, 'Patricia', commented later to the *Shepparton Advertiser*: 'In sport, for instance, for so many years a man's realm, woman can hold her own. In the recent cricket broadcasts girls were the keenest listeners-in, knowing a wealth of detail of the personnel of the team, appreciating the finer points of the game and able to argue with any man on the delicate points of "bodyline".'

But women were not just spectators at these events, letter writers or listeners via the radio, they were playing a wide range of sports themselves in increasing numbers. This included both amateur players as well as a growing number of professional sportswomen. It involved team sports, such as hockey and basketball, as well as individual sports, such as tennis and golf. Australian women had competed internationally at the Olympic Games since 1912 with a number of medals to show for it. By the early 1930s, sportswomen had formed their own associations in many sports and undertaken overseas tours as well as hosting international teams and players. With this growing involvement in international sport came practical experience and knowledge of the game, its tactics and its rivals. Alert sports journalist Pat Jarrett, writing for the *Melbourne Herald*, canvassed the views on bodyline of Victoria's leading sportswomen to inform her readers. According to Jarrett, who better to ask than sportswomen themselves, 'many of whom have played against English tennis, golf and hockey teams here and abroad' and who are 'keenly interested in the leg-theory controversy which has caused such a commotion in the present series of Tests'.

Many of the women she interviewed disagreed as much with the cable and its timing, as with the bowling. Eleanor Gatehouse, President of the Victorian Ladies Golf Union and a member at the Royal Melbourne Golf Club, thought the cable to the MCC was incautious: 'I feel ashamed of Australia for sending that cable to England. The mention of the word "unsportsmanlike" was particularly unfortunate. If a protest had to be sent it should have been at the end of the Tests ... As for leg-theory, I think a lot of the talk about it being so dangerous is spread about by hearsay.' Mona McLeod, Australian international golf champion said:

'I think it is a great pity that the Board's protest was not made at the end of the second Test. It seems to me that the trouble is not leg theory so much, as the short bumping ball. That certainly seems to be rather dangerous, but I do not see any reason to protest against legitimate theory.' Australian international lawn tennis player Sylvia Harper stated: 'I think a round-table conference as suggested by [Arthur] Mailey would have been much better than the cable that was sent abroad. As for legitimate leg-theory, I suppose something had to be done to stop batsmen making huge scores. It is the short bumping ball that seems to be the trouble, not legitimate leg theory.' International hockey player Alison Ramsay said: 'Perhaps Australia went rather quickly with the protest. Still, it is easy to criticise. We do not have to stand up and take the bruises.'

As well as seeking the opinions of sportswomen generally, Pat Jarrett also interviewed a number of Victorian cricketers for the *Melbourne Herald*. Victorian state captain Dot Debnam said: 'Women cricketers look up to the internationals, and we were looking forward to what promised to be a wonderful season of cricket, but all these distressing accidents tend to mar the game from the feminine viewpoint.' Despite this, Debnam still felt positive 'that it will all be overcome, as players on both sides are far too good sportsmen to spoil the relationship that has existed'. Secretary of the Victorian Women's Cricket Association, cricketer Joan Reeve, told Jarrett: 'We should have waited until the finish of the Tests before making a protest. I certainly think we should play out the series before trying to make a change. Personally, I think leg-theory is quite all right but do not agree with body-line bowling.'

Unlike the other sportswomen in golf and tennis, Reeve had to field questions about the possibility of bodyline in cricket played by women: 'Women cricketers are not adopting leg-theory, but the variety of our bowling is still a little limited. Anyhow, I do not think Victorian women cricketers are likely to take it up!' When reading her statement, it should be remembered that in an era dominated by men's sport, sportswomen were often willing, when challenged, to make vocal compromises, either by choice or by necessity, to gain access and acceptance in sport. Reeve's defensive statement early in the bodyline controversy was to prove one of the compelling questions throughout the next twelve months – were women capable of bowling bodyline, and if they could, should they?

Victorian spin bowler Peggy Antonio recalled: 'I don't think the women had that idea in mind, that we'd have to bowl bodyline, that we have to knock them out and all that sort of thing. No, two entirely different games I would have said.' Fast bowler Nell McLarty recalled, 'Never entered my head. I'm sure no one thought of bowling bodyline in women's cricket.' Nell had been to every match: 'I never missed a game, never missed a ball, it was so tense when you were there, screaming and yelling and then Larwood come on and he'd run and you could hear a pin drop it was so tense. I lived through all that, oh my word, I did.'

There were two major avenues that were needed to fix the bodyline controversy. One was through official channels, committees of enquiry that saw the Australian Board of Control, the International Cricket Council and the Marylebone Cricket Club meet and explore options to change the rules to prevent short-pitched bowling with a stacked leg-side field. This was achieved before the women themselves played an international Test. But the other way, just as important as the official role, was to restore the game of cricket back to its pedestal, among not only the cricket-watching public, but also among the general public.

*The bowling action of Australian pace bowler Mollie Flaherty.
By 1936 she was lauded as 'Australia's greatest fast bowler' and
captured fifty-four wickets in the grade season. She possessed a
strong throwing arm, easily returning the ball over the stumps from
the boundary, and was also the Australian baseball pitcher.*

Chapter 3
National Hysteria

'It was sheer national hysteria.'
— Gilbert Mant, Reuters correspondent, 1933

One bowler who did have the ability to bowl bodyline in Australia was Queensland Sheffield Shield fast bowler Eddie Gilbert. Gilbert was born at Durundur Aboriginal Reserve and had grown up incarcerated at Barambah (later Cherbourg). Asked his opinion, Gilbert told the Hobart *Mercury* newspaper: 'I have absolutely no objection to bowling leg theory, and further, I will get more wickets by doing so.' Gilbert was a likely selection to play for Queensland against the visiting English men's team scheduled for February 1933. His response raised another point troubling many Australian commentators and former players: should they move to ban a tactic that Australia could itself use in retaliation?

The public cable war between the Australia Board of Control and the MCC did nothing to quell the growing public controversy over the series; in fact it inflamed the situation. Five days after the Australian officials sent their provocative cable, and after England had claimed victory in the third Test, the MCC committee, consisting of twenty-two members, returned fire:

> We, Marylebone Cricket Club, deplore your cable. We deprecate the opinion that there has been unsportsmanlike play. We have the fullest confidence in the captain, the

team, and the managers, and are convinced that they would do nothing to infringe the laws of cricket and the spirit of the game. We have no evidence that our confidence is misplaced. Much as we regret the accidents to Woodfull and Oldfield, understanding that in neither case was the bowler to blame, if the Board wishes to propose a new law or rule it shall receive our careful consideration in due course. We hope that the situation is not now as serious as your cable appears to indicate; but if it is such as to jeopardise the good relations of English and Australian cricketers and you consider it desirable to cancel the remainder of the programme, we would consent, with great reluctance.

This response was described as 'an iron hand in a velvet glove'. *Smith's Weekly* went for the man itself, decrying the members of the MCC committee 'elderly dukes, barons, knights, and other dignitaries' who 'have not the faintest idea of the technique of the body-liner' and accused them of being 'sound asleep' during the last cricket season in England when they might have 'scotched the menace'. Even former cricketers backed this opinion. Recently retired English international player Jack Hobbs wrote: 'I deprecate the greybeards arguing that they in their youth would have scored freely from bodyline bowling. I say definitely that they would not have done so against Larwood in Australia.'

There were more cables to come. The rejoinder to the MCC cable by the Australian Board of Control was delivered on Monday 30 January 1933, reiterating its protest, and appointing a committee to report on the action necessary to eliminate such bowling from all cricket in Australia from the beginning of the 1933–34 season. However, under pressure from the Australian Government, the committee withdrew the charge of 'unsportsmanlike', allowing the fourth Test to proceed and dispelling a government fear that Britain might not renew essential loans to Australia for Depression recovery projects. The controversy also threatened the existence and planning for the forthcoming 1934 tour to England by the Australian men's cricket team.

Meanwhile, through all the controversy, there were more matches to play. England won the two remaining Test matches in the series, at Brisbane (10–16 February 1933) and Sydney (23–28 February 1933), with Bradman being dismissed by Larwood in three of his four innings, his fourth and final dismissal by Verity after Larwood had broken down with an ankle injury. The Ashes returned to England, but the cables and controversy didn't cease.

Smith's Weekly claimed in February 1933 that 'the whole sorry business is discussed with intense feeling wherever two or three men (and women, too) are gathered together'. The parenthetical addition of 'and women, too' was designed to convey just how widespread the general public feelings were. They claimed the controversy had 'reverberated and re-echoed into the remotest corners of Australia and of every cricket-playing country in the world'. Why, even a German newspaper had dispatched a special correspondent to London to cover 'the threatened dismemberment of the British Empire'. The Dee brothers from Nelson, New Zealand, were keen spectators at the Tests in Adelaide, Brisbane and Sydney, and wrote home to the *Nelson Evening Mail* to share their observations on the Australian Tests. They claimed that women spectators in Sydney were equal to men in attendance and 'counted out' Jardine each ball. One Dee brother wrote:

> What surprised Bert and myself was the interest of the ladies and the way they scream on a catch or a run out. You can hear them from one side of the ground to the other and they are as bitter as the men. One day I heard one next to me say 'Oh! The brute. Why do they allow it?' This was when Larwood hit McCabe ... Nothing else was talked [about] in trams, buses, hotels etc. but the

leg theory or body bowling. Dangerous ball is the correct
word ... I feel sure they won't play this in New Zealand.

Immediately after the controversial third men's Test in Adelaide,
where Woodfull and Oldfield had been struck, an altogether
unlikely controversy erupted in the cricket world. It was no
coincidence that it was also centred in Adelaide. The incident
ran for a number of months and received extensive newspaper
coverage and stirred strong emotions. The international became
local when members of the Adelaide-based Waratah Girls Cricket
Club announced midweek (about Wednesday 25 January 1933)
that they too would 'try leg theory' in their weekend match
against their opponents, the Myers team. Cricket played by
women had been steadily growing in popularity with regular
teams popping up throughout the country and state associations
coming together, leading to women forming the Australian
Women's Cricket Council in 1931 to both oversee the game
and to provide a structure for the regular interstate matches
held annually between women players. It followed on from the
formation of the English Women's Cricket Association in 1926.

The provocative statement from the Waratah Girls Cricket
Club prompted a personal visit to the cricket ground from Miss
A.E. Kubank, President of the South Australian Women's Cricket
Association. Arriving on a Saturday, too late to intervene before
the start of play, she strode out onto the ground during the match
to call the two opposing captains together to hear her views and
ban the practice. Echoing the sentiment of the Australian Board
of Control's earlier and decisive mid-Test series cable message
to the MCC, she later told the press: 'I would resign sooner
than assent to such unsportsmanlike tactics ... leg theory was
undesirable because girls were supposed to play for clean sport
and comradeship ... I can't see this theory helps either.'

Later, the male umpire of the match, Mr C. Rusk, described
as 'the oldest umpire in the women's association', stated that he
would have personally intervened in the game. 'Although there

is no rule against leg-theory bowling, had it been practised I should have felt it my duty to suggest disqualifying it straight away, even though the women players might not have been able to inflict much damage on one another. Leg-theory bowling is poor sportsmanship.' President Kubank, however, didn't need the male umpire's support, she acted alone in delivering a missive on behalf of the South Australian Women's Cricket Association and introduced the motion: 'leg-theory bowling [will] be banned in all matches played under the auspices of the South Australian Women's Cricket Association'. She claimed to feel that she had the backing of 'most of the delegates'.

By Monday the issues had come to a head, a full meeting of the South Australian Women's Cricket Association was quickly called for at the YWCA rooms in Adelaide on 1 February. Waratah's secretary and bowler Hilda Randell put the association on notice with the challenge: 'The Committee has no right to ban the leg theory. It is interfering with the bowler's right to place her field. And no committee member has a right to enter the playing arena during play, as was done last Saturday.'

Both sides took their views to the hungry media. Randell, perhaps sensing the approaching storm landing on her head, became more conciliatory and issued a clarifying statement: 'It seems to me that some committee members are confusing the simple leg theory with bodyline bowling, which has never been tried by players and never will be tried. For one reason we have no bowlers of sufficient pace.' She added, 'I personally have often bowled at the leg stump with a leg field of three never more.' Seeking to be even more conciliatory, despite her charge against Kubank, she said: 'I have a great regard for the association president and I feel that her influence over the girls is for good. Should the committee ban leg theory, then I shall recommend our members abide by its decision.' She added, 'We are in cricket for the sport itself.'

The South Australian Association secretary, Mrs R. Miller, came out in support of President Kubank: 'I am wholly in favor of the president's attitude towards the leg theory. Persistence in any kind of bowling which would leave the batsman open to injury would kill the sport.' Miller thought the injuries would be minor but nevertheless career-ending: 'an injured finger might mean loss of employment to a typist-player, and no girl will risk that for the sake of any game.' She added a moral aspect to the argument:

> We wish our girls to keep their cricket clean and refined. We do not want them to lose their femininity – that is the reason why we insist on their wearing white frocks, instead of trousers, on the field. We want cricket to be a real force in clean sport among women, leading perhaps, in a few years' time, to international cricket for women. We want to feel that it is a good influence on the girls; leg theory tactics would ruin the game straight away.

So, if women were to bowl fast-leg theory, it might jeopardise both their femininity and their growing push for international cricket.

Randell stood her ground, ready to take on both the president and secretary about leg theory: 'I still feel that they are confusing it with bodyline bowling which has no part in our cricket. I shall point out that there is nothing injurious in our style of leg-theory bowling.' In the end, Kubank rejected the term 'leg theory', instead introducing a censure motion that sought to ban 'all dangerous body-line bowling'. Her opposition was to the 'ball aimed deliberately at the batswoman with the object of intimidating her'. She received unanimous support for her motion from all the delegates, even Randell.

The censure motion was thought necessary, as the secretary noted, there were 'at least two bowlers playing in the matches who were fast enough to intimidate the batswoman if they exploited such tactics'. Miller stated: 'We did not want the girls hurt and we took that precaution in case any girl attempted to try out that type of bowling.' Kubank avoided the need to invade the pitch again, leaving it to the umpire to warn the offending bowler 'under the rule of the association which provides that no player shall behave in an undesirable manner on the field'. Despite having effectively been banned by the South Australian Women's Cricket Association, bodyline was still a hot topic in the ongoing men's Test series.

As Miller articulated, bodyline tactics jeopardised women and girls' right to play cricket at all. Historian Rafaelle Nicholson has argued persuasively that in exchange for the right to play cricket, English women, from the formation of the English Women's Cricket Association in 1926, had laid down a number of measures designed to make their cricket acceptable and non-threatening to the men who controlled the game, the grounds and the traditions, as well as to the general public. These included contesting no cups, prizes or trophies, playing with an amateur ethos, using women as umpires, strict uniform regulations ensuring players never wore anything that looked 'male', such as trousers or caps, and a ban on mixed frivolous cricket matches.

Following the men's bodyline series in Australia in 1932–33, the MCC team travelled on to New Zealand for a series of matches. Gilbert Mant, one of four newspaper men travelling with the MCC team and a Reuters correspondent, expressed his relief at arriving in New Zealand: 'After storm cometh sunshine, after war cometh peace ... none of us knew that soon we would be war correspondents ... The great bodyline war broke out in Adelaide during the third Test and it did not let up until we boarded the Maunganui for Wellington.' He continued:

> Few New Zealanders can realise what that Adelaide Test was like. It was a test of good temper and tolerance rather than of cricket ... an incredible atmosphere of bitterness and acrimony marked that week. Nerves were on edge; tempers were frayed. The mere mention of 'bodyline

bowling' was tantamount to a punch on the nose. It was sheer national hysteria.

He claimed the forty correspondents covering the Tests never went to bed before 2 am, and together they wrote 'millions of words':

> Adjectives burst like bombs around various Australian press boxes. Our hands ached, and our brains reeled in trying to chronicle the most astounding developments of the most tragically astounding cricket tour in history. I repeat we came to New Zealand mental and physical wrecks; mere husks of the cheerful men who left London. And in the haven that is Christchurch our nerves and tottering bodies are being restored amid the stately poplars, the delicately trailing willow trees that line the placid Avon.

Amid his recuperation he remarked on the 'cathedral-like crowd' but noted a striking contrast between New Zealand and Australian spectators – a noticeable lack of women at the ground. 'I missed the colourful feminine crowds of Melbourne and Adelaide,' he stated, and then followed with the unnecessary remark: 'One could always look at them when the cricket was dull.'

Just as bodyline proved an injection of interest into reporting on the Ashes Test series, just one month after the conclusion of the series it was reported that the term bodyline quickly came to have a wider meaning in society. Just like 'Is it cricket?' had meant fair play in the past, now 'bodyline' acquired the means by which unfairness could be tagged. The *Shepparton Advertiser* reported the farewell of one of its town councillors, described as capable in sport and a good bowler. Questioned whether he was a 'bodyline bowler' his supporters replied, 'He played cricket in the true sense of the term just as he played straight in business and life'. Reportedly, the term was also spreading throughout the world: 'A Liberal member of the House of Commons referred a few weeks ago to the "bodyline" tactics of political opponents, a clergyman used it as an expression of opprobrium in a sermon, and a German professor in a controversy at Berlin hurled it at an adversary.' The term was spreading throughout the world as a 'reflection upon their sportsmanship of any man [sic] whether he is engaged in cricket, business, politics, or science'.

Bodyline continued to stir emotions. It was polarising. Cricket was perceived by many as a manly sport. In the Australian Board of Control's initial cable protest and its subsequent rejoinder, many saw a weakening, and such a weakening signified a resultant increase in effeminacy – of men becoming or acting like women. 'Anzac Spirit', a letter writer who still regarded himself as British, wrote to the Brisbane *Telegraph* in May 1933 in protest. He was livid and emotional:

> The recommendation adopted by the Board of Cricket Control … is, to my mind, weak, effeminate and almost childish. It would appear to the average normal, red-blooded Britisher that cricket is now to be controlled by a body of effeminate-minded weaklings, and, if the introduction of this recommendation takes actual shape in the future of the game of cricket, the sooner cricket is relegated to the female species the better. Could anyone imagine that the British Empire would have been built and maintained by men of the calibre of the cricketers of the future if these childish and effeminate rules are to obtain? During the last few years cricket has tended more and more to the effeminate. In past years all sorts of trifling arguments and disputes over afternoon tea and other respites during the game have called forth columns of criticism in newspapers and other publications, which, to the average healthy, vigorous minded man must be nauseating. Just imagine if it was possible to adopt in football these silly effeminacies. The British Empire was

> never built up by men who were afraid to take a knock
> or obliged to stand up to hot opposition … If the Board
> of Control in London endorses the recommendation
> discussed herein the sooner we decide to make it
> a schoolboys' and women's game the better for the
> manhood of the British Empire.

So 'Anzac Spirit' thought that, without bodyline, cricket should be played only by children and women. Larwood later wrote about the protest during the Adelaide Test: 'If certain critics had not made such an effeminate outcry after the third Test the whole bother would be too childishly ludicrous to merit further consideration by grown-up men.'

A.P.H., writing in the *London Punch* with advice to his son, noted:

> Cricket … is played with a hard ball; and if this ball
> comes into violent contact with the human body it may
> hurt. That is why cricket is a manly game (as opposed to
> lawn-tennis in which the ball is so effeminate and soft
> that, if it violently strikes you in the eye, it causes no
> discomfort at all).

No number of placating cables and committees of enquiry could quell the ballooning interest in bodyline. As well as driving the sale of newspapers, books on cricket had a ready market in the 1930s and enjoyed widespread popularity, especially in serialised form. As soon as the bodyline controversy erupted, tales of pre-existing instances of 'bodyline' tactics were dredged up, and people held to account for previously expressed views. *The Worker* in Brisbane was one of the newspapers that looked immediately to English manager Plum Warner's 1930 book *The Fight for the Ashes*, in which he denounced the tactics. In May 1933, only three months after the conclusion of the men's series, the English fast bowler Larwood published his book *Body-Line* in response to the Ashes series in Australia. The book was immediately serialised in instalments in Australian newspapers, spreading his story quickly and widely. A situation that further inflamed the controversy, coming as it did just as the MCC was considering reports from the Ashes series and the ICC was meeting to discuss the international issue.

In Larwood's book he claimed (despite all well-documented instances of past practice) to have invented true bodyline, previous exponents having neither his accuracy nor pace. He stated: 'The term "body-line bowling" was maliciously coined by a cute Australian journalist for the express purpose of misleading and obscuring the issue. It was meant to damn me and damn me it did.' He made detailed allegations of what he called 'larrikinism' in Australia during the series. The *Melbourne Herald* reported: 'larrikinism in the streets, molestation during train journeys, and the throwing of missiles through windows, jeering at theatre entrances, and abuse during the Tests and elsewhere, including foul epithets.' The abuse was directed at Larwood, including 'several letters written anonymously ... of an offensive nature ... which contained veiled threats of reprisals'. Larwood's book and his statements were not universally well received, with the *Daily Telegraph* claiming perhaps a third meaning for the word bodyline as 'that on which cricketers may hang their dirty linen'.

By July 1933, Larwood's book was quickly followed by one from English captain Douglas Jardine, entitled *In Search of the Ashes: A Skipper's Log*, citing further instances of Australian crowd misbehaviour and highlighting what he saw as the obsessive preoccupation of Australians with sportsmanship – more than in any other country. He laid bare the Australian addiction to gambling on cricket, and questioned why the Australian cricket authorities had not done more to suppress barracking and ill manners. He declared the 'hackneyed legend' about the 'good nature and fairness' of barrackers to be 'threadbare'. Australians could not get enough of the syndicated book instalments (carried for example in Sydney by *The Sun* and the *Daily Telegraph*) and they kept the bodyline controversy firmly in the public eye.

Soon after, Australian test cricketer Alan Kippax (1925–1934) turned radio commentator, and state cricketer Dr Eric Barbour, published their 1933 book *Anti Body-Line*, in which they called bodyline 'the cricket sensation of the century'. It was aimed at an English readership. Kippax wrote in the preface: 'Certain newspapers, both in England and Australia, whose news sense is developed more highly than their Imperialism, have featured the dispute with scare headlines.'

Rarely missing a publicity opportunity, it nevertheless took Don Bradman another five years before he released a book on his life story, in which he discussed bodyline in detail. Back in England, Plum Warner continued to comment on the implications and repercussions of bodyline: 'International cricket has drifted in a somewhat perilous direction impairing the relations between Australia and England.'

Just as the Waratah Girls Cricket Club in South Australia had created their own controversy around bodyline in grade cricket, at cricket clubs across Australia, as well as other parts of the British Empire, cricketers were alert to and attracted by the new bodyline tactic. It carried with it a sense of menace, bravado and swagger, long the stock-in-trade for any aspiring fast bowler. *Smith's Weekly* contended that 'Every kid bowler has had a try-out with it, and every Saturday afternoon has brought its crop of casualties'. Reports of bodyline spreading to near neighbour New Zealand reached the press by March 1933, when a fast bowler in Auckland placed a leg field and made the ball bump disconcertingly at the batsman. At this the informed spectators at the ground reportedly shouted, 'Cut it out. You've been reading the Australian papers,' and the practice was abandoned on the advice of the bowler's captain.

Australian cricketers Kippax and Barbour in their book *Anti Body-Line* detailed the impact of bodyline on the 30,000 juniors playing every Saturday in Sydney alone, practically all on concrete wickets. The repercussions were a mixture of violent retaliation and threats, as well as injuries. On Moore Park a batsman walked down the pitch and threatened to hit the bodyline bowler over the head with the bat; on the Domain a match was abandoned after a fight between the opposing teams; and at Centennial Park an ambulance officer on duty reported that his casualty list was four times its usual length, the vast majority being head injuries. 'Such is body-line bowling, in practice,' the authors wrote.

Across the world, it came as no surprise when the English Women's Cricket Association decided to follow the lead of the South Australian women and articulate a bar on 'leg theory' during the first so-called all women's 'Test' between England and 'The Rest' at Leicester, England, in August 1933. Rather than bodyline, the enthusiastic crowds really came to see the legendary Mabel Bryant play for the England team. Bryant had first played the game in 1903 when she scored 224 not out, and taken all wickets at Eastbourne. Australian newspapers featured the wire story with the sensational (and largely irrelevant) headline 'Bodyline Barred'. The story, however, came with a suggestion that this 'Test' 'should be a forerunner of a visit to Australia of an English women's eleven'.

Australian women had met annually, since 1906, to contest interstate matches, and by the 1930s many of these women, in Victoria at least, had formed themselves into what they called the Pioneer Victorian Ladies Cricket Association, predating the concept of 'masters' competitions by decades. Women who played cricket continued to emphatically state their opposition to bodyline. Anticipating the forthcoming next interstate carnival scheduled in Brisbane in March 1933, the players were canvassed for their opinions on bodyline. Journalist Pat Jarrett again sought the thoughts of Dot Debnam, a member of the Victorian team. Debnam reiterated that no leg theory or bodyline bowling would develop in cricket played by women. 'It is against women's ideas. Victorian bowlers are too good at the orthodox methods to resort to packing the leg field.' She was a traditionalist: 'The girls in my team love the game too well as it always has been played to want to see it altered in any manner that might cast a reflection on the game.' Similar statements were made on behalf of the Victorian team, where 'Body-line bowling finds no advocates among women cricketers'.

Despite members of the Victorian team's stance against bodyline, the Sydney women at the interstate carnival were wary of Victorian fast bowler Nell McLarty, in particular, who certainly possessed the pace to emulate Larwood. Her reputation was well known among all interstate teams. Jean Sutton, a champion Victorian batswoman, picked up on a rumour going around the New South Wales team that McLarty had adopted bodyline bowling. She knew the rumour was false: 'It was really comic to see their quick movements and scared expressions when she bowled the first few balls at the interstate matches in Brisbane. But they need not have worried. Nell McLarty disapproves strongly of body-line bowling.' Disapproved yes, but capable of bowling bodyline – undoubtedly. A bowler didn't need to bowl bodyline to be intimidating, you just needed the potential to be a threat.

In welcoming women to the interstate carnival in March 1933, the Lady Mayoress of Brisbane, Phyllis Greene, declared herself not a fan of bodyline bowling, having received a 'rather nasty knock on the face' during her own cricketing career. A successful bowler and fieldswoman in her youth, she recounted her participation in interschool contests until an injury brought parental protests and abandonment of her cricketing career.

We have already seen how the occasional male newspaper columnist eagerly latched on to the term 'bodyline' in cricket and could think only of women's bodies, but it was during the women's interstate carnival played in Brisbane in March 1933, immediately following the bodyline series, that the press coverage explicitly linked cricket played by women with the sleazy double entendre of bodyline. Similarly, no mention could be made of leg theory without male journalists thinking of women's legs. In a derogatory article on the carnival, 'All Leg – No Theory', published in the Brisbane *Sunday Mail*, it is evident that women playing cricket was a long way from acceptable in the eyes of some male journalists:

> ... occasionally the girls packed the slips – and mostly slipped ... these sweet young things who patted the ball hither and thither with apparent graceful abandon ... Mr. Hillsider ... more often than not he forgot his usual instructive vocabulary, and was too polite to shout 'Get a bag,' when some sweet young thing fumbled the ball, or 'put on a new record,' when a dainty bats-girl stonewalled with monotonous regularity ... He had expected to see an array of bloomers, but of a different variety ... And, after all, a leg in a cricket pad is no longer a thing of beauty or a joy for ever.

Concentrating on women's legs and undergarments may have been excused as male 'humour' in 1933, and was no doubt useful in selling newspapers, but the women who were passionate about the sport would not be deterred; if anything it drew more girls and women to the sport than ever before.

Strong opening or middle-order bat, Amy Hudson executes a perfect cut shot at the 1933 Interstate Championships in Brisbane. She earned her first Australian selection in the third Test in Melbourne in 1935, toured England in 1937 and was the only player from that team to make a return to England for the 1951 series. She finished her long career with a Test batting average of 32.31 and bowling average of 16.25.

Chapter 4
The Great Leg Pull

'Nothing in the world of things that interest
the reading public has perhaps a bigger or
more consistent public than cricket.'
— W.G. Grace, 1909

The number of women and girls playing cricket, and the standards they had reached, progressed so quickly that a mere three months after the conclusion of the men's bodyline Ashes series in 1934, there was earnest talk of a cricket Test between Australian and English women. Records show that it was Englishwoman Vera Cox, secretary of the English Women's Cricket Association, while holidaying in Australia in 1931, who first discussed with Elsie Bennett of the YWCA in Melbourne the possibility of English women embarking on a cricket tour of Australia, modelled on previous hockey tours. The two women kept in constant touch, especially after Elsie Bennett's move to England. This was an ambitious proposal in the early years of the establishment of the Australian Women's Cricket Council.

Margaret Peden, foundation member and secretary of the New South Wales and national associations, raised the issue again at the all-Australia meeting in Brisbane in March 1933 and sought to have the invitation sent immediately. However, Victorian and Queensland delegates cautiously rejected the notion, citing financial reasons. But then the *Daily Telegraph* headline jumped in with their own take on the debate: 'Finance,

Not Body-Line Bar to Women's Cricket Tour'. *The Australian Women's Weekly* quickly followed with the statement: 'Of course, body-line bowling would be barred.' It seemed a tour of Australia by the English team could not be discussed in the press without the spectre of bodyline. And this begged the question: how could such a Test match proceed in a world obsessed with bodyline? Even so, for a proposal that lacked official paperwork, endorsement or agreement, the England–Australia Test matches quickly snowballed and took on a life of their own. Information was exchanged through the news wire services with press interviews in both countries providing the other with the most up-to-date information.

Marjorie Pollard, assistant-secretary of the English Women's Cricket Association, suggested the tour might involve fourteen or fifteen players, all of whom could and would pay their own expenses. She expressly stated in the *Telegraph* that the women's tour could fix English–Australian cricketing relations: 'We are not interested in silly bodyline or leg theory, but would play cricket as it should be played.' The newspaper stated: 'In view of the existing ill feeling a friendly visit by women cricketers ought to improve sporting relations.' There it was out in the open: women could fix bodyline.

How much had the bodyline controversy encouraged women in Australia to take up cricket? At the end of the 1933 season, hundreds of women were reported to be playing the game. Country player Jean Sutton remarked that 'public interest has increased surprisingly this season. Our galleries have grown. Of course, many come through curiosity. They seem surprised at our professional equipment and trim white frocks. Next season we will have many new players, judging by the inquiries made already.'

The momentum for the tour continued to build before the eyes of the public, in which the women cricket backers and administrators probably had a guiding hand. A judicious, well-placed and well-written letter to the editor (called 'What People

Think') by 'Mrs X' proposed that it would now 'be a good idea to have women's test matches with other countries'. Mrs X was very knowledgeable:

> I see that the number of women cricketers in England is growing rapidly, so perhaps matches could be arranged between representatives of both countries. The so-called bodyline bowling will of course not be seen in women's matches, and this will do much to restore the harmonious relations between England and Australia which were ruffled somewhat recently, beside putting the sport back on the pinnacle which it previously occupied.

Mrs X finished her letter with some practical advice: 'Our women cricket officials should get in touch with those in England and discuss the proposal.' Today we would call that kind of letter 'kite flying', but it served to put the notion squarely before the public and create the conversations that a series between Australian and English women could both 'restore harmonious relations' and put the sport back on its pinnacle. In other words, it could be the bodyline fix.

But such positive messages and energy did not go unchallenged. Throughout history, whenever women threaten to stray from their assigned gender roles, especially in the worlds of sport and politics, an inevitable, highly orchestrated public backlash ensues. This can be in the form of newspaper editorials, letters to the editor, opinion pieces, newsreel commentary, or from the pulpit, parliament or any public platform largely controlled by men. In 1933 it came from male newspaper cartoonists.

Cartoonist Percy Leason (1889–1959) was a controversial figure who, following bad reviews for his depictions of Aboriginal portraits, would later emigrate to America in 1938 to escape the criticism. Accompanying just one sentence about aspirations of the English women's team to tour Australia, Leason was given a full page in *Table Talk* under the title: 'More Bodyline!' In it he depicted English players on the field with a stacked leg side and a muscly mannish bowler being thrown the ball, while two frail Australian batswomen cower at the wickets and the English team all laugh. The cartoon wasn't even funny.

In England, following years of bad press, trivialisation, sexualisation, overt sexism and ridicule, women had taken steps to take back control of their own messages about cricket. They refused to passively accept the public judgement. As early as June 1929, the editors of the popular magazine *Hockey Field and Lacrosse* made available three summer editions to be devoted solely to cricket, and player–author Marjorie Pollard took responsibility for them. In her first editorial she claimed the move was aimed at providing the 'right kind of publicity'. Pollard solicited endorsements from well-known male cricketers, with Plum Warner contributing: 'I feel certain that all the best and highest traditions of Cricket will be safe in the women's hands.' It quickly became a reliable and alternative source of information and entertainment on the women's game in that country and it challenged the mainstream media. After three editions it became the standalone magazine *Women's Cricket*. The magazine was financed by subscription (6d an issue) and advertising drawn from a range of sports goods manufacturers, holiday companies and physical training colleges. The magazine carried Women's Cricket Association and club news, as well as articles on skills and knowledge of the game.

In Australia, without the playing numbers and readership to sustain their own mainstream magazine, Australian women journalists, including Pat Jarrett and Ruth Preddey (both cricketers themselves), used what resources they could to provide a positive dialogue about the sport, free from ridicule. Following its establishment in June 1933, *The Australian Women's Weekly* contained two pages per issue devoted to sport played by women written by Ruth Preddey. Fortunately for women, *The Australian Women's Weekly* was a fortuitous and timely partner in their quest for international Test cricket. The popularity of the *Weekly*'s sport pages led to *The Sydney Morning Herald*'s women's supplement also featuring articles on sport written by cricketer and journalist Kathleen Commins from November 1933. Other sportswomen, including journalists Pat Hansen, Pat Jarrett and Dot Debnam, wrote for the Sydney *Sun*, *Woman's Budget*, *Sporting Globe* and the Melbourne *Herald*, among others.

As a result of this extensive press coverage across multiple publications, cities and sports, many sportswomen from the 1930s possess expansive scrapbooks of their sporting exploits. Nance Clements in Melbourne remembered:

> There's some good headlines, Dot Debnam I think it was wrote them ... it wasn't bad publicity at all, it was not too bad for those days, and that goes for club cricket, every team, you got results in the old *Argus* green, *The Star* or the *Herald* ... there'd be odd write-ups about different girls, but all the results were always printed in the paper.

Anne Palmer remembered: 'They had a paper called *The Star* and Dot Debnam, who was our skipper in Clarendon, she had a roving commission job for women's sport writing for them. It was nothing to see a full-page spread on women's cricket, there was always something about cricket, it was amazing.' She also read articles by Pat Jarrett: 'Well, she was very cricket minded. She became a great friend of mine subsequently. Yes, she was very fond of cricket.'

It seems remarkable today that a cohort of women were welcomed into sports reporting in the 1930s. As we have seen, Pat Jarrett had taken the opportunity in 1933 to quiz Australian sportswomen on their attitude to the bodyline controversy. Jarrett was born in 1911 and had grown up in Kyneton, Victoria, and learnt to ride and shoot on her family's country property. An all-round sportswoman, she described herself as a 'natural ball player' and by the time the family moved to Albert Park in Melbourne she had spent more time on the school sports fields than in class. By the time she left school at sixteen, she had developed into a talented swimmer and surf lifesaver, training alongside Frank Beaurepaire at Middle Park Surf Club. With an uncle, Charles Herschell, working at the Pathé film laboratory, her first job was to write captions for *The Herald* newsreels.

Her contacts at *The Herald* suggested she write about championship swimming as a freelancer for the *Sporting Globe*, where Fred Laby employed her and she enjoyed her own byline. Encouraged to expand her sports reporting, she wrote directly to Keith Murdoch at *The Herald*, who placed her on a four-year cadetship as a sports reporter at £5 per week. She produced a full page on women and sport once a week, learning also the technical side of producing newspaper copy. She described her covering of sports 'as pretty strenuous because I was competing as well as reporting'. Jarrett participated in swimming, surf lifesaving, athletics, javelin, discus and shot-put, cricket and rowing – 'I thought if I was writing about a sport I had to know what it was all about.'

These pieces were not simply results of games, but full articles and opinion pieces canvassing a range of sports and issues. One of the issues was, of course, the ongoing resolution of the bodyline question. In this vein, Ruth Preddey reported at the end of September 1933 that the Australian Board of Control had agreed to adopt the new bodyline bowling law for the Sheffield Shield competitions. Because the women played their interstate cricket matches according to the laws that govern Sheffield Shield, the new rule applied to their matches as well. Preddey added: 'Although it is quite unnecessary to allude to this form of bowling in connection with women's cricket, it is perhaps advisable to refer to it, so that a greater knowledge of the game may be gained.' Preddey outlined the new rule that would be adopted in Australia:

> Any ball delivered, which, in the opinion of the umpire at the bowler's end, is bowled at the batsman with intent

to intimidate or injure him, shall be considered unfair, and 'No-ball' shall be called, and the bowler notified of the reason. If the offence be repeated by the same bowler, in the same innings, he shall be immediately instructed by the umpire to cease bowling, and the over shall be regarded as completed. Such bowler shall not again be permitted to bowl during the course of the innings then in progress.

Although the women journalists took their task to provide comprehensive and informative coverage of cricket and other sports seriously, that did not mean that they did not use humour to do so. Turning any criticism on its head, *The Australian Women's Weekly* in a light-hearted piece in October 1933 asked that if the English women's cricket team comes to Australia 'Will Husbands be Allowed?' They imagined the reverse of all the rules governing men's cricket and also wanted to know: 'Will husbands be forbidden to accompany their wives?'; 'Will the members stands be placed at the exclusive disposal of women players and ticket holders?'; 'Will the men occupy the ladies stand and be forbidden to smoke?'

On the 'deplorable' subject of bodyline bowling they posited: 'Because the Australian women's cricket team includes something in the nature of a surplus of fast bowlers [it] might act as a deterrent in the matter'.

But, of course, despite the presence of so many women writing on sport, women didn't control large swathes of the press that, in turn, stepped up their criticism of cricket played by women. The Brisbane *Telegraph* reprinted a story from an English journal under the extraordinary headline: 'No Bodyline for Women. "Hardihood for Men and Amazons"'. Bodyline aside, they noted the writer of the original article 'M.P.S.' 'does not seem to consider cricket even under normal circumstances, suitable for women'. The article contained 'biting criticism of women's bowling', 'their weather beaten faces', 'more than ordinary risks

of injury', 'facial scars', 'blows on the chest', 'destroying the
femininity which will be their main charm and road to success
when grown up'. It pointed out the dangers of 'stooping and
standing', the enlargement of the hands due to gripping a bat
and cricket ball, and the general muscle building. And concluded
with, 'in our hearts we know that hardihood is for men and
Amazons, not for potential mothers'. No one called for women
to stop all factory and housework. In England this style of press
reporting was referred to by women as 'tittle-tattle columns', a
term coined to describe derogatory and dismissive reporting on
their cricket.

Sports journalist Pat Jarrett sought to counter such views, but
in doing so ran the danger of tipping the scales too far in the
opposite direction. She evoked images of 'carefree, sun-tanned
girls' in 'spotless white tunics'. She quoted former Victorian
state player Myrtle Elvins, who played the game 'for the love of
outdoor exercise'. To Elvins, 'It is not a strenuous game if played
with proper equipment and under correct supervision' (hard to
imagine it otherwise!) and she believed she 'owed her continued
good health to activity on the cricket field'. Jarrett reported that
the Victorian association by 1933 had five hundred girls playing
in weekly competitions, 'all of whom hold a distinctly feminine
attitude to the game'. She doesn't say so, but this differed from
the English, as they 'enjoy the thrill of competition' and are ready
'to uphold the prestige of their club ... they play in true feminine
sporting spirit and take defeat with a smile'. Couldn't women just
play cricket and enjoy the game? It didn't give them big hands
or make them more graceful or beautiful. It seems emphasis on
femininity was required in public and mainstream discourse.

Still, the concession to not bowl bodyline was gathering
momentum across Australia and England as the price women
were prepared to pay for the right to play cricket. But was that
a ruse? Was the reassurance necessary or was it just another way
for the media to use bodyline to spice up all stories about cricket
and sell newspapers. Cables from London continued to quote

Women's Cricket Association officials reassuring Australia, 'We don't bowl bodyline and do not pack a leg field. We haven't a bowler sufficiently fast for effective leg theory.' Mudgee, in the Central West of New South Wales, hoped to be one of the country centres to host the English players. The *Mudgee Guardian* declared, 'If they do come our way, we hope there will be no recurrence of the body-line business.' The Adelaide *Mail* reassured its readers: 'Body-line bowling has not been taken up by women.'

Meanwhile, in the lead-up to the 1934 Australian men's cricket tour of England, a tour put in jeopardy by the ongoing bodyline controversy and the efforts to resolve it, cables seeking reassurance from the MCC that the Australian men would be welcomed were exchanged back and forth. That Australia had to keep repeating its request for the elimination of bodyline from the series drew the ire of *The Referee* newspaper, which labelled an individual male member of the Australian Board of Control 'a garrulous and obstinate old woman'. The newspaper clarified: 'One is not suggesting that the board members most concerned are figuratively old women. They are one and all, sincere lovers of cricket.' Such was the gendered nature of the language and gratuitous references to women. Thus, the men's tour was to go ahead despite risks of cancellation.

In an era when quick communication between countries was nigh on impossible, and letters crossed each other at sea, the news came in March 1934 that the English Women's Cricket Association had accepted Australia's invitation to tour at the end of 1934, even though that invitation had not yet been sent. The invitation had not been sent because the proposed program needed to include an itinerary for the two-month tour, and negotiations needed to be completed with both state associations and country centres that would act as hosts. It helped that the English players were able to pay their own way. It was thought by the Brisbane *Telegraph* that the only expenses would be for entertainment and these 'will be divided between the three States [Queensland, New South Wales and Victoria], who will surely not be at any loss'. The newspaper stressed, 'The Britishers are players of no mean ability ... the first Test matches will be well-fought contests, with, of course, no body-line.' Of course. Again, the reassurance was there.

Discussions of bodyline, leg theory and the Australian propensity for barracking still preoccupied English newspapers concerning the proposed tour to Australia. The 'English correspondent' of *The Australian Women's Weekly*, Muriel Segal, reported in April 1934 that 'the English Press considers that a note of warning should be sounded'. She quoted an opinion published in the London *Daily Mirror*:

> No, I don't like the idea of sending an English women's cricket team to Australia as has been suggested. And I don't think that Jardine would like it either. Haven't we enough trouble with the Southern Cross without a Maggie Murphy being barracked for hitting Don Bradman in the slats? Let's keep the fight to the men. You never could tell which side those old boys from the sheep stations would take.

Segal thought the comments that she passed on would amuse her Australian readers, and added: 'Anyone familiar with the atmosphere of sportsmanship and keen enjoyment of the game that attend our women's interstate matches will find a certain humor in the paragraph from the *Mirror*.'

Reflection on, and repercussions from the bodyline series continued to occupy public opinion especially in the press. W.G. Grace, writing in *WG's Little Book* in 1909, had stated, 'Nothing in the world of things that interest the reading public has perhaps a bigger or more consistent public than cricket.' He continued: 'Very rarely indeed can a man who has not played first class cricket criticise, with success, the man who does.' He lamented, 'It is a pity all cricket reports and criticisms are not signed. The reader would then know just which description to read and which to avoid.' Such sentiments were reprised in cricketing circles by mid 1934 when the bodyline controversy was turned into a blame game. Arthur Mailey stated, 'That men writing cricket who didn't know a googly from a long hop, gave a twist to the Larwood exploits that caused people on the terraced seats to adopt an attitude that might not otherwise have been.'

Others also criticised the encroachment into cricket commentary by former cricketers, and spoke to a demarcation dispute over whom was qualified to write about cricket:

> The real trouble in cricket today is not the legitimate staff men, but the ex-cricketers who have butted in on the pressman's job. They write ponderously, and in their efforts to appear learned upset the equal tenor of the game. They advise everybody what to do, or what not to do. With their advice they bewilder players and officials. The present bodyline controversy might never have arisen, but for the ex-cricketers or nearly played out cricketers wanting to also indulge in journalism.

One correspondent to the Brisbane *Telegraph* even suggested that 'a couple of business men would settle the whole matter in five minutes'.

Looking back over the whole bodyline scenario, the *Daily Standard* in Brisbane labelled it 'The Great Leg Pull', and with their view from the northern state of Queensland, that it was no doubt concocted in the southern states:

> The great leg pull has finished. Or, as others put it, the bodyline controversy has been ended. The whole thing started with the big southern newspapers stampeding the Board of Control into sending that now famous cable reflecting on the sportsmanship of Jardine's team. What board members didn't realise was that the more audacious of the pressmen saw in the leg-packed field

and the thunderbolts of Larwood a good story. They
played on it – and the ballyhoo had success far greater
than they had ever imagined.

A good story? Ballyhoo? All caused by the southern newspapers!
The article continued:

> Anybody who followed the controversy closely must
> have noticed how some of these papers shifted their
> ground. Demanding action from the board in December,
> they got a shock when the board did the very thing they
> demanded. So another angle to the story was sought.
> It presented itself in the language of the cable. So that
> was attacked. It was all good copy – and the board kept
> on falling for the bait, hook, line and sinker. Then
> the public showed signs of being bored of the whole
> affair. Keener readers of the signs than the Board of
> Control members, the newspapers sensed this – and
> they sensed, too, that a continuation of the demand for
> a complete climb down by the M.C.C. would only end
> in an abandonment of the cricket tour of England. That
> would have meant no stories about the run-getting feats
> of Bradman, or, better still, duels between Don and his
> friend Larwood. So there was still further shifting of
> ground by some newspapers, and those who demanded
> that England should cease bodyline attacked the board
> members because they demanded that guarantees should
> be given that England would not let anybody bowl the
> leg stump delivery at Bradman – or anybody else.

The *Daily Standard* predicted the outcome:

> In it all should be a lesson for the board. That lesson is
> to refuse to be stampeded by the passion of the moment,
> no matter how powerful the press behind the stirring up

of the passion may be. The board was let down by many journals on bodyline. It merits a little sympathy for that, and it is to be complimented on, even at this late hour, deciding to drop the whole business. Big qualities are necessary in the swallowing of one's pride.

Between June and August 1934, the Australian men's cricket team played a return five Test Ashes series in England. Without Larwood and Voce, the English 'hurricane bowlers', the first match at Trent Bridge was won by Australia. England won the second Test, with the third and fourth drawn. During the tour, some newspapers in Australia returned to their old themes, 'Well the body-line question looks like developing into another big battle of hate and acrimony. Anyhow most Australians knew it would come once England found out the "Ashes" were in danger.' Although Bradman started the series not in the best of health, by the fourth Test at Leeds he contributed an innings of 304, together with Ponsford's 181. In the fifth and final Test at the Oval, Bradman and Ponsford again fired, Ponsford scoring 266 and Bradman 244 to guide Australia to a 2–1 Ashes series win.

Bradman remarked later, 'By the end of the tour, to a large extent, we had got over the unpleasantness that happened in Australia in 1932–33.' Not all agreed. In his 1934 book, *The Fight for the Ashes*, Surrey batsman Jack Hobbs recognised that there was 'some semblance of Bodyline bowling in the Tests in England this year'. Speculation arose that England might even have thrown a Test series to hold the Empire together. Ever a newspaper to sniff out a conspiracy theory regarding Empire relations or the establishment, the *Labor Call*'s 'Scrutator' quoted a 'budget of news' received from a London friend in which he claimed in October 1934 that the victory by Australia in England had been orchestrated:

In the present cricketing situation, it is not a question of the British prestige being at stake. It is a question of

placating a Dominion of whose 100 per cent loyalty
there are considerable doubts. Therefore the authorities
here realised that the quarrel with Australia must at all
costs be patched up. Throughout the Australian tour
the MCC did everything beyond publicly condemning
the tactics of Jardine and Larwood to meet the visitors'
wishes. It was only at Nottingham that the MCC was
flouted, and Voce allowed to indulge in bodyline. His
subsequent shin trouble was a purely diplomatic reason
for his sudden removal from the game. Though a
pretence was made by the England Selection Committee
to consider Voce's claims for the final Test, those in the
know are aware that he never had the ghost of a chance
of playing.

The left-leaning *Labor Call* had every reason, in the great class
struggle, to imagine that Australia's loyalty to Empire was
in doubt and to promote that idea with conspiracy theories
and speculation. By November 1934, the MCC placed the
onus on umpires to intervene following their redefinition of
what constituted a direct attack on the batsman in an action
that newspapers were calling 'The Death of Bodyline'. While
the cricketers may have got over what Bradman called the
'unpleasantness', bodyline was still at the forefront of the press,
commentators and popular culture. Leg pull or not, the bodyline
genie was out of the bottle, and it wasn't going away any time
soon. Something at the very heart of cricket had been shaken
to its core. Fixing it could not be achieved in one game or
one series. It needed a reset. Cricket needed to go back to its
grassroots and re-establish what had made it into the game that
was synonymous with fair play. Who better to do that than
women who played the game 'as it should be played'?

With a three-Test series to be played between Australian
and English women in December 1934 and January 1935 – in
Brisbane, Melbourne and Sydney – the necessary arrangements

progressed quickly. As the English women got closer to arriving in Australia for their Test, the press was obsessed about two aspects of the tour: would bodyline be part of it, and what would the women wear?

Marjorie Pollard, 'the well-known English authority on women's cricket' commented, 'There is no possibility of bodyline bowling being exploited by the English women's team. Anyway, leg theory is too clever for us, and we haven't the super bowlers that this type of cricket demands.' Betty Archdale who would captain the English team remarked to the press that not only had she never seen bodyline bowling, but also 'the field will be placed in such a way that there will be not the slightest suggestion that bodyline is being used'. She added, 'It does not exist with us.' Muriel Segal, writing for the readers of *The Australian Women's Weekly*, claimed, 'From an Australian point of view, bodyline bowling will not be put into practice, inasmuch as there are few women bowlers of the fast variety who can make the ball rise dangerously.' Few, but not none. She singled out Australians Nell McLarty and Amy Hudson, both state players, who could make the ball rise sharply off the pitch. She reassured her readers:

> Neither of these bowlers would deliberately aim to injure the batsman. Leg theory is perfectly legitimate, and there would be no objection coming from the Australian Women's Cricket Council if it were used in the forthcoming Test matches against England. But the fast rising ball, bowled with no other object than to hit the batsman, is as divorced from women's cricket as the batsman who would swing her bat in an endeavor to hit the wicket-keeper.

In a further interview, Betty Archdale stressed, 'You can take it from me that there will be no unpleasantness in our Tests.' It seemed Archdale could not be interviewed about the forthcoming tour to Australia without bodyline being headlined by the press. At the English Women's Cricket Association farewell to the team at Caxton Hall, Archdale reiterated, 'They were going determined to play the game, while doing their best to win. They hoped to preserve the friendliest spirit, and not get too solemn about it.' She 'laughingly denied her intention of using bodyline, or even a suggestion of leg theory'. This news article was carried across many Australian city and regional newspapers, but with one change. *The Courier-Mail* in Brisbane was the only newspaper to replace Archdale's word 'solemn' with the word 'serious'. An important change, with those in Queensland reading the headline 'Women's Cricket Team will not be too serious over game', an entirely different matter from 'solemn'. Women would indeed be serious in the forthcoming matches.

With the constant denials of bodyline bowling having a place in the women's matches, rumours started to circulate that women bowlers who were capable of producing bodyline bowling were being actively omitted from selection in Australian teams. Scheduled during the English tour, with the dual aim of aiding in the selection of the Australian Test team to meet the English, was the annual women's interstate cricket carnival to be held in Melbourne in January 1933. Hilda Randell, the secretary and captain of the Adelaide-based Waratah Girls Cricket Club, was back in the news accusing the South Australian selectors of omitting bowler Molly Dutton from the South Australian team: 'I would like to know why Molly Dutton has not been chosen.' The Adelaide *News* speculated that, 'It is not known whether the selectors feared a "body-line" rumpus in the women's cricket world, but Molly Dutton, who besides being the Bradman of women's cricket here, is a fast bowler, who bumps the ball in true Larwood style has been unaccountably omitted.' (Molly could have held her own bodyline series, being both Bradman and Larwood in one!) Pat Jarrett backed Randell's view, writing in the Melbourne *Herald*, 'Bodyline Bowler Omitted from SA Women's Team'.

Rumours and references to bodyline bowling among English women also began appearing in Marjorie Pollard's monthly magazine *Women's Cricket*. The first mention of bodyline is an extract from the *Yorkshire Observer* in June 1933: 'I hear that the Bradford and District Newspaper Team have strengthened their bowling considerably by the addition of Miss M. Atkinson, a Yorkshire player. In her debut at Highcliffe she was accused of body-line bowling, and dubbed as a feminine counterpart of Larwood by the disgruntled supporters of the visitors'. Bodyline did not necessarily have the negative connotations in England that were present in Australia. The same issue of *Women's Cricket* featured an extract from Country Vicar (the pseudonym of Randolph L. Hodgson) in an article titled 'Cricket Again', in which he extolled the 'great performance' of Larwood because 'lately the batsman has had the better of the contest and cricket-matches have been burdened with huge scores'. Country Vicar enthused, 'it is this mode that I most want to see – the "leg trap" – baited and set, with the fieldsmen standing close in ... I take my hat off to Harold Larwood!'

In the following issue of *Women's Cricket* in July 1933, Marjorie Pollard reviewed the latest four books published on the bodyline series:

> How many of us have, I wonder, really formed any clear opinions about the last series of matches played in Australia. Even after reading carefully the above-mentioned four books on the subject, which do present both and every side of the case, I must admit that I am bewildered. One thing is very very clear – and that is that the Australian Barracker is a nasty customer indeed.

The four books were J.B. Hobbs's, *The Fight for the Ashes 1932–33*; Bruce Harris's, *Jardine Justified*; Arthur Mailey's, *And then came Larwood*; and Harold Larwood's *Body-line*. The latter described by Pollard as 'a fast furious, and virile piece of work – full of criticism of Australia and Australians, but also full of much sound advice for bowlers and players'. In the September 1933 issue of *Women's Cricket*, Pollard accompanied a report on English bowler Carol Valentine taking 5 for 10 in a match during Cricket Week with a pen sketch captioned, 'C. Valentine for the Larwood touch'. Marjorie Pollard continued her provocation over bodyline. Prior to the English team leaving for Australia, the cover of *Women's Cricket* in July 1934 featured a photograph from the *News Chronicle* in Adelaide of a wicketkeeper with a full face-covering grille behind the stumps with the caption: 'What they would have us believe our players will find in Australia. Is it protection against their own bowlers – or our leg side hitting players?'

In November 1934 *The Sydney Morning Herald* stated: 'In spite of body-line and other occasional impediments, the cricket Tests … have played a great and enduring part in cementing the Empire tie. And now the women are taking a hand in it.'

Victorian state cricketers (left to right) Nance Clements who played for Clarendon, Ivy Cooksley (Semco) and Peggy Antonio (Raymonds) depart Melbourne by train for the 1933 Interstate series in Brisbane. Both Clements and outstanding leg-spin bowler Antonio were selected in the Australian team in 1934 and 1937.

Chapter 5

Old Rivalries

*'The majority of them were real class, I don't
mean playing cricket, but I mean in their lifestyle.'*
— Amy Hudson on the 1934 English team

It was a big jump for any cricketer from playing in a club or state team, to the possibility of being considered for an Australian team. Such a scenario is every cricketer's dream come true. No Australian team, whether women or men, no matter the sport, can ever escape the controversies associated with interstate rivalry, in particular the rivalry between New South Wales and Victoria. Such competitiveness dates from colonial times and its impact is felt in areas as diverse as economic policy, geographic borders, governance and culture. But in sports, especially team sports where numbers can be counted and statistics proffered, the rivalry is fierce. The controversies go deep, the divides are ingrained in Australian sports and sportspeople. Within a sporting code it bubbles away, sometimes overtly, sometimes behind the scenes, and invades all levels, from selection, governance and captaincy to crowd support and barracking.

From time to time, individual players move states to better their opportunities for selection. In the 1932–33 bodyline men's Test series there were nineteen Australian players in all – ten Victorians (although at least four of these had begun their state career elsewhere, including in Queensland and Western Australia), six from New South Wales and three from South

Australia. Their ages in 1932 ranged from twenty-year-old
Ernest Bromley to fifty-year-old Herbert Ironmonger, although
the latter had lied about his age on debut, and 'selectors no
doubt kept picking him because they lost track of his age amid
all the moves he made'. The average age of the men's team was
just over thirty, with the majority in their twenties, although it
is interesting to note that the two batsmen who sustained the
most serious injuries from bodyline were Bill Woodfull, aged
thirty-five, and Bert Oldfield, aged thirty-eight. New South
Wales and Victoria came to dominate the women's game, too.
This interstate rivalry did not escape the notice of the visiting
English captain, Betty Archdale, who saw its effect on the series:
'We knew each other and were a united group, whereas the
Australians, I think there was a bit of trouble between Victoria
and New South Wales, one sort of sensed, you know, that there
was a bit.'

As the English were visiting during the annual Australian
interstate series, selection could be closely tied to current form
and the correct processes followed. But, like any selection, there
were controversies, especially around the balance of players
from each state. Three experienced Australian selectors were
appointed and included one from each of the three main states –
Violet Hilliard from Victoria, Ruth Preddey from New South
Wales and Dorothy Waldron from Queensland.

Some players needed to work hard in order to catch the
selector's eye. Seventeen years old and not at school or in
work, part of Ruby Monaghan's commitment and dedication
to furthering her cricket had been her weekly travel by train
from Wollongong to play for the Annandale club in suburban
Sydney. Such a situation was not uncommon among male
cricketers trying to break into the state or national men's team.
Ruby recalled how she had set her sights on selection in the
New South Wales and Australian teams for the forthcoming
tour by the English team. To qualify she knew she needed more
than just weekly runs on the board and features in the Illawarra

newspapers; she needed to be noticed in Sydney. She recalled: 'I played a year in Illawarra and you weren't recognised much up in Sydney – the country girls – and we had a reporter from Port Kembla and he used to write up things then, you know, "lady cricketer was unrecognised" and say why I should have been in the team … that got me in.' Journalist and selector Ruth Preddey also stood by Ruby, as she 'was good for the country players, she stuck for them'.

When a benefit match was put on in Sydney for New South Wales teammate Peggy Knight, who had broken her leg, Ruby took her chance. 'They just had to pick me because there was so much in the paper about me not being picked. So, I went up and they put me in opening bat and they couldn't get me out, so from then on I stayed, played in the team.' Although primarily in the team as an opening batter, Ruby regarded herself as an all-rounder – 'just a medium bowler, got a few wickets' – in Illawarra and Sydney. She could also field in any position – 'I played everywhere, in close, outfield, in slips. I could go anywhere.' When she was picked for the Australian team at sixteen years of age her parents were excited – 'Me dad went mad!' As the only country player in the team, travelling up to Sydney to practise was difficult. 'See, it was all right for the girls who already lived up in Sydney, they were there, where I had to travel all the time. I couldn't get up all the time.'

Amy Hudson was working at McKenzie's, a food manufacturer in Bay Street, Glebe. It was factory work and, when it was announced that she was selected for the Australian team, her workmates 'were really pleased and bought me a beautiful suitcase'. The company gave her time off work – although unpaid, it was appreciated during the Depression. She didn't get the opportunity to practise much, but that was in part due to her team spirit. At club training:

> If I did go to practice, I'd rather bowl to my club mates
> you know, I'd bowl full tosses for them to learn strokes

around or so they could play. It wasn't a case of me supposedly being a star and that I owned the bat and the ball and I had to do all the batting. I liked to see the others getting a fair go, too. A lot of people are different to that, that was just my attitude.

The new suitcase was required as Amy hadn't travelled out of the Annandale district: 'I'd never been out of Sydney, you might as well say out of Annandale or just around the Sydney areas.' As a factory worker, the teenager did not have the same opportunities as some of the other players and was not part of the Peden set:

> The first time I went to Melbourne, you know, I felt real out of it, because the other people … seemed to be a lot more experienced than I was in all ways, all walks of life, if you can understand what I mean. And I think that was why I always used to sit in the back, in the dressing room, and people would think I was stuck up. But I wasn't stuck up. I was just, you know, shy.

What was to be a long career in the Australian team began with a false start:

> I went up to Brisbane. There were thirteen chosen but I was the thirteenth man, so we had all this hullabaloo and everything for sort of nothing. And then when we came back the Test was in Sydney. I didn't play there at all … they brought a Victorian girl up to be twelfth man, which was sort of stupid, and then we had the interstate and I did really well at the interstate. Then I was chosen in the third Test.

Nance Clements was the Victorian player called up to Sydney to be twelfth person instead of local Sydneysider Amy Hudson. Twenty-year-old Nance was on holidays with her family at

Hepburn Springs in Daylesford when the cricket selectors wanted to contact her. With few other options, the police were called to help – 'The police came looking for me.' Once located she still had to get from her holiday in Daylesford to Sydney. The logistics were confounding:

> The train service wasn't that hot in those days. My father had to find somebody with a car – and a lot of people didn't have cars – that was going to Melbourne. And finally my father contacted someone up in the hills that was going to Melbourne in a car, so we did about 90 miles an hour from Hepburn Springs to Spencer Street. I had to ring the lady next door, or my mother I think rang the lady next door, to get the key to get the cricket case and everything in it and get it to Spencer Street, and I remember stepping on that train and it moved off. But I was twelfth man; I never made the team.

Nance chose not to recount the controversy, featured widely in the newspapers at the time, regarding her rushed trip to Sydney only to be replaced in the Australian team by Barbara Peden, the captain's sister.

Other than for cricket games, Nance had never travelled within Australia. She worked as a typist at the Australian Paper Company – 'I got the job on my own, it was what you call today girl Friday, where you do everything and anything and it was a paper company and it was only the boss and the carrier and me. Well, you were inwards and outwards clerk, you did a bit of shorthand, interviewed and so forth.' Nance got her opportunity early in the English tour when selected for the Victoria versus England match held at the MCG on 7–8 December 1934. She remembered the excitement of making that team: 'You don't make a big deal about anything like that but it got around and the phone started ringing congratulating me and all that. That was really exciting getting in to the Victorian side.'

Victorian batswoman Lorna Kettels also had a chequered start to her Test career. Originally playing cricket for the Youldens team, she was selected to represent Victoria for an interstate series in Queensland. After this carnival an 'Australian' team was selected, which included Lorna, but of course there was not yet any opposition to play against. Once it was announced that England was touring in 1934–35, Lorna was selected in the first Australian team – 'the family thought it was fantastic' – and the players in her club 'rallied round, and if you went anywhere they sort of raised the money for you – more or less you had to finance yourself, sort of thing. And they got together, they'd raise finance for you, to help you along the way.' Lorna was working as a sales assistant, which she described as a 'counter jumper', at Love and Pollards, a drapery establishment in Sydney Road, Brunswick. 'Fortunately I used to have annual leave, they used to allow me my annual leave to coincide with the cricket.' But that support didn't last: 'It did interfere in the finish and I was asked to leave, sort of thing – it was too much time off.' Jobs were still hard to find:

> I was lucky enough there was a man that used to work for the Economic Cash Order Company in Melbourne and he was interested in women's cricket. He was secretary of that firm and he got me employed in it, and I finished up doing office work. He was very interested in all the girls in cricket, actually, especially the state and the English side, and he used to go along and help coach them. He was very good, Mr Richardson. He came from out Hawthorn way. He was very good and he helped quite a lot of us along.

Her club and local community also held social dances and ran raffles to support her interstate travel.

Outstanding Victorian spin bowlers Peggy Antonio and Anne Palmer hoped for selection in all three Tests. Both had been putting in long hours of private practice away from their club and state teams. Peggy thought she hadn't really focused on selection in the Australian team in 1934 but, when it happened, her family and friends were 'thrilled to bits. They thought a lot more about it than I did, it just seemed to be going over my head. Oh, yes you're going to play cricket for Australia, that's it, but they were all keen.' With their enthusiasm, however, came some unwanted pressure on the seventeen-year-old Peggy: 'I think it was their keenness that took a little bit of the shine off it for me, because the pressure became a bit intense, that you had to do something and I don't like pressure, or I didn't.' Peggy worked at Raymonds cardboard box factory (the sponsors of the women's team Raymonds) and found her co-workers and management supportive: 'The bosses were thrilled to bits, so were quite a lot of the personnel, and they did all kinds of things to help me ... from the money side of it.'

Left-arm wrist spinner Anne Palmer was nineteen years old in 1934 and working at Hartley's Sports store on Friday nights and Saturday mornings, 'which gave me pocket money, and my parents subsidised me at home, it was terribly hard'. When the English tour was announced, she had been playing cricket for a number of years and now set her sights on selection: 'I think it was the ambition of all girls who played for their state, and I think I played 1930–31, my first year [for the state side], and I feel it was Peggy's, too. And we played, and then you naturally felt you'd made the state side, well, you felt like you would like to play for your country as well.' Her parents were 'elated' with her selection in the team but 'money came into it in those days and we were not in very affluent circumstances at all – the Depression had started to find its way through'. Fortunately, Anne had an aunt and uncle who promised her £100 if she made the final selection for Australia 'to buy equipment, pads, bat, gloves, uniform. So that took a lot of pressure off my family, but they just happened to be in a position where they could at that stage – and £100 was a lot of money.'

The woman appointed as the Australian team manager was the selector, Sydney-based Ruth Preddey (born 1891). At forty-three years of age, she was considerably older than the average age of the players in her charge. Twenty-year-old Hilda Hills, the Australian wicketkeeper, described Preddey as 'very strict'. Sports editor of *The Australian Women's Weekly* from its inception in 1933, Preddey was a foundation member of the New South Wales and Australian Women's Cricket Council. She was a driving force in cricket in Australia, coaching and even developing a cricket bat for women that Slazenger manufactured and sold as the Ruth Preddey Model. The close relationship between cricketers who were also sports journalists for major city newspapers and magazines – notably Ruth Preddey, Pat Jarrett, Kathleen Commins, Dot Debnam – and the Australian team, certainly impacted on the cachet that the sport received and earned in the 1930s in Australia.

Like New South Wales and Victoria, England too had some internal divides. In the north of England the game was most popular with girls working in factories and industrial offices. In the south, most of the players were drawn from the large schools and training colleges for women. Reportedly there were over a hundred teams playing cricket throughout the country. No prizes for guessing where the first representative Test team was largely drawn from. Each player needed to meet a number of criteria to be selected, the minimum being proficiency at cricket, the financial means to fund the trip, and the ability to take six months out of their usual lives to make the 13,000 mile trip to Australia and then on to New Zealand. Other factors were also considered, such as a general fitness, and the desire to tour with a group of friends and like-minded women. Obvious issues of the complex English class system were also at play, just as they were in the Australian team.

The woman appointed to captain the travelling English team was Betty Archdale, who would later migrate to Australia following World War II and make her home outside Sydney.

Betty Archdale (born 1907) played cricket from the age of six at Bedales, the first co-educational school in England, located in Hampshire. Her mother, Helen Archdale, was a suffragette, who was arrested in 1912 for breaking windows in an act of civil disobedience, and was subsequently imprisoned for two months in Holloway Prison. At twelve years of age, Betty was sent to St Leonards School in St Andrews, Scotland:

> You know, the golf place, which was one of the girls' schools started along the line of the boys' schools – no nonsense. We had prefects and fags [younger pupils who acted as servants to older pupils]. Sport was compulsory and we played whatever we had to play according to the term – lacrosse one term, hockey the next and cricket the next, and those you blank well played every afternoon!

Of St Leonards, she said:

> We had very good [cricket] coaching ... and I played regularly.
>
> One of the reasons that I liked cricket [is that] I could throw. I was one of the few girls in those days who had a pretty good throw. I couldn't bowl so I was always – I fielded out in the deep – and it wasn't the cricket, it was just being able to stand there ... and think about all the things that were happening. It makes me laugh when I think of it now, but I used to love cricket because that was when I really had a bit of time to myself, because we were kept on the double all day.

Of course, social class and proximity to a cricket ground played a large part in Betty's continued involvement with cricket after graduation:

> I lived out in Kent, roughly 30 miles from London, and we had golf, of course, and we were very lucky the women's cricket, the chairman and secretary, a couple of dear old ladies, they lived just a few miles away and in their grounds they had a farm [with] a lovely little cricket ground and a hockey ground, so we played hockey there in winter and cricket in summer and, of course, there was plenty of tennis and golf.

According to Archdale, the Women's Cricket Association in England had been started by women 'who were all, I think you would call them upper class, they were certainly upper middle-class, and very keen on behaviour and your dress being correct. You know, they set a standard that I think was good.' The English model was non-competitive: 'We weren't allowed to have a cup or a competition, and each club, Comp was the one I played for down in Kent, we just decided what other club we would like to play and we organised to play them and if we didn't like them, well, we didn't play them again'. She added, 'I mean you could be a factory worker and still play cricket ... but the sort of traditions of non-competition, it didn't matter whether you won or lost, the great thing was to have fun. Them were the days!'

Most of the Australian cricketers spoke fondly and respectfully of Betty Archdale. Nell McLarty described her as 'absolutely superb, in fact she was more like an Australian person than an English person. She fraternised with us and was so friendly and a beautiful sense of humour and a great leader.' Nance Clements retained a friendship with Archdale throughout her life, not overly close but the type of friendship that can be picked up and rekindled via a phone call at any time. Ruby Monaghan judged her as a marvellous and good opposition captain. Amy Hudson remarked, 'You couldn't help but like Betty Archdale.'

Of the other women in the English team, less was known, and few of the Australians knew what to expect. Amy Hudson remembered: 'I didn't know a thing, but they were a good team.'

The class difference with many of the Australians was profound. Amy said, 'The majority of them were real class. I don't mean playing cricket, but I mean in their lifestyle.' She named Mary Spear as one of their good bowlers. Amy's shyness was both a positive and a negative in this situation: 'I just kept to myself. There's an old saying, "The looker on sees most", and so I was sitting in the back and I could pick who I liked and who I didn't like. But there wasn't too many of them that I didn't like.'

Anne Palmer found the English team:

> Very professional, very friendly nice people, delightful people but most professional and they seemed to be, they had had so much practice as a team, which had a distinct advantage over us. Individually, probably, we were better but, as a team, they were far superior and I think it was because they had had so much time together.

Lorna Kettels agreed: 'They were a team and they were sort of together the whole time. But I think travel does that to you, doesn't it, brings you together.' Lorna recalled being impressed by some of the English players, including Betty Archdale and Betty Snowball, and 'the girl [Mary] Taylor, the fast bowler, she was a vivacious sort of a person, she was one of the youngest in the team.' She recalled Myrtle Maclagan as 'a very quiet type of person ... but on the whole they were all quite a nice group of people'.

If the Australian women didn't know much about the English cricketers, how much did the English know about the Australians? Betty Archdale had a rather serendipitous introduction to Australia. At school in Scotland she had completed a project in geography on the Gulf of Carpentaria, which she had done well in – 'I got 98 per cent, so I was favourably inclined towards Australia'. The feeling was cemented with the arrival of an Australian girl, Mavis Mackenzie, at her boarding school. 'We got on like a house on fire. She was a real shocker – we had a whale of a time, always in the wrong place doing the wrong thing, you know.' As a result, Betty thought that Australia 'was a long way away, but it was fun'.

The selection of the English team was primarily decided on an individual's ability to pay. Archdale recalled: 'We were given the dates, you know roughly, and I think we were told the cost, which really makes me blush – it was something like eighty pounds round the world – Australia, New Zealand and home by sea. Of course, there was no flying in those days, but you wouldn't get far now [on that money], would you?' Archdale submitted her name: 'I worked out I was living in a flat in London, studying for the bar, but I worked out it would cost me eighty pounds to live there for six months anyway.' She also figured she could easily take time off: 'I held up being called for the bar. I thought, oh well, I better wait until I get back. So yes, I was in a very good position – a student – and what's six months?' She recalled:

> The others were a mixed group. There were some teachers – Grace Morgan was a public servant, Betty Snowball was a teacher, Molly Hide in those days ran her own farm; I think her father was probably still alive and she was his assistant. An awful lot of them were what we now call 'leisured women' ... or they were young enough for their parents to say, you can take six months or nine months off from a course, it's fairly easy. But we sent our names in, had a selection committee and we were very lucky. We had Peta Taylor, I think she taught, she was a fast bowler, she was excellent. Little Burletson, who would never have been in any representative team, she was a sweetie ... she was a nice kid.

With the need for a contribution of eighty pounds each, the team was not strictly representative of the best talent available in England. Archdale estimated that well over half the women would have been selected for England on merit:

We weren't a complete lot of rabbits, but we did have a tail end that would never have really represented England. But they had fun out here and they played in the local matches. But there was a little bit of comment when we got back to England, [that] we weren't really an English side. I wonder what they were complaining about – we didn't lose a match!

Like the feeling between Victoria and New South Wales, Archdale detected 'there was a bit of feeling between the north and the south of England':

It's that social class business isn't it, it's priceless. There were quite a few clubs that were factory clubs, they'd have a cricket team, we used to play them, it was fun. At Comp we were on the edges of London and there was a lot of industry ... further up north, Grey's End ... it was quite extraordinary. I think the sort of social background was much stronger there. Here [in Australia], it doesn't mean two pins.

The voyage out to Australia cemented the English team bonding. Archdale considered they were successful:

... merely because we were a touring team and we'd had that lovely time on board ship ... A few of us knew each other quite well, but on the whole we didn't. By the time we got here we knew each other absolutely back to front ... whereas the Australian team, I don't know how long before a match it was picked, not very long.

The English team practised on board: 'We were pretty fit and we played a lot on the ship. We had nets, we used to play and, of course, we swam in the pool. Oh yes, I think we were pretty fit and, of course, we were all pretty young.'

Entrusting the captaincy to Archdale came as a surprise to the young lawyer:

> I have always been a bit puzzled …I wasn't captain of my club, you know. I captained occasionally when someone was away or something, but …. I didn't expect to be chosen as captain, I was surprised … There was some much better cricketers in the team than I was, but for some reason the powers that be, who really boiled down to Miss Cox and Mrs Heron-Maxwell, must have thought I'd keep it steady.

Unlike the Australian team that had the luxury of playing at home and could be selected on form from the interstate series and state matches, the English touring team of 1934–35 was selected months in advance. The touring party included: Myrtle Maclagan, Betty Snowball (vice-captain), Molly Hide, Mollie Child, Joy Partridge, Betty Archdale (captain), Doris Turner, Joy Liebert, Mary (Peta) Taylor, Mary Spear, Carol Valentine, Mary Richards, Grace Morgan, Mary Burletson and manager and player Betty Green.

Marjorie Pollard, writing in the English magazine *Women's Cricket*, devoted a page to the cricket profiles of the English women who were selected for the tour:

> It was a difficult job to choose the fifteen players who are to go to Australia. There were applications from many more players than fifteen – and all were 'good and true'. But fifteen was the limit, and so fifteen had to be chosen. On another page will be found the itinerary, vastly exciting and exhausting. The players will live together for six months. They will have to endure heat, dust, travelling; but the fifteen chosen are more than equal to such a trip.

She referred to each woman by their surname and initials only, preserving the formality and traditions of cricket writing. In her descriptions, Pollard deliberately concentrates solely on their cricketing ability. Many of the women would already have been known to the faithful and regular readers of *Women's Cricket*. The team had a lot of promise. She described captain Betty Archdale as 'an experienced and travelled person. Sane, sensible, level-headed and broad minded. A good bat, a willing field, and an enthusiast.' Vice-captain Betty Snowball, also the wicketkeeper, would open the batting with Myrtle Maclagan, and they would 'make a perfect opening pair'. Myrtle Maclagan, Pollard was sure, 'is going to be a thorn in the side of the Australian teams. The two- and three-day matches will suit her admirably. Maclagan is a wonderful bat – she never fails to make runs, but she must make them in her own time. She will do really well in Australia.' Molly Hide she described as 'a far more dashing run getter, and thinks she is doing badly if she cannot get a four in every over; a beautiful field and a good bowler'. Joy Partridge, she wrote 'is a sound, careful bat and a brilliant field, and a slow bowler whom one is apt to treat too lightly'. She claimed that fast bowler Mary Taylor on hard Australian wickets should make the ball 'talk. Length must be her watchword and then she will do great things.' Doris Turner, she said, 'is another bowler determined and persevering, a batsman who has improved enormously this season; always a trier and always dead keen'. All-rounder Joy Liebert she described as 'an extraordinarily useful player to have on a side, as she can do most things well'. Bowler Carol Valentine was as 'fast off the pitch, with a ball that swings in from the leg side and then straightens out – a nightmare to play if it comes early in an innings'. Bowler Mary Spear she said, 'keeps a length and bowls accurately for long spells'. Grace Morgan the reserve wicketkeeper was 'quiet and refined in all she does, and her batting, if not forceful, is accurate and neat, and good for 50 any day'. Mollie Child she described as 'a forcing bat, always a joy to watch, plays the game with terrific zest and has a beautiful straight drive'. Regarding all-rounder Mary Richards she claimed, 'her fielding is superb and her batting careful and correct'. The inexperienced Mary Burletson she described as an 'all-rounder who will no doubt improve on the tour'. She thought player and manager Betty Green had a difficult task, 'that she will carry out with grace and efficiency. As a player, Green is a keen, beautiful field, and a steady bat. Her ability as an entertainer will no doubt give a great deal of pleasure on many occasions'. Pollard farewelled the team with, 'There then, are the players. There are plenty of bowlers – they will be needed, the tour is long. While envying them, we wish them the best of luck, and give them the assurance that we have utter and implicit faith in their ability to represent English Women's Cricket.'

The Australian press was less interested in the women's cricket profiles and more interested in their personal profiles. Manager Betty Green, a former hockey player with experience of overseas tours, was close in age to the players themselves, and she and Captain Betty Archdale were the only team members authorised to deal with the Australian press. Speaking to the Perth *Daily News* on arrival in Australia, Green profiled the English players for the newspaper and, like Pollard, attempted to control the message, refraining from any physical descriptions of the players. Instead, she outlined their employment status, noting that Valentine and Maclagan were the only two without jobs: 'Some of them have secured six-months' leave from their work for the trip, but others have had to give up good jobs and try for others when they return to England.' Seven members of the team were sports mistresses:

> or rather, games-mistresses, as they are called in England …
> One member of the team, Miss G.A. Morgan, holds a position in the Civil Service and is captain of the Civil Service Women's cricket team. Miss Betty Archdale, B.A., L.L.D., is a law student, and Miss J. Liebert – the baby of the team – is studying at an art school in Bushey.

The *Daily News* noted that Green had informed them 'that the team have no mascots — but they do carry around with them a huge model English lion, and a sailor-boy doll, presented to them by the officers of the *Cathay*. But they do not officially pin any faith whatsoever to mascots.'

The newspaper wanted more personal descriptions, and made their own judgements based on physical appearance, especially hair colour and clothing style:

> Probably the smartest frocker and acknowledged to be the best dancer in the team is Miss E.P. Snowball, the vice-captain, who, quaintly enough, is a brunette. Miss M. Hide, a young agricultural student, celebrated her 21st birthday on the ship in the Bay of Biscay. There was appropriate celebration. The brownest-faced of the team is the captain, Betty Archdale, who favors in headdress a straight Eton crop, the long forelock of which is held back with a clip-pin. Probably the most vivacious of them is Miss Tyler [Turner]. She has fair hair and is often confused with Miss Taylor, but not in appearance. Miss Taylor is a brunette. She is a photography enthusiast, and usually has a camera slung across her shoulder.

The voyage report given to the team on their disembarkation from the *Cathay* stated: 'The English Ladies' Cricket Team, who have been favorite personalities of the voyage, are out to teach Australian ladies how cricket should be played.'

While the English team was united on their long sea voyage, many of the Australians keenly felt the impact of the interstate rivalry within their own team. Victorian Lorna Kettels reflected: 'You were sort of segregated. The Victorians, in my estimation, stayed with Victorians, the New South Wales with the New South Wales, and that's how it was.' As ever in cricket, part of the issue lay in the selection of the captain.

Betty Archdale spoke about her rival captain (and later good friend) Margaret Peden:

> I thought she had a pretty rough time. I may be wrong but I had a feeling that the so and sos down in Victoria, for some reason, thought that somebody else should be captain. I don't know enough about the local [scene]. Margaret seemed to have done a very good job, but it was quite obvious to me that she wasn't popular. You could sort of sense that with the others.

Archdale considered that part of Margaret's trouble was 'she wasn't a good enough player, you know. I mean she was a good cricketer, but she wasn't – the captain wants to have something a bit more and I don't think she ever made a score and she didn't bowl, did she? So I think she had a rough trot.'

Such was Archdale's opinion of Margaret Peden remembered fifty-six years after the event. Yet in her summary of the tour in her 1936 report published in the *Women's Cricket* magazine, Archdale described Peden as the 'much needed steadying influence on the Australian batting'.

The English team brought with them a large black scorebook to begin the chronicle of matches between the countries. Embossed on the front cover was 'The Empire Cumulative Cricket Scoring Book'. Inside, the blank pages would record the tour and held the promise of restoring cricket to its rightful place in the Empire, back to its pedestal, unsullied by bodyline. To live up to the promise of being once again a 'humanising game', the game desperately needed the participation of women. The Australian summer awaited.

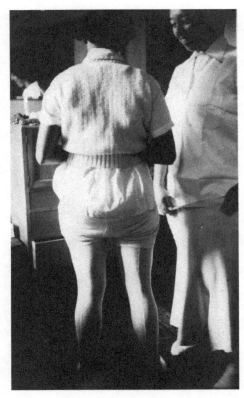

Did women wear cricket clothing that allowed the greatest possible freedom of action? A candid image of Australian teammates Peggy Antonio (left) and Amy Hudson dressing for a match that reveals their many layers. Antonio was scornful of the white lisle stockings: 'They would have looked better on a corpse,' she quipped.

Chapter 6
The Clothing Divide

'then ye contented your souls
With the flannelled fools at the wicket
Or the muddied oafs at the goals.'
— Rudyard Kipling, 'The Islander', 1902

'Flannelled fools', Kipling wrote in 1902 to deplore and ridicule those cricketers who shirked military service for their country during the Boer War. Controversy has long accompanied sports clothing, with cricketing attire undergoing many changes and adaptations over the years. Indeed, pads and gloves were once both frowned upon. When Lord Frederick Beauclerk (born 1773) first saw leg pads he declared them 'unfair to the bowler', while Charles Cowden Clarke (born 1787) writing on the use of gloves referred to 'the dandyism which the gentlemen of the present day have been compelled to resort to, in order to preserve their precious fingers from the fury of the bowler: I mean that of playing in stuffed mittens!' Invited to contribute because he was the oldest living member of the MCC, Sir Spencer Ponsonby-Fane (born 1824) wrote in the introduction to Lord Harris's 1920 chronicle of the MCC:

I once saw Mr Budd, a wonderfully good-looking man, perfectly dressed in breeches and stockings, bowling fast underhand. The ordinary dress of the day included a flannel jacket of short cut and a tall hat, and I can say that the latter was no more uncomfortable than the hard billycock which succeeded it as headwear. Wisden was the first professional who wore a straw hat before the introduction of the cricket cap ... There were no such things as pads or finger-guards in those days ... When leg-pads were first introduced they were worn under trousers, as though the hardy cricketer was ashamed of his cowardice in wearing them.

White or cream was also not the sport's original colour. W.G. Grace recounted some style changes by 1909:

> At one time all cricketers wore top hats ... and when I began playing cricket nearly everyone wore caps, and the few exceptions wore 'bowlers' ... At this time nearly everyone wore coloured shirts and black boots or shoes, then brown boots were worn, until everyone by degrees took to wearing white ones. It was also the custom to wear belts with clasps in place of the scarfs which are now generally worn ... Pads or gloves were not so generally used as they are now.

What women wore on the cricket field played a major part in their delicate negotiations to play the game. In this instance their cricket clothing can be viewed as a compromise. The clothing, or outward appearance of women and girls, was designed to reinforce femininity and not challenge the status quo. But what did men wear on the cricket field in the 1930s? Their clothing was dictated by a number of elements – comfort, safety, tradition, fashion, official rules and personal preference. Most information can only be surmised from photographs, because the subject was rarely thought worthy of discussion in newspapers, biographies or similar sources, except when it was an object of derision by Australian crowds, as had been the case when Jardine sported his harlequin cap on the field. The harlequin cap was earned at Oxford where no more than twelve were given to men in residence at the university each year.

Men generally wore long-sleeved cricket shirts, with many rolling up the sleeves to free their arms for batting or bowling. During the bodyline tour of 1932–33, Australian cricketers, like Victor Richardson and Bill Ponsford, often wore their long sleeves rolled up. English bowler Harold Larwood rolled his sleeves up to bowl. At least three of the MCC English cricketers on that tour, including Douglas Jardine and Nawab of Pataudi, wore white neckerchiefs inside their shirts, probably for extra protection from the sun. Don Bradman is often photographed with his sleeves neatly rolled up tightly to just above his elbows, and the collar turned up, possibly to protect his neck from the sun, even in official portraits. It was a signature look, and no doubt copied by many school children, backyard and grade cricketers across the country. Short-sleeved shirts were frowned upon in men's cricket.

When they toured Australia in 1932–33, the English men cricketers wore Sea Island cotton shirts, the cotton grown in the British West Indies and manufactured in Lancashire, a fitting confluence of Empire. Tariff protection and free trade were hot topics as countries began to come out of the Depression. While in Australia, the English men's team were presented with woollen ties in the hope that the 'wearing of these ties overseas by the Englishmen will undoubtedly be a good advertisement for Australia' and its wool industry. It was known that male cricketers shined the cricket ball on their woollen socks, or on the inside of their caps to take advantage of any hair oil present. As for the fashions in facial hair, none wore beards or mutton chops – as in the days of Dave Gregory (full beard), Fred Spofforth (moustache) and Charlie Bannerman (moustache and mutton chops) – all looking boyish 'clean faced' as the day they 'entered the world'.

Bradman wore loose trousers with no belt or coloured scarf or braces to keep them up, but with a mechanism to bring them in at the waist. He neatly tucked his shirt into the trousers. In fact, these trousers were most likely the Selfixo beltless trouser, which had gained popularity among male cricketers because it featured no buttons and 'fit neatly and trimly and prevent the shirt from riding up'. Described as fitting:

> Comfortably and neatly on the hips – no buttons, belts, buckles or braces – the patent elastic waistband ensures comfort with smart appearance no matter how the wearer bends or twists, and prevents the shirt riding up. Selfixo trousers are thoroughly comfortable for any sport or for general wear; in fact they represent the only real improvement in trouser construction for years. The non-perishing elastic of the waistband is unconditionally guaranteed against washing and cleaning.

The Selfixo trousers were manufactured in Perth and made in cream gabardine and offered 'the greatest possible freedom of action in every movement in any game'. They were recommended for men in golf, tennis, cricket, bowling, fishing, sailing, hiking and cycling. In Queensland the Elasta-Strap, self-supporting trouser, was on sale, ranging from 14s.6d to 30s. a pair, depending on material. Washing cream cricket trousers in hot water was recommended to remove ergot, a fungi picked up through grass stains – 'cold water bachelor methods are of no avail'. Male cricketers in the hot summer days of Queensland, at least, with the exception of schoolboys under sixteen, were not permitted to wear shorts, but rather 'correct cricket costume', defined according to established custom as 'white boots or shoes, white socks, long cream or white trousers, a white shirt with collar and sleeves, and a cap or white hat', and a 'kind smile' in case Jardine throws the ball to Larwood, 'in the hope that the heart of the body-liner will melt'.

As we have seen, Australian batsmen did begin to wear some form of chest and forearm protection against the English fast-bowling attack. In the England versus West Indies cricket series played in England in May 1933, English batsman Elias 'Patsy' Hendren wore a prototype style of helmet, described as a three peak cap, designed and made by his wife Minnie Hendren, against the bowling of the West Indies, notably Learie Constantine. Hendren had himself been hit by Larwood in 1931. 'The West Indies match was a good test for the cap,' Hendren said:

> One of Constantine's deliveries was like a bullet and if it had hit me on the head I would have gone to kingdom come. The wife made the cap of cloth and lined it with rubber. It is a very fine job, but a little heavy on a hot day. Nevertheless, it protects the temples. I don't mind having my face altered and my teeth knocked out if my head is protected. I don't think other players will get similar caps. They will wear pads and abdominal and chest protectors, but they haven't courage to wear a head protector.

Concern for the safety of the head was not new. During a match in 1870 between Nottinghamshire and the MCC, batsman George Summers was struck so severely on the head by a ball that the injury proved fatal. The next batter, Richard Daft, came to the wicket with a towel wrapped round his head for protection. More amusingly, in the days before safety matches, there was a report of a male cricketer called Parnell catching fire at a match in Dartmouth in England, when a ball struck his thigh while he was batting and ignited a box of matches in his pocket. He was stumped when he jumped and clasped his leg, but later ruled not out.

Arriving in London for the Test matches in 1934 the Australian men's team ordered over £800 worth of clothing from David Wax, a tailor in the East End of London, who had also fitted out the team during the 1930 Test series. Wax, who was not interested in cricket and when invited 'was bored and did not stay long at Lord's', stated, 'I found the Australians a totally different physical type from English cricketers; they are longer in the arm, broader in the shoulders, and strangely different in muscular development. They presented a new and absorbing tailoring problem,' which Wax solved by 'getting them to parade slowly past me naked, after practice in the dressing room at Lord's, enabling me to sketch each'. An absorbing tailoring problem indeed.

So, did women wear cricket clothing that allowed 'the greatest possible freedom of action'? Prior to their arrival in Australia, news of what the English women would wear preceded them. The team had already debuted their new uniform – divided skirts and short-sleeved blouses – during a practice match against 'The Rest' at Northampton. *The Referee* noted: 'The English women cricketers coming to Australia next summer will present a very natty appearance on the field. The cricketing uniform is a dress of white with a divided skirt, blouse, sleeves to the elbow, and stockings.' Betty Archdale later commented, 'The stockings themselves were quite all right, they were no trouble, but, oh dear, the suspender belts we used to have to wear to keep them up, they were sheer murder.' A report in the *Albany Advertiser* added that they would also be wearing 'a shady hat' and that 'several of the players did not want to wear stockings'. One of these was most likely the English captain Betty Archdale:

> I got into an awful lot of trouble. Miss Cox was secretary and Mrs Heron-Maxwell was, I think, president – I'm not certain and they just happened to live nearby – the ground I played on was on their field. But they used to go over to Switzerland every summer holidays for a couple of months, and I'm afraid one year when they were away I argued very effectively that knee-length stockings were long stockings, and when they came back they found us wearing these knee stockings. Oh, they were angry. But, of course, I was quite right.

It was idiotic. We played in quite short skirts but we still had these wretched – it wasn't the stockings that were a nuisance, it was the suspender belt to keep them up! Oh, Miss Cox was furious, she was very rude to Mother about that.

Archdale further reminisced, 'I wouldn't say the stockings actually made any difference to our play. They were a nuisance. They used to take a long time to put on, keeping them up was always a bit of a problem, you could feel the belt.'

The English magazine *Women's Cricket*, written and published by player–author Marjorie Pollard, carried advertising from many sporting goods and clothing manufacturers promoting appropriate cricket shoes, stockings, dresses, skirts, shirts, ties, blazers, cricket balls and bats and, what was deemed, the 'Svelte Belt' for holding up the stockings. In the Australian team's final match in England in 1937 against Surrey, reportedly Mollie Flaherty 'bowled so hard that one stocking descended, and she then rolled both stockings down and they became ankle socks'.

Some controversy and debates in this era centred around appropriate clothing for all sportswomen. In 1932 a local official in Collingwood, Melbourne, Councillor Marshall, declared that women's cricket was a 'burlesque and a leg show', and that the girls 'should be rocking cradles instead of running around cricket ovals'. This statement was challenged by the Sans Souci women's cricket club in Sydney, where women wore cream trousers and where the average age of women playing cricket was eighteen. Captain Doreen Blake commented, 'There is more leg show in the street than at a girls' cricket match.' Hazel Pritchard replied to the Melbourne councillor, 'We won't neglect the cradle when our time comes.' Together the women declared Councillor Marshall 'nasty-minded'.

One Australian woman didn't get the memo about the need to maintain a strict uniform policy when she presided over a dinner in February 1934, held for visiting interstate players in

the Girls Secondary Schools cricket tournament. Dr Constance
D'Arcy, a renowned obstetrician and gynaecologist, rose to
speak to the girls:

> I may be walking where angels fear to tread, but I was
> surprised to find that skirts are still worn by cricketers.
> On my way to the university on Saturday, to view my
> first women's cricket match, I passed two sports girls clad
> in red slacks and neat white shirts, and I thought that it
> would certainly brighten up the university if I was to see
> two elevens in similar garb. Your skirts look neat, but I
> think slacks are the normal and better cricket garb, and,
> since the Duchess of York has cast her vote in favour of
> shorts for tennis, I feel that I am in good company.

Dr D'Arcy was not without a sense of humour when she told
the girls, 'I was not quite sure upon what I should talk to you,
and when I consulted a friend on the matter I was warned not
to mention "body-line". I promised to be as silent as an "oyster"
about it, but was informed that it would be sufficient if I was as
silent as Jardine.' English captain Douglas Jardine, of course, had
just published his book on the Ashes bodyline tour.

The Australian women also had some firm ideas as to the
suitability of their cricket attire. Nell McLarty recalled the
Australian women 'were about the first team to go into culottes'.
'We were really smart,' she said:

> but the thing was those terrible stockings we had to
> wear. They were lisle and they were long, and we had to
> wear a suspender belt to keep them up and Peggy and I
> couldn't stand them and we'd take ours and put them on
> at the last minute before we went out, because we played
> in tennis socks and you have more freedom, oh it was
> really terrible.

Peggy Antonio dryly added her view on the white stockings: 'Shall we say, they would have looked better on a corpse.'

Ruby Monaghan in Wollongong was used to playing in long trousers in her local competition: 'I liked the long trousers myself. They were like just a bib in the front, long trousers with a bib.' When selected for the Australian team she had to wear the divided skirt and white stockings – 'Oh, they're terrible,' she recalled. Amy Hudson remembered, 'you were playing in white cotton stockings and a dress down past, nearly past down to your ankles'.

One of the impacts of English and other overseas women's teams touring Australia was that they brought with them different uniform styles. Betty Archdale stated: 'My recollection is people thought our uniform was pretty hot stuff.'

By the first Test in Brisbane, the Australian team had rethought their uniform. Margaret Peden had submitted a new cricket costume to the national association at a meeting in early December 1934, 'in the style of a divided skirt in linen material ... to replace the present knee-length frock'. Nance Clements commented, 'I liked the divided skirt, they were a great idea, the divided skirts. The white stockings – no.' Lorna Kettels recalled she played in a skirt that was:

> ... an inch or two inches below your knee, white cotton stockings and you had a cap – yes, we had white caps in those days too. And then, of course, when we got to the Test, when the English girls played in culottes – that's what they're called, I think – we got the idea that we'd like culottes too, and that's when they were all measured and [they were] made by David Jones. And when they were delivered, sort of, everybody had everybody else's outfit and by the time we sorted ourselves out some of them were too big, some were too small, sort of thing, you know, but still white stockings ... We used to wear boots, boots with sprigs in them – [but] only for batting

on turf. You couldn't bat on the coir matting with them because you would get stuck.

It was thought the English women had an advantage, as they were used to playing on turf in boots that were suitable. Australian women, usually playing on concrete and malthoid and coir, only played in boots when at the University of Sydney turfed 'square', or at interstate carnivals on the turf wickets of major cricket grounds.

The newspapers reported:

> The news that members of the Australian team will wear short divided skirts and short-sleeved blouses, instead of the usual one-piece frocks below the knees, is not surprising to sportswomen. England is sponsoring much of the movement towards divided skirts for team games. The English cricket team won much approval when the girls appeared at the Melbourne Cricket-ground recently in their trim Aertex divided skirts well above their knees, with long white stockings and short-sleeved blouses.

Aertex fabric, a British invention, was a woven fabric designed on a cellular pattern that permitted free circulation of air through the fabric. It utilised the same Sea Island Cotton as worn by the English male cricketers in 1932–33. Although it could be imported, it was not manufactured in Australia until 1939.

The touring English manager–player Betty Green reflected on the English uniform: 'Our uniform (specially thought out by Miss Hatten and her committee) was on the whole satisfactory and was much admired everywhere.' Admiration was one thing but practicality for a manager was another, she continued, saying, 'The divided skirts, being made of Cellular naturally lost their shape because they were either washed hurriedly by us or sent haphazard to the nearest laundry, little time being allowed in our programmes for domestic matters.' She saw other issues too, including 'the possibility of a gap between skirt and shirt', and the need for a larger brim on the hats. Despite these issues, at least the clothes 'didn't really need ironing' and 'no one was laid out by the sun'.

Australian women officials were prepared to follow their English sisters in enforcing a strict uniform policy for women playing cricket. Betty Archdale said, 'I think we were probably, both here and in England, very anxious not to offend anyone, you know, by being too daring.' Marjorie Pollard in an editorial in *Women's Cricket* held the line through 1936, when she railed against the push for socks rather than stockings: 'I am fearful of a future that brings change too rapidly.' Her conservatism was supported by knowledge of the historic struggle, she reminded her readers, that 'it is not those who were in the fight for women's cricket when it was fiercest and most difficult who are anxious to appear as if dressed for tennis or soft-ball and party games'. She warned, 'caution at the right moment can never be misplaced'.

As they toured around Australia the English team provoked many comments regarding their attire. When the English arrived in Perth, Western Australia, for the first of their warm-up matches against state sides, they featured on the front page of the Perth *Daily News*. What they wore to practise at the ground caused comment:

> A hybrid kind of one-piece garment, which could not be classified as frock suit, shirt and shorts or divided skirt, yet appears to embody the features of all, was worn by the members of the English Women's Cricket Association Touring Team (their official title) when they practised on the W.A.C.A ground yesterday and today. It was a kind of 'romper' suit, tailored and one-piece with a shirt top, and a lower part which was either pleated shorts or divided skirt, worn very short, and giving the appearance of a kilt. It could not have been more suitably devised for the Australian climate. The garment has short

sleeves well above the elbow, and open neck, while long
white stockings, white shoes with spiked leather soles
and white hats (rarely worn) of Aertex lined with green
gauze, make up a suitable and becoming sub-tropical
cricket garb for women. Cream flannel blazers with the
monogram W.C.A.T.T. on the pocket, were worn to and
from the ground.

It was noted that the average age of the team was twenty-four;
'The members care more about cricket than clothes, but they
all like dancing, and they all like ice-cream.' The local Western
Australian team would wear slacks in their match against the
English women, despite slacks being banned in England, and
Western Australia being the only state side to wear them.
The local newspaper stated: 'for years, women's costume on
the cricket field has been the subject of keen controversy ... the
English will wear regulation skirts and blouses ... somehow we
fancy that our girls will look smarter in their slacks.'

Playing in Sydney at the SCG, Amy Hudson noted the
comments were not restricted to their cricketing attire, with the
women's hair provoking reactions among the all-male members
of the SCG, who were shocked by what they witnessed and
demanded conformity:

> I remember when we played on the cricket ground,
> because I had long hair, we didn't get allowed in the
> members stand, we were all put over in the Sheridan
> Stand, but some of the old members there were saying,
> 'Oh, women with long hair!' ... but then you finally had
> to get a hair net and put your hair up because 'women
> with long hair!'

When the English team arrived in Queensland, Carlie Hansen
of *The Courier-Mail* commented, 'The English girls will wear
the divided skirt which has also been adopted by the New South

Wales team, but, according to reports, does not appeal to the masculine sense of beauty, although most admit it is most sensible. The Queensland team will wear pleated tunics, finishing 2 in. above the knee.'

The English team arrived in Brisbane by the Kyogle mail train and the Queensland weather gave them a 'stewing welcome'. *The Courier-Mail* described 'The English girl cricketers, sun-browned, sleeveless, and stockingless laughed and made the best of the heat when they came into Brisbane on the Sydney express yesterday. They were cheered by the crowd on the platform, and hurried off to their hotel, to look for the coldest baths they've got.' Carlie Hansen reported, 'Clad in summer frocks, with stockingless brown legs, they tried their best to defy the heat, which one member of the team cheerfully said was "not as hot as the Red Sea".' Captain and lawyer Betty Archdale refused to be drawn by the press on the topic of shorts for women playing cricket:

> 'Ah, no, I'm not going to be dragged into that controversy. We have met teams in greatly varied costumes since we came to Australia, where there seems to be no fixed rule for individual club attire, particularly in the country. One country team even turned out in slacks ... I have no opinion on slacks or shorts, or shirts or skirts. I believe you've had some arguments here about these things, and I'm keeping out of controversies'.

The English team, she added, wore divided skirts, with shirts and hats all made of Aertex. The divided skirt gave all the freedom of movement a cricketer could need. Archdale confirmed: 'And we think they look well, too.'

Photographs taken by Betty Green and possibly Doris Turner of the English and Australian women playing cricket on this tour are quite revealing. Many of the Australian women photographed while batting against England in 1934 didn't wear batting gloves, including the players across the three main states – Ruby Monaghan, Nell McLarty, Essie Shevill, Hazel Pritchard and Joyce Brewer – although Kath Smith from Queensland did wear batting gloves. Both Ruby Monaghan and Essie Shevill, who were both short of stature, wore cricket dresses or skirts way too long for them that seemed to get caught in the top of their batting pads. Ruby also wore a white peaked cap. Without exception, all the white stockings on every woman in every photograph are always bunched and wrinkled at the knees. The Victorian team all wore sheer rather than white stockings, together with white ankle socks, and white cloth caps.

After the English toured Australia and New Zealand, player–manager Betty Green reflected on the variety of uniforms she had encountered:

> The Australian and NSW XI's copied our skirts, making them longer and in linen which hung well but crushed. As for the other state teams – Western Australia looked somewhat irregular in 'slacks' (white trousers, not all of the same material), Victoria had cotton dresses, and Queensland tunics, all very long. Stockings were worn by every team except the country ones, as were caps, a small percentage having white hats which looked nice but blew off.

In New Zealand, she remarked, the types of uniform were the same, except she noted no one had stockings, until the Test match when the New Zealand Test team wore divided skirts 'and put on white stockings in our honour, and hated them!'. The Australian women persisted, according to the English, with divided skirts that were too long for comfortable cricket. By 1936–37 advertisements for divided skirts worn at least six inches above the knee were appearing in clothing advertisements in the English magazine *Women's Cricket*.

The Australian women's uniforms for the 1934 Tests against England had been hastily made at David Jones. As we shall see, in preparation for the Australian women's return tour to England and Holland in 1937, the women were sent patterns to make, or have made, their own shirts and divided skirts. These were made at the players' own expense. Nance Clements had two lots made, plus a tunic to wear during early morning practice on the boat. Amy Hudson appreciated that the skirts were no longer 'nearly down past your ankles' but they still 'couldn't be above the knees'. Working at exclusive clothing manufacturers Henry Bucks in Melbourne in their shirt factory in Stewart Street, Richmond, opposite the Richmond railway station, Nell McLarty had help from her co-workers in the factory: 'We had six shirts and they made them at the factory for me. I paid for the material and they cut them out and the girls, they did parts, and they all took a part to do, and they made the shirts for me. Instead of getting six I got eight out of the material, that was pretty fortunate.' As both women had working-class origins, Peggy Antonio quipped about Nell's Henry Bucks shirt: 'That would put you in the exclusive line!'

Clothing worn by sportswomen in this era performed both a liberating and restrictive role as the players sought to gain access to more vigorous sports. The uniform of male cricketers was also evolving and subject to some, although lesser, regulations.

*Victorian captain Elsie Deane (left) and English captain Betty Archdale toss
the coin at the start of the Victoria versus England match at the MCG in
December 1934. The press reported that the large crowd of over five thousand
in attendance each day was treated to 'a delightful exposition of the game'.*

Chapter 7

Summer Tests, Australia, 1934–35

'Imagine Larwood and Bradman
helping one another to drinks!'
— *Sydney Morning Herald*, 17 December 1934

The summer of 1934–35 was ripe with all the promise and anticipation of past cricketing summers. For the young Australian women selected in their local, state and national teams, who would get the opportunity to play against the English team, it was a season overflowing with possibilities and challenges.

The English touring itinerary was extensive; they would be in Australia for two months. The visitors agreed to play fourteen matches in all, including four two-day games against state sides (Western Australia, Victoria, New South Wales, Queensland); seven one-day games against regional towns in New South Wales, and Canberra; and three three-day Test matches against the national team in Brisbane, Sydney and Melbourne. Just like the Bradman Chevrolet snub by General Motors the year before, Tasmania missed out on a match against the visitors and was joined in their disappointment by South Australia, even though the English team was scheduled to stay in Adelaide en route to the eastern states.

The cricket would be solemn and keenly contested, but the itinerary allowed for plenty of social interaction between the visiting team and their hosts. The English players would pay their own fare, but Australia would contribute the cost of their entertainment. The states and regional towns had bid for the right to be included in the itinerary and were ready with civic receptions, sightseeing and souvenirs. The English would be treated to an Australian experience replete with Indigenous encounters, sheep stations and native animals.

The Empire itself had been created through formal parliamentary, judicial, military and civic institutions. Its practical maintenance relied on people and events – from governors to regular royal visits. But the bonds that held the dominions to the Empire depended heavily on individual ties, personal commitment and public sentiment. These bonds of Empire and commonalities of purpose would be reinforced through friendship and hospitality by local mayors and councillors in regional centres, and through dignitaries and special guests in cities and towns. Many women involved in administrative positions in sport and other organisations, such as the Peden sisters, had extensive contacts within Australia's middle- and upper-class society. They were 'public women' with existing links to Great Britain through ancestry, birth, education and travel. Some of these women had participated in overseas conferences and represented Australia on the international stage. Cricket would play its part in reinforcing, restoring and strengthening Empire ties that had been fractured during the bodyline series and other events of the Great Depression. The new *Empire Cumulative Cricket Scoring Book* the English women brought with them was unpacked, pencils sharpened and the scorers ready.

But before any play could get underway, English captain and lawyer Betty Archdale had a few things to clear up. In fact, in a move that once again jeopardised the bonds of Empire, she threatened to take the team straight home. The fuss was over the hours of play for the upcoming major matches. England usually played matches from 10.30 am to 6 pm with a break for lunch and tea, but Betty 'discovered when we got to Perth we weren't starting until after lunch and nothing had been said to us. This was really where they made the mistake. They should have organised this before. I immediately said, you know, because obviously we can't [just] play three afternoons, you won't get anywhere.'

Archdale suspected that the Australian officials were limiting play times to prevent decisive results early in the tour: 'They were anxious that these matches should be drawn so there'd be more interest in the Tests. This is what they told us, and of course I rather coldly told them we haven't come umpteen thousand miles, or however far we'd come, to play a lot of drawn matches. I was extremely rude.' The English team arrived at the cricket ground with captain Archdale saying, 'I wasn't certain we'd play'. Betty Archdale clashed with the Australian manager Ruth Preddey: 'She was a very nice woman but she had slightly different ideas than we did as to what sport was.' A compromise of an 11 am start was reached – 'We were really not interested in winning or losing, you know, but I did feel we shouldn't come all that way just to play a lot of drawn matches.' Archdale also convinced Australia to adopt the six-ball over instead of their usual eight-ball, and in return agreed to a heavier weighted cricket ball than that used in England. The same game, but seemingly worlds apart.

The English Women's Cricket Association Touring Team were not the only English visitors that summer. The Duke of Gloucester arrived in Australia to attend the Centenary celebrations in Melbourne, landing first in Fremantle, Western Australia, and beginning a transcontinental journey that concluded in Brisbane. Despite a rumour circulating in other parts of the Empire that his visit was a pre-arranged mission 'to clean up the bodyline bad feeling', the topic of bodyline was reportedly a taboo subject with the royal party in Australia. The visit was instrumental in demonstrating, according to *The Sydney Morning Herald*, 'that the loyalty and devotion of our people to the Throne stand sure and fast'. The *Sunday Mail* in Brisbane

published the words to a special song composed to welcome the
Duke to that city:

> He symbolises Throne and Crown
> And far-flung smiling lands.
> He welds the Kingdom closer still
> In firm and loyal bands.

Just don't mention bodyline to the royal visitor.

England versus Western Australia, Perth, 24, 26 November 1934

When the English team arrived in Fremantle aboard the *Cathay*,
only Archdale and player–manager Betty Green were authorised
to speak to the press in what was called a player–writer ban –
'They do not wish to withhold information that might benefit
women's cricket, but at the same time prefer that the team
should not be troubled.' With all players over twenty-one years
of age, the women were free to socialise in Australia and were
not subjected to any onerous rules and regulations. The only
general rule was to be in bed by ten o'clock before a match. The
fact that Betty Green was a keen photographer added another
dimension to the tour, her candid photographs revealing much
that is missing from the official records.

Press interest in the game was indeed high and, remarkably,
the *Melbourne Herald* sent sportswoman and journalist Pat Jarrett
on the four-day train trip to Perth to cover this first match on
Australian soil. In her first report, Jarrett praised the English
women, noting their 'vivacious personalities, quiet manners, and
a pleasant method of speech'. Archdale impressed upon Jarrett
that she was leading 'a fine team of girls, with their charm and
intellect they will prove real sporting ambassadors'. Jarrett was
immediately awestruck and described Archdale as 'a striking
personality. She wears her hair in a severe Eton crop which
may set a new fashion for women cricketers.' Archdale told the

journalist Carlie Hansen, writing for the Brisbane *Courier-Mail*: 'We have come to Australia to play the game for the game's sake, and there is no talk of taking back the "Ashes".'

With unpleasantness between officials out of the way over hours of play, ball weight and length of overs, sections of the Western Australian press immediately began to niggle over bodyline. The Western Australian team was coached by Alan Evans, who told the press the team 'was shaping very nicely and are showing plenty of promise', triggering the double entendre headline, 'Girl Cricketers Shaping Well'. In an otherwise positive and supportive article that described the cricketing attributes of the Western Australian players, including the captain and century-maker Jean Cameron, who 'has a good knowledge of the finer points of the game', the article stated: 'There's no danger of bodyline with these girls, as no fast bowler has been included in the side.' An accompanying photograph of local cricketer Marie Jegust batting in the nets was captioned, 'Now bring out your Larwood!' The Perth *Mirror* noted:

> There's no lack of enthusiasm in the camp, and the practice nights have been well attended. Alan Evans has found them to be a keen band of girls, who are always ready to learn, and he is confident that by the time the English girls arrive the locals will have moulded themselves into a good side. And here's where a few of the 'A' grade masculine clubs could sit up and take notice. The girls don't just have a hit and a bowl, but every practice night they have organised fielding training, and have shown that they are just as adept at holding catches and cutting off runs as making them.

The women proved keener than their male counterparts. When English captain Betty Archdale first saw the Western Australian women practising in the nets prior to the first game of the series, she later admitted to being 'rather pensive'.

A civic reception was held in Fremantle with a welcome by the Mayor. Jarrett thought it went well: 'Both Miss Archdale and Miss Green proved cultured and entertaining speakers when responding to the welcome.' A luncheon reception was held at the Women's Service Guild, and members of the English and Western Australian teams were hosted by women from many service organisations across the state; 'nearly every branch of Western Australian women's activities was represented'. In her speech, Betty Archdale noted that the work of some of these women was already known to her through connections in London. The president of the Women's Service Guild, Ethel Joyner, stated: 'The team was welding a link between England and Australia through cricket and all its ideals.' She had been a cricketer and practised with Clem Hill. The English team also took the opportunity to swim at Yanchep and attend the trots at Richmond Park.

Despite feeling pensive about the Western Australian team's ability, after playing them Betty Archdale considered that she had 'overestimated their ability'. In the two-day game England won the toss and batted with Molly Hide scoring a century in front of a crowd numbering 3500 at the WACA. England declared at 3 for 201 and dismissed Western Australia for 82, and asked them to follow on. At stumps on the second day Western Australia was 3 for 59, the match ended in a draw. The English cricketers had their first introduction to the Australian barrackers who invented nicknames for the players, and repeatedly implored the captain to 'Put Larwood on' – Larwood being the name given to England's fast bowler Mary Taylor. 'Taylor later said she had no desire to emulate her male model and raise a howl from the hill, but she took the barracking she received with good grace.'

At dinner that night Betty Archdale recalled: 'We sang and sang and sang until nearly midnight.'

The English team left Perth and travelled by sea to South Australia on the SS *Balranald*. Along for the return journey was Australian journalist Pat Jarrett, photographed by Betty Green relaxing on board with Carol Valentine and Molly Hide. On arrival in Adelaide, *The Australian Women's Weekly* reported they were greeted by a 'seething mass of people ... Seldom in the history of South Australia has a reception to a sports team caused more commotion than that tendered by the Lord Mayor of Adelaide to the English girls.' The reception was followed by a drive through the Adelaide Hills and a picnic lunch at Mount Lofty, with manager Betty Green later writing, 'you are treating us like royalty'.

England versus Victoria, Melbourne, 7–8 December 1934

Arriving in Melbourne, the English team stayed at the Hotel Esplanade in St Kilda. Immediate arrangements included an official welcome, a civic reception at the town hall, and an official luncheon hosted by the Melbourne Cricket Club (MCC). Betty Archdale recalled, 'Our first day in Melbourne we were staggered to find ourselves entertained by the MCC in the MCC Pavilion. It was a magnificent lunch and we looked at the ground and surroundings with great awe.' The team was driven around Melbourne in a fleet of luxurious cars lent by a private firm and decorated, to their surprise, with the Marylebone Cricket Club colours. Other events during their brief stay included: an afternoon tea at Parliament House as guests of the Speaker; a lunch at the Myer Emporium; a dance and supper at Earl's Court in St Kilda; a gala performance hosted by J.C. Williamson Ltd of 'Blue Mountain Melody'; a visit to Black Rock, where they were entertained by management of the Semco factory; and cricket practice every morning at the MCG. And, of course, a cricket match that *The Age* newspaper loftily described as 'the opening match of the English tour', discounting the match in Perth, which it said 'could not be regarded as a first-class contest'.

The match was at the MCG against the Victorian state side, perhaps one of the strongest in the country, especially when it came to spin bowlers. It soon became clear that this time the

English had in fact underestimated their opponents. Archdale recalled: 'Peggy Antonio and Anne Palmer were bowlers with whom we had no idea how to deal.' The wickets were also a challenge: 'We must get used to the fast and perfect Australian wickets.' The Victorian players also had a challenge getting used to playing on turf wickets.

England again won the toss and batted. Anne Palmer struck first; Peggy Antonio followed with five wickets. The long arm and sharp reflexes of Nell McLarty snatched a catch close to the wicket and England was all out for 115. Palmer and Antonio, batting in Victoria's middle order, held up the side with 75 runs between them. Anne Palmer recalled:

> It was fabulous on your own ground, to walk out there and see all those faces from the middle, I have never seen anything like it, it was so unreal. I've never been the sort of person who gets butterflies in the tummy to any great degree, although it was very awe-inspiring, but Peggy and I overcame it and we batted, and those English girls had a strong bowling line-up, they really did.

The press reported: 'The large crowd which was present – including many women – was treated to a delightful exposition of the game, the visitors in particular revealing a splendid knowledge of the rules of cricket ... Snowball possesses a stentorian "Howzatt" reminiscent of Duckworth's famous cry.'

Nance Clements batting at number 10 was delighted to see her name come up on the MCG scoreboard as she strode to the wicket. She batted for forty-six minutes, working the ball around the field for twos and ones as she scored a respectable 21 runs to help Victoria to finish all out for 151. In England's second innings, Antonio snared another five wickets leaving England at 6 for 73 at stumps. Another draw. Close to five thousand people had witnessed the game each day, the crowds a surprise to the visitors. Archdale recalled: 'They staggered us. We were used to playing in England, most of our matches were club matches, we didn't have any spectators at all, except perhaps a few parents or something.' Looking back on the two teams, Archdale said: 'As players there really wasn't anything to choose between us. I mean, you think of Peggy Antonio and all that lot, McLarty, oh boy!' Before she left the ground Nance Clements walked over and visited the scoreboard attendants and came away with a treasured souvenir that would firmly link her to the bodyline series in the years to come.

England versus Deniliquin, New South Wales, 10 December 1934

The Deniliquin Women's Cricket Association had offered to pay the expenses of a visit by the English team and promised to 'give them an opportunity of enjoying station life'. The bus, described as a parlour car and loaded with English cricketers and their gear, was delayed when it suffered a tyre puncture en route from Melbourne to Deniliquin. The cricketers would stay for three days at the Globe Hotel, attend several functions, including a visit to two large sheep properties providing 'an intimate glimpse of Australia's real station country life'. Betty Green's camera captured the rough ride by cars through long grass tracks out to the Deniliquin stations. She captioned the photograph: 'Deniliquin: the type of country over which we drove at 40 m.p.h. after kangaroos!' Emus, kangaroos and a fox were chased, sheep shearing witnessed, and a brown snake killed with the tail souvenired.

The town declared a holiday for the cricket match. Betty Archdale later wrote that during their first taste of country life 'clouds of grasshoppers rose as fielders ran after the ball'. One break in the match proved to be a cultural experience – 'the tea interval was enlivened by a display of boomerang throwing and singing by the Aboriginals who presented us with boomerangs and flowers, beautifully made from feathers'. The Indigenous Australians were from the Moonahcullah Mission Station. Betty

Green photographed a gum leaf band playing tunes on gum leaves surrounded by the crowd. The English beat Deniliquin by an innings and 39 runs, the locals only managing two scores under 50. From Deniliquin the English team was driven by car to Albury in time to catch the express train to Sydney.

England versus New South Wales, Sydney, 14–15 December 1934

The English team arrived in Sydney on 13 December to attend a scheduled practice on the University of Sydney's turf square; however, wet weather forced the team indoors to train at the women's cricket coaching school in Elizabeth Street. Betty Green's photographs captured the team unloading their large suitcases and trunks to stay at Women's College at the university. That afternoon they attended a reception at the Hotel Australia and at night were entertained at the Queen's Club. The next day after practice, they were guests at the David Jones Business Girls luncheon, and in the afternoon entertained by the women's amateur sports council president, Lady Elsie Walder, at her home.

The next match was against the New South Wales state side, which possessed the standout batswomen Hazel Pritchard and Ruby Monaghan. Archdale was impressed. She described Pritchard as 'the most attractive bat in Australia' and Monaghan as 'an attractive and perky bat with a nice stroke past point and slips'. The New South Wales team, especially the slow bowlers, needed to transfer their skills from their regular games on concrete wickets to the turf pitch at the SCG. Only the University of Sydney's square had provided women with the experience of playing on turf. They hadn't had too much experience, however, of the barracking from 'hillites' of the SCG. *The Sydney Morning Herald* declared:

> Women cricketers, playing their first international
> match, completely won the hearts and admiration of

these hard-hearted barrackers. Many men and youths went there, as they openly confessed, to 'see the women players make fools of themselves' in their efforts to emulate man in his prowess with the bat and ball, but they left the ground expressing astonishment at the remarkably high standard of play, and feeling satisfied that they had had 'the best bob's worth of cricket for many a day'. It was real cricket, they said, worth half a dozen ordinary men's matches. Opinion was expressed all round the ground that the girls had introduced to Sydney spectators a brighter cricket; making it a vastly more interesting and entertaining spectacle.

'The women play the game just as well as the men, and they do not waste any time on the field, or resort to scheming tactics' said one spectator. Most of the 'know-alls' of cricket were present, including Yabba and many of his big-throated mates, and, of course, the well-known inebriates, whose continual and unprovoked bellowing of nasty epithets proved so unpleasant to the ears and the temperament of the English test players on the ground last year … When drinks were brought out, and two English girls walked over to the batswomen with refreshments, the crowd thought it was a wonderful gesture. 'That is sportsmanship,' they muttered. 'Yes,' added someone, 'It is a knock to men's international cricket, all right. Imagine Larwood and Bradman helping one another to drinks!'

Betty Archdale later recalled an incident during this game and the presence of barrackers at the SCG: 'one man, having lunched rather too well made a long speech on the theme that a woman's place was in the home – "You ought to be at home looking after your children," the drunk shouted at the single, childless players.'

Describing the New South Wales match Charlie Macartney wrote:

> The entertainment they provided, and the ability they revealed, are still spoken of in Sydney by the man in the street ... Many spectators wandered off to the Sydney Cricket Ground to scoff and enjoy a laugh at the expense of women cricketers. Every one of those people returned home thoroughly respecting the ability of the women players. All were unanimous that for years they had not enjoyed such a cricket treat. Personally I was not surprised at the displays throughout the game. I have watched the women cricketers of New South Wales in action on many occasions.

England won this match after a sporting declaration by New South Wales captain Margaret Peden, who asked the visitors to score 57 in 30 minutes in their second innings, which they duly achieved. Again, it was the social side of the game that cemented the ties and 'welded' the two sides and countries together.

The teams lunched at Women's College hosted by the governor's wife, Lady Gwendolen Game, who was attracted back to the SCG 'to see a little of the play'. Lady Game may or may not have been enchanted by the cricket, but she wanted to prolong her contact with the English team. English-born, she and her husband had been in Australia since 1930, and she was homesick for news of her young daughter sent back to England for school – 'As Miss Partridge, one of the English team, was games mistress at Wickham, where Miss Rosemary Game is at school, Lady Game was anxious to hear news of her small daughter.'

The sporting declaration by Peden attracted favourable comment in the press. Comparisons were made with men's cricket and the lingering bodyline controversy by diverse sections of the media. The *Catholic Freeman's Journal* observed: 'From a cricketing point of view the match was more enjoyable than any of our Interstate matches. Why? Because the girls played the game for the game's sake. There were no Jardine touches about the business.' The English women in their summer frocks and swimming costumes were entertained to a picnic at Palm Beach – 'The English cricketing girls had the greatest day in their lives when they were motored to Palm Beach and raced down to the surf.' They were accompanied at Palm Beach, according to Betty Green's candid photographs, by Lady Elsie Walder, president of the NSW Women's Amateur Sports Council, and whose husband, Sir Samuel Walder, was a conservative member of the NSW Legislative Council (with Sir John Peden) and described as 'an Imperial patriot'. Lady Walder may not necessarily have shared her husband's politics, but she shared his contacts. Also photographed with the group at Palm Beach was noted feminist and activist Linda Littlejohn. Such were the private connections to Australia, that the English women had a free day in Sydney to allow them to accept 'private invitations'.

Leaving Sydney, the women's cricket association arranged for the English team to be taken to Wollongong and back by car, in order to give them the opportunity of seeing some of the South Coast of New South Wales.

England versus Wollongong, New South Wales, 18 December 1934

The English team was welcomed in Wollongong with a civic reception from the Mayor followed by a dinner and dance at night. Wollongong invited three 'metropolitan' players to strengthen their team, including state bowler Dorothy Morecroft. The English team batted first and 'appeared troubled by the matting wicket', declaring at 9 for 110. In reply Wollongong was 6 for 44 at stumps, the match resulted in a draw. Bowlers dominated the game with Morecroft taking 5 for 25. After the match, the association hosted a dinner for the visiting team. Betty Archdale said the team had already received many souvenirs of Australia, and thanked the Wollongong Association for their gift of boomerangs. She diplomatically refrained from mentioning that by now the English women had at least two boomerangs each.

England versus Newcastle, New South Wales, 19 December 1934

Returning late to Sydney by car from Wollongong, the English team flew the next morning to Newcastle, but as only a couple of the team had ever flown before, 'several of the members are somewhat dubious as to how they will appreciate the journey'. Again, the team was welcomed by the Mayor and Mayoress and entertained at dinner and a dance after the game.

In a preview of the match 'Onlooker', writing in the *Newcastle Morning Herald and Miner's Advocate*, stated: 'The list of sports that man, perhaps foolishly, regarded as being in his own domain, is dwindling.' The article highlighted for readers the historical instances of women playing cricket in England since the 1780s. This time the match was played on Newcastle's 'No. 1 Sports Ground', with a turf wicket, which the paper reported, 'The wicket is in splendid condition and will doubtless assist the English team's "Larwood", the be-shingled Miss Edna [sic] Taylor, a young lady who bowls at great pace and who delivers the ball with perfect action'. 'Be-shingled', presumably, referred to the short, tapered haircut of English fast-bowler Mary Taylor. English openers Myrtle Maclagan (103 not out) and Grace Morgan (78) registered their biggest opening partnership of the tour and declared at 1 for 184. In reply, the Newcastle team made 6 for 33 when thunder and lightning made conditions 'unnerving' and rain stopped play and a draw declared.

England versus Queensland, Brisbane, 22, 24 December 1934

The English team came to Brisbane with increased purpose. They were scheduled to play a match against the Queensland state side to be followed by the first Test match against Australia. With three days before the next match, the team arrived in Brisbane by the Kyogle Mail Train, which followed the North Coast Line. When the train stopped for thirty minutes in Coffs Harbour at 8 am for breakfast, Betty Green's camera snapped three English players sprinting along the train platform in their bathing suits for a quick surf at nearby Jetty Beach, a two-minute dash away.

In a match preview, Brisbane sports journalist Carlie Hansen predicted: 'The Queensland girls are bound to be somewhat handicapped at first by insufficient match experience on turf.' The match was scheduled on the smaller Exhibition Ground, rather than the Gabba. The rain from Newcastle had followed the women up north, and a wet wicket delayed the start of play. The cricketers, however, had not left the double entendres behind. As soon as the English women entered the field, male journalists' attention and focus changed to bodyline, or rather women's bodies. F. Ricketts, who usually reported on Australian Rules, wrote in Brisbane's *Sunday Mail* under the headline 'Body-Line of a Different Kind', and reported on the game between Queensland and England:

> Hard-crusted devotees of man-cricket who occupied the stands on Saturday ... took an intense interest in the game – particularly in the players. More long-range spectacles than ever were in use, and even field glasses, when the visions in white began to flit about in the inspiring cause of women's cricket. Man was obsessed, for there were other phases of body line than those which caused him such deep concern not so long ago. Many of the players are physical models.

Man-cricket? Physical models? Among his focus on women's bodies, Ricketts noted that:

> The English girls who opened their match against Queensland yesterday have done so much, and have

travelled so far that they leave the conviction that they mean business. In other words, the ladies are staying in the game – and Queensland has become strongly infected with the same spirit … They all looked extremely neat and athletic … To them cricket is a game not a business.

Queensland was coached by Mr L.L. Gill, former captain of the Queensland state men's team, who 'earned encomiums for his efforts, and to those who have aspirations for the position the kindly word is passed that he has no intentions of resigning it'.

The attendance at this game was smaller than expected, seven hundred on the first day and nine hundred on the second, mainly due to the weather. The start of the game was delayed until after 2.30 pm due to rain. The English lost the toss and were sent in. By the morning session of the following day, they were all out for 181, with middle order batter Joy Partridge contributing 63, six more runs than the Queensland team managed in their reply. Remarkably, the Queensland team included nineteen-year-old slow bowler Edna Crouch, an Indigenous Ngugi woman who took 5 for 25. Asked to follow-on, Queensland were all out for 83, with Joyce Brewer top scoring on 36. England won decisively by an innings and 41 runs. The *Sunday Mail* noted:

> The idol was B. Snowball. She hooked, leg glanced, and drove without a fault … Her opening partner, M. Maclagan, was the Woodfull, patient, but punishing when the right ball came. Snowball has the shoulders, and there was music from her bat in the driving … The attack was sound, but the batting sounder, and the most exacting judge could not fault the play. There would have been much sparkle in it had the wicket been good. It was wonderful how the strength of that English batting had pumiced man's early partisanship down to smoothness. He had looked at stylist cricket for one hour with 40 up, and not a wicket lost.

Another article described Snowball as the 'dancing, daring, and skillful Betty Snowball'. Top scorer 'Partridge was solid and sure, and was cheered often'.

The English women had been welcomed to Brisbane at an afternoon tea hosted by the Lady Mayoress Martha Jones in the mayoral reception room. Australian poems spoken by Elsie Byth, the president of the Brisbane Women's Club, were a feature of the morning tea. In welcoming the cricketers, Jones said that she had happy recollections of her visit to England some years earlier. Jessie Beames rendered vocal solos to accompaniments by Elsie Byth.

In the few days between the end of the match against Queensland and the first Test against Australia, which included the Christmas break, the English team again embarked upon a whirlwind social calendar that served to strengthen and reinforce local ties. A morning tea was hosted at Bishopsbourne by Amy Wand, wife of the Anglican Archbishop of Brisbane, and her daughter, Kathleen. The Archbishop and Kathleen later posed for Betty Green's photograph at the cricket standing against a white picket boundary fence. Again, strong connections to Empire were explored at the morning tea, as Kathleen had attended Bedford, a physical culture training college in England, as had many of the English cricket team who had trained as games mistresses. Happy reminiscences of days spent in Bedford were discussed. Even if they hadn't trained there, all cricketers knew of Bedford, the institution being a regular paid advertiser in Marjorie Pollard's monthly magazine *Women's Cricket*.

Other events in addition to the reception by the Lady Mayoress, included a welcome from the National Council of Women, dinner at the Belle Vue Hotel, and entertainment at the Regent Theatre. On a less formal note, the pull of the Queensland surf beaches proved irresistible to the English women. In January, Betty Green photographed scenes on Southport Beach, including lifesavers undertaking a rescue, and she noted in her handwritten captions the rubber surf mattresses popular with swimmers.

First Test, England versus Australia, Brisbane, 28, 29, 31 December 1934

The Victorians in the Australian team – Nell McLarty, Peggy Antonio, Anne Palmer, Hilda Hills and Lorna Kettels – travelled by train from Melbourne to Brisbane for the first Test in a second-class carriage – 'There has been some criticism of the decision that they should travel second class such a long distance in the heat and before a strenuous match.' Lorna Kettels recalled, 'It was a real eye opener. The travelling was shocking. You had to sit up from the time you left Melbourne to the time you got to Queensland.' To try and increase their comfort, 'We used to take the card tables out and put them under the cushions and you'd lay on those ... it was fun. There was no jealousy or anything about it, you were out for a good time. I really enjoyed it.'

While the Australian team was travelling up the coast on the train, the English team was treated to more entertainment in Brisbane. They had attended the trots in Fremantle, and were now welcomed to the races at Ascot. Betty Archdale recalled, 'Having been advised to take garden party frocks to Australia, we were thrilled to have a chance to wear them. Fifteen visions in flowing frocks and picture hats appeared at the race course.' Excited by the imminent arrival of the Australian team, the English women decamped from the races to the train station. Archdale continued, 'The Australian team arrived that afternoon and we went to welcome them at the station with an arch of cricket bats. We were still in our party clothes so the effect was a bit incongruous.' The Australian team stayed together at Anne Hathaway House, a private residential hotel in George Street, Brisbane, which featured 'hot and cold water in all bedrooms at all hours' and a 'cool well-ventilated roof garden'.

Some controversy broke out in Brisbane, with Queensland cricket supporters upset that the Australian team had been selected, and players secretly notified of their selection in the first Test prior to the England versus Queensland game, apparently giving the local women no opportunity to impress their claims on the selectors. Albert Bonwick, sportsman and professional runner, wrote in complaint to *The Courier-Mail* on their behalf, but in an explanatory note national selector Dot Waldron claimed that five Queenslanders were available and nominated for selection with two appointed – Kath Smith and Joyce Brewer.

The first Test match was scheduled at the Brisbane Exhibition Ground, rather than the city's larger more iconic cricket venue, the Gabba. Archdale was keen to win the first Test. She recalled: 'the day before this match many anxious consultations took place. How could we get rid of Pritchard, Monaghan and Shevill?' Sports journalist Stan Phillips previewed the match in the *Brisbane Telegraph* and described the English women as a 'goodwill side' who preserved the 'correct cricket atmosphere', while the Test series 'should do much to link in closer bonds the women of the Mother country and those of her youngest Dominion'. In a preview of the Test match *The Courier-Mail* invoked the Dr Johnson quote of 'a woman preaching is like a dog walking on his hind legs. It is not done well but you are surprised to find it done at all' in their introduction to the match. But they would also go on to invoke what would become standard fare across the country as the women played cricket – that men came to scoff and stayed to praise. *The Courier-Mail* continued:

> Elderly gentlemen who look back longingly to the good old days of cricket – 'Dash it, sir, we took our knocks like men and never whined about bodyline!' – probably feel much the same way about the intrusion of women into the game. The real matter for surprise, however, is that young ladies, having gate-crashed into what used to be an exclusively masculine field of sport, should have mastered so thoroughly the art of wielding the bat and ball ... Now they have changed all that. They have cut off their hair, donned a uniform which would have been looked at askance in Aunt Tabitha's day, and marched

boldly on to the cricket field, there to astonish male
sceptics by their skill and prowess. The elderly gentlemen
aforesaid, if they were to attend a women's cricket match
to scoff, would probably remain to applaud. Today's Test
match, the first between English and Australian women's
teams, promises not only to make history but to provide
good cricket. And it is on the merits of the play, and not
for the novelty of seeing women at the wickets, that such
matches will attract the sport-loving crowds.

Despite the weather the crowds came out to watch the game.
The Brisbane *Daily Standard* reported the many men who
thought they would have a quick look at the cricket before going
to the races, ended up staying at the ground, 'Our men have
been surprised by the way the girls can play cricket'. Bodyline
and women's bodies were not completely forgotten. *The Courier-
Mail* wrote, 'As they stood at the wickets with padded legs their
"bodyline" simplicity resembled Grecian statues.'

Australia won the toss and chose to bat. Opening batter Ruby
Monaghan recalled, 'I was never ever nervous. I like to take
the first ball, you know, and if it was on the wicket or not,
I would still hit it to the boundary. I wouldn't play my way
in, if it was a ball I liked I would hit it.' Ruby fell to English
slow bowler Myrtle Maclagan, who was in great form, some
said 'unplayable', snaring 7 for 10. Queenslander Kath Smith was
the only Australian to offer any resistance, scoring 25 runs in a
total of 47. Australia's wicketkeeper Hilda Hills was hit in the
face while batting and retired hurt, 'she jumped out to the slow
bowler and the ball hit the shoulder of her bat and struck her a
nasty blow on the face'. A nasty blow, but no bodyline intended.

It took England only thirty-eight minutes to pass Australia's
first-innings score. Maclagan opened the batting and worked
the ball around the Exhibition Ground for over two hours,
contributing 72 runs before she became one of Anne Palmer's
many victims. Hazel Pritchard deputised for Hills as wicketkeeper.

The English were dismissed for 154, with Anne Palmer taking 7 for 18 and Nell McLarty's long arm and sharp reflexes close to the wicket snaring three catches. The two bowlers were used together effectively; Palmer's slow left armers alternated with McLarty's fast bowling. The imagined threats from Pritchard, who played a 'sturdy innings' and Shevill materialised in the second innings with scores of 20 and 63 respectively in an Australian total of 138. England batted again and scored the required 34 runs in just over half an hour to record a 9-wicket victory in this first Test match.

Batting at number eight for Australia in the first Test in Brisbane, Lorna Kettels made 9 in the first innings and a duck in the second, and found herself dropped for the second Test in Sydney due to start in a few days' time. In Brisbane she was told to 'pack up' and travel back to Melbourne by herself: 'That's when the manageress said you're not going, you're staying. So I would have had a long trip back by myself, thanks to her I stayed.' Lorna was not alone in failing to make a score – captain Margaret Peden, for instance, made 1 and 11 – but her disappointment made Lorna 'all the keener to try and get back in to the third Test, which I did'. The itinerary made for difficult and challenging cricket. Lorna noted, 'We never had time; there was no time to practise. See you played up in Queensland, you came back to Sydney, there was no practice. You didn't go out and practise on the ground before you played the next Test, you were into the next Test; you didn't get to know anybody.'

The first Test match was over, the English tourists had won decisively. While the women had not yet been permitted to play on all of Australia's hallowed cricket grounds, they had been permitted into cricket's flowery hyperbole. Brisbane journalist Stan Phillips invoked Shakespeare's *Henry V*'s speech before the Battle of Agincourt on St Crispin's Day:

> The English and Australian teams in the first Test match
> ever played in women's cricket will be able to say, with
> Shakespeare's exemplar of patriotism – that 'then shall

our names, familiar as household words ... be in their
flowing cups freshly remembered.'

Pity they weren't playing the French. His prediction was not far
off the mark. Anne Palmer, who had achieved the remarkable
bowling figures of 7 for 18 in this match, later recalled:
'Somebody told me the following year that whilst the men were
playing cricket against England in Queensland and they were
having difficulty getting the Englishmen out, a voice from the
outer said, "Send for Anne Palmer!" and they wrote it up in the
newspaper here in Melbourne. It created a great laugh.'

Second Test, England versus Australia, Sydney, 4, 7, 8 January 1935

A few days later, with New Year out of the way, the second
Test was played in Sydney. Staying at the now familiar Women's
College at the University of Sydney, Archdale recalled the
English women found the iconic grounds of the SCG and
the MCG, 'like billiard tables'. Lady Gwendolen Game, the
governor's wife, was keen to keep contact with the English
cricketers and invited them to Government House for morning
tea prior to their practice on the SCG. The English team also
spent their free time at Bondi Beach, where Betty Green again
photographed the latest surf craze – the rubber surf mattresses –
and they motored to picnics up the Hawkesbury River and over
the Spit Bridge. The English touring team visited Koala Park in
Sydney, with Mary Richards photographed holding two koalas.

The crowd at the Test match at the SCG built steadily to its
peak of over five thousand on the first morning to watch Margaret
Peden again win the toss for Australia and elect to bat. Opener
Ruby Monaghan got off to a bright start scoring a couple of twos,
a four and a single – 'Beautiful, you couldn't miss the ball on
there,' she recalled – only to be bowled by Maclagan for 9. She
remembered being allowed to mix with her family at the ground:

'We used to sit around with me mum and, you know, people that went up to watch us. You could go and sit with them if you wanted to, but you could go and sit with the team.'

Despite some early wickets the Queensland middle order in the Australian team of Kath Smith and Joyce Brewer built a solid innings. Smith scored 47, including six fours, with Brewer contributing 34. Archdale later recalled Kath Smith 'played a grand innings, being one of the few Australians with a good drive'. The Australian tail of Peggy Antonio and Anne Palmer contributed 32 runs for the last wicket to see the side all out for 162. The match was set up nicely before rain intervened in the game and the second and third days' play was quickly rescheduled. Charlie Macartney wrote in the *Sydney Sportsman*, 'It was a sad blow that rain fell last Saturday. Had the weather been fine, in my opinion 10,000 people at least would have watched England bat, and what a thrill they would have enjoyed.'

Two thousand turned up on the Monday and were treated to a quick-fire opening stand of 145 by the English with Myrtle Maclagan 119 and Betty Snowball 73. England declared at 5 for 301. Batting in their second innings, Australia, through their two tailenders, this time captain Margaret Peden and Anne Palmer, held out the English bowlers long enough to score 24 in their partnership (all out for 148) to force England to bat again. It was an exciting struggle for runs, and the crowd showed its appreciation. But it was a lost cause, and England wiped out the deficit of 10 runs and won the second Test by eight wickets. That gave England the series 2–0 with only one Test to play. Charlie Macartney again writing in the *Sydney Sportsman* summed up the second Test:

> The scoffers who came to the Sydney Cricket Ground to get a laugh out of the feeble efforts of women cricketers, have again left the playing ground paying a respectful tribute to their prowess. I have heard it said that the idea

of women cricketers ever reaching a high plane in our national game was ridiculous and impossible. That idea has been completely exploded by the skilful entertainment provided by both English and Australian women on the cricket field. There is little chance of the circus entering into women's cricket, as they play the game too well. In fact, so pluckily and so skilfully do they perform in every department, that many comparisons have been made between them and male players of note.

England's player–manager Betty Green commented on the crowds in Australia:

> The fact that there were several thousand more spectators at our 2nd Test Match in Sydney than at the men's shield match the same week speaks for itself, as do the numerous full-page cuttings we have brought back from the Australian and New Zealand papers. Men who interpreted 'women's cricket' as a soft-ball caricature of the game, watched out of curiosity the first day and out of interest the second and reported it as 'good cricket played by women'. Officials, umpires and members of the famous clubs were most complimentary as to the standard of the play, the knowledge of the finer points and the etiquette of the game, and the conduct of the matches, and critical crowds were well satisfied.

A farewell 'costume' party was held at the YWCA for the English touring team, keen to meet as many Sydney women cricketers as possible before heading off to Canberra. The Sydney *Daily Telegraph* reported on the party: 'It was a happy thought. Representatives of all the metropolitan clubs donned sports costume and came to join the fun to make their last night in Sydney one that the tourists will never forget.' To celebrate the birth of international cricket for women a large birthday cake was provided on the supper table, 'proudly flaunting one candle, and bearing on its surface a replica of the Cricket Ground, complete with tiny figures representing the members of the English team and the umpires'. Time to have your cake and eat it, too.

England versus Canberra, 9 January 1935

With the Sydney Test delayed by rain, the English whirlwind schedule became tight. The team arrived by train in Canberra on the next leg of their 'country tour' at 7.30 am. For the first time they were hosted in private houses, a change from the hotels and women's colleges. Archdale thought the accommodation was 'agreeable'. By 11 am that day the English team was at Manuka Oval for photographs, with the match against Canberra commencing at 11.30 am. In preparation for the English arrival, several trial games had been held on Manuka and Northbourne ovals to aid selection of the Canberra team and give the players experience on turf pitches.

Governor-General Sir Isaac Isaacs (the first Australian-born governor-general) and his wife, Lady Daisy Isaacs, were official patrons of the match, which also included invitations to Prime Minister Joseph Lyons and Minister for the Interior, English-born Thomas Paterson. In true Canberra fashion, public servants in some departments, in this era a small contingent, requested but were denied permission to attend the match on work time. The Canberra team won the toss and batted, scoring a total of 72, with six of their wickets falling to Maclagan. Archdale later thought they had put up little opposition: 'Most of the players held their bats like croquet mallets,' she dismissively recalled.

A picnic lunch was held in the shade at Manuka Oval. In the party was Canberra identity and YWCA and hockey association president, the English-born Pattie Tillyard and her husband, Robin Tillyard, both of whom were graduates of Cambridge University, as well as cricket enthusiasts and sport patrons Sheila James and her husband Dr John James, Superintendent of

Canberra Hospital. Manuka Oval had some seating but patrons, including many small boys, sat on the grass.

In reply England were 2 for 47 when a heavy storm caused play to be abandoned. That evening, the English women attended Manuka Pool and participated in races hosted by the Canberra Swimming Club, where 'their appearance in one or two events was a novelty for the audience'. The following day the team was met at Parliament House (in this era, a solitary building surrounded by sheep paddocks) and photographed at Cotter Dam with Sheila and John James, and outside the James's Braddon home, presumably one of the private home billets. After a dinner hosted at the YWCA in Civic, the English team left Canberra by the night train at 8.30 pm for nearby Goulburn.

England versus Goulburn, New South Wales, 11 January 1935

The team arrived by train in Goulburn at 10 pm, where they were welcomed by the local brass band (the first of the tour), and escorted and transported by four private cars to the Alcestan Hotel. They were up bright and early the next morning for a civic welcome at the Town Hall, with the match due to commence at 11 am at the sportsground. The Mayor of Goulburn welcomed the team:

> As the people felt that it was visits such as these which tended to create an even better feeling between the Motherland and Australia. This was undoubtedly the result of the matches played between England and Australia by the men, and the girls were now showing that they wished to foster that friendship and kinship between the two countries.

Friendship and kinship? He followed his clumsy reference by adding, 'jocularly that he had no doubt that body-line bowling would be kept in the background'.

Goulburn was keen to use the visit to raise money for a new ambulance wagon, and after rain had dogged a couple of matches, including that of neighbouring Canberra, the town took out £50 of rain insurance. But the match against the Goulburn club team Revellers was played in pleasant weather, despite threatening clouds and a cool breeze, and in front of a large crowd of over one thousand two hundred, even though it was held on a Friday and not a public holiday. England won the toss, batted first and declared at 6 for 248, with Snowball scoring 82 and Hide 64. The morning edition of the *Goulburn Evening Penny Post* reported, 'A noticeable feature of the morning crowd was the large number of men and youths present. There was an absence of barracking and it is doubtful if either team has ever played to a more appreciative throng of enthusiasts. The game was played with a happy sporting spirit.'

In reply to the English declaration, Goulburn offered strong resistance, despite being all out for 49 in their first innings, with local opener Peterson carrying her bat. Compliments flowed that night at the social held at Liedertafel Hall, with Archdale and Green both commenting on their enjoyment of the game and the town. The Goulburn Mayor responded to their toasts:

> Goulburn had seen the English men in action, but had never seen a better exhibition of cricket than that provided by the English women. The visitors had no apologies to offer to their men-folk at home when it came to the standard of cricket. The Mayor said that if the visitors had derived one half the pleasure that the people of Goulburn and the players had, then Goulburn was doubly pleased. The exhibition was an education and the visit would help to cement the bonds of friendship between the Old Country and Australia.

He presented the English side with 'handsomely mounted views of Goulburn as souvenirs of the visit'.

Later that night the visitors left for Leeton. Months after the English women visited Goulburn, the *Penny Post* editorialised:

> It is very necessary that women should be trained to play team games and to acquire the team spirit. This is necessary because, if this country is to be held by the British race with the small handful of people who inhabit it, there is work to be done, and only by team training, such as can be acquired by playing games like cricket and hockey will we succeed in holding on to our heritage.

England versus Leeton, New South Wales, 12 January 1935

The forthcoming visit of the England cricketers was reportedly 'causing quite a stir among the women cricketers in Riverina, and practice matches have been held in various country centres in order that the cream of the talent may be skimmed from the various clubs'. The nearest the area came to cream was all-rounder Vera Treweek, who was brought from Junee to strengthen Leeton, and local Grong Grong cricketer Ivy Chisholm, whom residents from the nearby town travelled to Leeton to see, although reportedly 'she was very nervous and failed to make a name for herself'. The English women arrived on the midday train, followed by an obligatory civic reception held at the Hotel Hydro, where the Shire President, who had himself emigrated from England, told them that their presence 'would help to bind closer the ties between the old country and this new land of Australia'.

The match against Leeton began at 2 pm. More than a thousand turned up to sit under the palm trees and watch the game played on a turf wicket in 'splendid weather conditions'. Leeton won the toss and elected to bat, but within four minutes both openers, including Ivy Chisholm were out, and Treweek, batting at three, top scored on 7 in a total of only 25, despite

Leeton being permitted to play 14 batters. In reply, England, playing the manager Betty Green for the first time on tour, declared at 1 for 108. England won on first innings.

That night they were entertained at a dance on the Glideaway open air floor. The following day they swam at the Leeton Baths, visited a rice farm and the Yanco Creek Weir, and had a swim in the Murrumbidgee River. They also inspected a cannery, where they sampled tinned fruit at the quick lunch counter and spent an hour in English-born orchardist John Hetherington's orange grove at Wamoon, Leeton. They then boarded the afternoon train for Junee, each woman juggling a large quantity of oranges.

England versus Junee, New South Wales, 15 January 1935

The English players arrived in Junee at 6.15 pm and were met by a large crowd and driven to their hotels in private cars. That evening they were entertained at the pictures. The following morning, they attended a civic reception at 10 am with representatives from the shire and every sporting body, where they toasted the King and were lauded with comments from the officials gathered: 'Such a fine body of young women was a great credit to the nation they were representing.'

The cricket match against Junee began at 11 am. The Junee team included Vera Treweek with her two sisters Mary and Elma, and was boosted by women from the surrounding areas of Wagga, Cootamundra and Eurongilly. Captain Vera was described as a fine bat, who can 'dispatch drives and leg strokes to the boundary'. Together with her two sisters they were the best tennis players in the Riverina. Like Deniliquin, Junee also declared a holiday for the match. They were expecting a 'record crowd' to witness both the match and the opening of the new turf wicket, which had been improved by the recent rain. The match aroused 'great enthusiasm in the town' and the crowd was pleased that the English side included popular players Maclagan and Hide, although wicketkeeper Snowball was replaced by

Grace Morgan, who was usually relegated to the scoring duties.

England won the toss and sent Junee in to bat in front of two thousand spectators, each paying one shilling admittance to the ground. They scored only 29 runs on the new pitch with Maclagan, taking 4 for 6. In reply, England struggled and were all out for 63, which the local newspaper described as 'a poor score for a team of their undoubted ability'. Vera and Mary Treweek took three wickets each and the three sisters, with wicketkeeper Elma, featured in all but one of the dismissals. In Junee's second innings Maclagan took a hat-trick in her 6 for 12, the first of the series, and Junee were all out for 23, to give England an outright win. Funds from the gate takings enabled improvements to the turf wicket.

Following the match, the English team accepted the invitation of the local doctor Ronald Cuttle and Jean Cuttle to swim in their family's 'private swimming baths'. That night they were guests at a conversazione at the railway refreshment rooms.

Third Test, England versus Australia, Melbourne, 18, 19, 21 January 1935

The country leg of the tour and the local matches were concluded. All that remained was the final Test match against Australia at the MCG. The English team had already won the series with wins in the first two Tests in Brisbane and Sydney. The English cricketers arrived in Melbourne on the Sydney express train from Junee. They were met at the station by a fleet of cars 'gaily decorated with ribbon', but few noticed the cars or the scenery as they were driven to the Carlyon Hotel in St Kilda. Letters from home caught up with the team, and 'not one head was raised from the reading of letters'.

In between practice, the entertainment of the English cricketers continued apace. Members of the Pioneer Victorian Ladies Cricket Association, a group of cricketers who had been playing in the early years of the century, took them for what was described as a picnic in the hills. Stopping at Belgrave in the foothills of the Dandenong Ranges for morning tea, 'crowds of people lined the streets to see the visitors'. They had lunch at Red Mill at Kallista, and visited the home and spectacular gardens of the Nicholas family, Burnham Beeches, at Sherbrooke.

The cricketers were guests of Isabel Nicholas (of the family of aspirin brand Aspro fame), who had connections to the men's 1934 Test team, and her daughter Margery, also a cricketer. The family was well integrated in society, business, politics and cricket, with Prime Minister Robert Menzies a guest at Margery's wedding later in 1940.

Back on the cricket field at the MCG, England won the toss for the first time in the Test series and elected to bat in front of a crowd numbered at 4172. The wicket was perfect and the weather ideal – bright sunshine being tempered with a cooling southerly breeze. There were two changes to the Australian team. Victorian fast bowler Nell McLarty with one wicket in two Tests to her name and only a handful of runs with the bat, was dropped to twelfth. Australian opener Ruby Monaghan was also absent in the third Test: 'I had something wrong with me. I think I had itchy hives or something, you know, something was wrong that I couldn't play and that's when Sir John [Peden] rang down to Melbourne to see why I wasn't picked, he used to worry about me, Sir John.'

When play began, English opener Snowball was out cheaply, but her partner Maclagan scored 50, which with Archdale's 32 lifted the English total to all out for 162. Australian slow bowler Peggy Antonio once again proved difficult to play, taking 6 for 49. The non-Victorians in the home team were overwhelmed to be playing on the MCG and were fully aware of the traditions of the ground. Lorna Kettels, who opened the bowling for Australia in place of Nell McLarty, described playing at the MCG as 'absolutely fantastic ... the Long Room, when the English girls were here, the Melbourne Cricket Club gave us a dinner and we were in that room. And then to walk to the windows and look over the ground you think, oh gee, that can't be, you know, but it was really good.' Victorian Nance Clements took the opportunity to gather signatures of as many players as possible on her cricket bat.

Amy Hudson and Margaret Peden opened the batting for Australia. The second day saw a crowd of 7029 attend the match, described as 'a world record for a women's cricket match'. The Australian top order made moderate scores before tailenders Joyce Brewer and Anne Palmer added 65 runs 'in a much brighter partnership' for Australia to be all out just 12 shy of England's total.

In their second innings English wicketkeeper Betty Snowball scored 83, to enable Archdale to declare at 7 for 153 at tea. The Australians didn't take the challenge of scoring 165 runs in two and a half hours play when openers Amy Hudson and Hazel Pritchard, on instruction from the captain, 'showed no disposition to chase runs'. At stumps Australia was 8 for 104, with Barbara Peden and Joyce Brewer holding out the English bowlers for a draw.

The cricket in Australia had finished. In their descriptions of the matches, journalists, many of them former cricketers themselves, often at a loss to describe the feats of the women, had resorted to direct comparisons with male cricketers, calling them, among others, the Larwood, Woodfull, Bradman, Grimmett and Duckworth of the team. Irrespective of the crowd sizes and therefore the gate receipts, the tour was a financial success, with most of the money to support the English on tour being raised before they arrived. This had been done in the time-honoured ways of women's amateur sport – among them jumper-knitting, toffee-making and the holding of dances.

Arthur Goode, a sports journalist before he turned to stock broking, penned the newspaper story 'Women Wield the Willow' in February 1935 and proclaimed: 'The average Australian – you, me, and Mr Smith – has taken a lot of convincing that women's cricket must be regarded seriously. Probably it was only the fact that a team of women cricketers had travelled 14,000 miles to play the ancient game that finally decided him.' Interesting to note that in Goode's eyes, the average Australian didn't include women.

English players Betty Green and Doris Turner keenly documented the tour with their photographs, but at a price. Green commented later that the cost of photography added to the strain on her personal finances. Turner also took on the responsibility of liaising with Kodak to film parts of the Test matches in Brisbane, Sydney and Melbourne, but not all publicity and attention was good publicity. The women were eager to have themselves filmed in this historic series, but they soon realised their mistake in trusting that their games would be filmed and presented to the public in the right spirit. In February 1935, groups protested on their behalf against the newsreel commentators and 'their unchivalrous and belittling remarks about the players'. As one person complained: 'Women are putting good work into the organisation of good, clean, wholesome sport, and it is most disheartening to have their efforts ridiculed, and have facetious remarks made about the players when their game is shown on the screen.' Came to scoff, stayed to scoff.

As well as having accomplished speakers Green and Archdale at official events, many of the English women were talented artists, raconteurs and singers, skills honed and much encouraged no doubt at annual cricket weeks. With the Australian leg of the tour over, the teams met for dinner on the last night in a restaurant in Bourke Street, Melbourne, where Betty Archdale was presented with an opal. The team raconteur, Betty Snowball, delivered a well-received recitation of 'The Lion and Albert', a humorous poem by Marriott Edgar, made famous by Stanley Holloway in the early 1930s. The next day, Misses A. and M. Laing, principals of the Prahran College, hosted a tea party for the English and

Australian cricketers at the Lyceum Club. On arrival, each of the forty guests was presented with a posy of English lavender and red gum blossom. The flowers worked together and symbolised the links between the two countries.

Betty Archdale commented at the conclusion of the tour: 'All Australia,' she said, 'seemed to have done its best to make their tour happy. A sense of humour had helped them through less pleasant phases of the trip, such as wet weather in Southern cities and Brisbane's stewing welcome.' She noted: 'Australian women cricketers were great sports. Every match was played in a great spirit, and the visitors made many fine friends among their opponents.'

The English cricketers arrived back in Sydney on the *Wanganella* on 25 January and sailed for New Zealand that same day to continue their cricket tour. They were given a rousing send-off by officials and friends and pictured holding streamers connecting them to shore, which they had thrown 'with the sure cricketers aim'. Betty Green concluded: 'Our tour was a success ... our fifteen players established most friendly relations everywhere with opponents, officials and the general public ... a great service has been done to the game itself.' She recalled that crowds 'turned up in their hundreds to watch and encourage us'. Betty Archdale remarked upon the extraordinary number of little boys attracted to all the country matches. She said: 'The team has been nearly dead with tiredness at the end of some of these trips, but we wouldn't miss seeing anything, so we have ourselves to blame.' She added, 'Feelings regarding cricket in England and Australia were rather mixed when we started on our tour, and I hope that we succeeded in some small way to foster the relationships.'

The contrast with the 1932–33 men's bodyline Test series was there for all to see. Fifteen women from England had turned the feelings about cricket and gone a long way to restoring the game in the eyes of the public. On the field, the women had won over the crowd and the press with their high standard of play and their deep knowledge of the game. Off the field, they had charmed their way around Australia.

England tour to New Zealand, 1935

Up to this point Australian women had never played New Zealand in cricket, although Margaret Peden had suggested a match against the Kiwis prior to the invitation being issued to England, but it came to nothing. The first Australian international men's team had travelled to New Zealand in 1878 to prepare for their first-ever tour to England, playing seven matches starting in Invercargill. The MCC in England had sent a side to play the New Zealand's men's team in 1907. The New Zealand men's team made their first tour of England in 1927.

News of the bodyline tour had, of course, reached New Zealand, where the word bodyline had also entered the national consciousness. Movietone News featured Arthur Mailey giving his views on bodyline bowling in June 1933 and by October the picture shows in New Zealand featured footage of the bodyline controversy for all to see. By the time the English women arrived, even a New Zealand racehorse had been given the name Bodyline. Despite a speech by the president of the Auckland Cricket Association, Mr F. Earl, in September 1934 – 'the bodyline question has not yet thrust itself into New Zealand cricket' – the New Zealand newspapers' editors were ready with their copy. Reproducing a cable news report of the women's cricket week held in Malvern, Worcestershire, in the United Kingdom, the *Opunake Times*, commented on the 'ladylike attire' of the women cricketers and added:

> No mention is made of the other directions, in which it is hoped that girls will be girls – or rather ladies. Doubtless the bodyline theory will be sternly frowned upon, and anyway the cricket is sure to be bright and lively. No questionable tactics are to be permitted, and even silk

stockings are barred. The reason for this last one has not been made clear, but we can rest assured there is something at the bottom of it, even if it is only their notorious proneness to 'runs'.

The New Zealand newspapers received and published many of the same wire news items as the Australian press about the forthcoming tour of English cricketers, declaring emphatically that the English women 'don't bowl bodyline'.

After their tour of Australia, the English women arrived in New Zealand in January 1935 to play their first match against Auckland at Eden Park. It was a tight tour, the 'visitors arrived only this morning by the Wanganella from Sydney and practically stepped straight onto the ground'. More than two thousand spectators watched the game and the standard of the English 'was their all-round cricket ability which would have done credit to the best of the men's teams'. To the Auckland press, Betty Archdale discussed the 'wonderful time' the English team had in Australia and noted that the antipathy supposedly felt towards women playing cricket was noticeably absent: 'We do not play with men or strive in any way to emulate them, but they have helped us wonderfully in every possible way. We are not touring for the Ashes, but to play test cricket. It is very much against the principles of the association to play for trophies of any sort.' Had she at last left the questions about bodyline back in Australia?

An editorial in *The Auckland Star* entitled 'The Woman Cricketer' on Saturday 12 January 1935, stated:

> Men have gone to scoff at these women and their Australian opponents, but have remained to praise. These women can really play cricket. This upsets a rooted male conviction. To boys, girls are muffs at cricket. They cannot throw or bowl, and their bats are wickedly crooked ... One hope may be fervently expressed at the outset – that big cricket among women does not develop

the tense feeling, the distressing incidents and arguments that have wrought so much harm to the game among men. If it becomes so important that all the Empire holds its breath while matches are played, or if it produces a bodyline controversy, then there will be many who deplore the day that women's cricket escaped from the girls' schools.

Nancy Joy later wrote: 'New Zealand was no match for the England touring side, and in reply to their opponents' score of 503 for five, could only muster 44 and 122.'

A month later, a deputation to the local improvement board from the Papakura Cricket Club over turf wickets in the district acknowledged the growing number of cricketers in the district. C.S. Beechley remarked: 'Cricket is a game which is increasing widely. Now that women have entered the field it will increase still further. I don't want to touch on …' and then he hesitated just long enough for board member D. Weir to interrupt and insert, 'The bodyline', after which there was much general laughter. Good to see the New Zealand men had the same schoolboy sense of 'humour' about bodyline and women's bodies.

Back home in England in mid 1935, Betty Archdale was visited by the London correspondent of the *Melbourne Herald*, who noted she was busy unpacking her souvenirs: 'In her cosy flat in quaint old St. Peter's Square, Hammersmith, with its canary yellow painted stairs and air of bachelor girl freedom. Simple furniture, lots of books, and a carefree Bohemian atmosphere are the main characteristics of Miss Archdale's flat.' Surrounded by 'Slippers made from kangaroo hide; gum-nut toys, koalas, boomerangs, Maori head-dresses, and, above all, scores of photographs', the newspaper correspondent noted Archdale 'was looking bronzed and well after her long sea trip, and confessed that she did not feel a bit inclined to settle down to work again'.

CLEMENTS

LARWOOD

In the days before electronic scoreboards, a cricketer's name was painted on black cotton fabric and nailed to wooden planks for display to the crowd. After the game, the fabric was rolled up and put into storage. An extraordinary memento and example of re-use from the 1932–33 bodyline and the 1934 women's matches at the MCG. The banner featuring the names of Nance Clements and Harold Larwood symbolises the close connection between the two series.

Chapter 8

Larwood Lingers

'As cricket players we are now being taken for granted. We are no longer a stunt – a novelty – or a spectacle. Surely, surely that is what we have been working for.'
— Marjorie Pollard, 1933

The relationships between women's and men's cricket in the 1930s, interwoven around the bodyline incidents and their aftermath, have been forever and remarkably captured for history – if not in stone, in cotton at least. It is quite some story.

Cricketer Nance Clements lived in Melbourne. She had been born in 1914 in Noorat, a small township in south-western Victoria. She was a solid middle order bat and medium-pace bowler who was selected to play for Victoria in 1934 against the visiting English team. She was also selected in the 1934 Australian Test team but carried the drinks in the second Test at the SCG. Playing for Victoria against England at the MCG in 1934 was a highlight, as it would be for any cricketer in their hometown. In 1937, she was able to stake her claim for a position in the Australian team and travelled to England and Holland as both a selected player and the team's treasurer. She was again denied a Test match in this series but played in many county games. Nance, though, was a great collector. Often it is not the well-known star of the team who keeps and collects everything from their sport, but instead it is the twelfth person, the drinks carrier, the reserve player who has the time and inclination to assemble everything associated with their career and with a tour.

In 1990, I met Nance in the lounge room of her neat pre-World War I bungalow in Elsternwick, Melbourne.

The 76-year-old had played in the two-day game between Victoria and England at the MCG on 7–8 December 1934, in the wake of the bodyline controversy of 1932–33. When asked about the controversy in the men's game, particularly the role of English fast-bowler Larwood and the tactics of Captain Jardine she produced a tightly rolled length of black cotton fabric. Here was one object she had not originally put out for display. Dramatically but carefully, she flicked out the long roll onto the carpet across the lounge room, so that it extended its full length of over two metres. On the black material in large white capital letters was spelled the name CLEMENTS.

Nance explained how she came in possession of the original MCG scoreboard banner. In the match against the English women's team Nance had scored 21 runs batting for Victoria. In the days before electronic scoreboards, each player's name was painted on to lengths of black cotton fabric and nailed to wooden planks for display to the crowd on the giant scoreboard. When finished with, the roll was removed from the plank and rolled up and stored in the rooms behind the scoreboard for future use. Knowing that the appearance of her name was most likely a one-off, Nance had visited the scoreboard attendants after the game in December 1934 and convinced them to give her the banner as a souvenir.

Clearly, she had had to do some persuading at the time. Now, in 1990, she was having doubts – would she be getting the scoreboard attendant into trouble for giving away MCG property? Due to the passing of many years I assured her that the scoreboard attendant's job and reputation were safe. But that was not the end of the story. Without warning, Nance flipped the banner over to its verso to reveal more letters that now spelled another word: LARWOOD. Here was the scoreboard banner bearing the name of the infamous English men's bodyline bowler, Harold Larwood, from his last match at the MCG – a match at the height of the bodyline series.

The Clements side of the banner had sufficient cache to make this an object worthy of a national collection, to warrant its value and importance in cricket and to the nation. With the addition of the name Larwood and all its connotations, here was a rare object that spoke directly to one of the connections between men, women and the bodyline series of 1932–33. It was two sides to the one coin, the yin and yang of cricket in the empire writ large on a black and white banner.

No one looking at the banner on the scoreboard as Nance played at the MCG could imagine what was hidden behind, or yet foresee what the women's series against England would inadvertently do to reshape the memory of the bitter bodyline series and the animosity towards Larwood in the eyes of the Australian public.

Nance also possessed further testaments to the interrelationship between women's and men's cricket in the 1930s. An avid collector, she used her cricket bat to record the signatures of her English and Australian playing cohort in 1934. To these were added the signatures of nine Australian and four English male cricketers – Ross Gregory, Don Bradman, Jack Fingleton, Bert Oldfield, Stan McCabe and Bill O'Reilly, among the Australians.

Although some male members of the press and some former players treated cricket played by women with ridicule, the interaction between women and men cricketers in the 1930s in Australia was probably the closest that it would be for decades. This was not the case in England, where women had chosen to take a separate path. On arrival in Australia in 1934, Betty Archdale confessed to sports journalist Pat Jarrett that 'enthusiastic as she is about cricket, she did not attend any of the big matches in which Woodfull's men played in England this year. Although the game they played was fundamentally the same, she said, they did not mix their interest in cricket with the fortunes of the men's contests'. After interviewing Archdale, Jarrett emphasised: 'They called themselves women cricketers, not lady cricketers. They did not play with men, nor did they try to emulate them.'

The women's game in Australia developed alongside that of the men, albeit always negotiating the negative presence of a few dinosaur administrators and provocative male cartoonists and journalists. The attitude to women being accepted as cricketers was changing but pockets of open hostility remained, and these were often crystallised around the 1934–35 tour by the English women. 'Westerner' writing in the Perth *Daily News*, in a column titled 'With the Man in the Street', labelled the women 'invaders':

> The impending visit to Australia of a team of English women cricketers has roused the ire of a cynical friend of mine. 'Once women get into the game it's ruined. That's the end of cricket', he said to me. 'They should stick to croquet, rounders, tennis, if you like – among themselves, that can be made quite a womanly game without danger of fractured limbs or disfigured faces. But cricket and football, no. They're not women's games, and the intrusion of women into them will be a worse plague than bodyline.'

Another commented, 'They've robbed us of many of our jobs, half our clothes, and now want to grab our sports.'

The women were able to convince many of the onlookers and critics, however, that they were serious – they trained hard, they practised often, their batting was technically correct and they could be adroit as well as powerful, their bowling was inventive and canny, their close-in fielding was brave and their throws were strong and accurate. They understood captaincy and appreciated the traditions of the game. It was soon understood that cricket was in safe hands with women. But the one refrain that the women from the 1934–35 series came to despise more than any other was the 'came to mock, stayed to praise' line. The English captain Betty Archdale was fed up with hearing the patronising comment, the assumption that somehow women wouldn't be good at the game:

> Look, we got sick and tired of the men who came to watch, especially if we were playing at the Oval or something, and said over and over again: 'Oh we went to watch and scoff and we stayed to praise cause we liked it so much.' I expect you had the same here, we got sick to the back teeth with that.

In Australia, despite stories such as those told by Amy Hudson in Annandale, Sydney, of men taking over women's pitches, facilities could be shared, although often that meant women played on a Sunday rather than the more convenient Saturday. When the New South Wales Women's Cricket Association embarked upon opening an indoor cricket practice school at 140 Elizabeth Street, Sydney, the wickets were available for hire by any club, female or male. Dr Eric Barbour noted in his promotion of the facilities that coaching was arranged through the association: 'The official coach is George Guest, the Waverley all-rounder, who is not only one of the best of the younger players, but is proving worthy of his mentor, George Garnsey, in his coaching methods.' *The Australian Women's Weekly* promoted the indoor school as a first for women:

> In one respect, at least, the women cricketers in Sydney are ahead of the men, inasmuch as they have acquired room space in the heart of the city for the laying down of three wickets, on which cricketers and prospective cricketers may practise and be coached. The wickets will be laid in a similar fashion to that of the English school which Alan Fairfax started, and which has been such an outstanding success. There will be wickets for the

> fast bowler, and a special wicket, laid down with cork
> and matting, on which the slow and spin bowlers may
> practise. These indoor wickets should prove a popular
> and profitable concern for the women's association. It
> is expected that quite a number of the men's clubs will
> avail themselves of this opportunity of practising, too.
> Special lighting has been arranged, so that neither the
> batsman nor the bowler will be hampered by the glare.

At the official opening of the centre on 17 August 1934, some 'prominent women cricketers' gave an exhibition of play.

The contact between male and female players was highlighted partly through social functions. As women joined existing clubs, they were likely to come into close contact with male cricketers. At the end of June 1933, the first annual combined Cricketers' Ball was held in Sydney at the Mark Foy's Empress Ballroom, with a staggering one thousand attendees made up of male and female players, partners and officials. The cricket theme was delivered in spades. Sheffield Shield and representative players formed a guard of honour while '19 white-clad debutantes all carrying floral bat posies, and their partners, walked slowly down the cricket pitch for presentation to Lady Isaacs', the wife of the governor-general. Bill O'Reilly, the talented leg-break bowler from the bodyline series, trundled a great floral cricket ball down the 'pitch', just missing the floral stumps.

The tables were decorated with miniature stumps, cricket grounds, pavilions, scoreboards, turf and tiny players. The dances were 'interspersed with community singing of cricket parodies of well-known songs, bodyline bowling being the favourite theme'. Not among the debutantes, the evening was nevertheless attended by women players and club officials from many metropolitan clubs and the NSW Women's Cricket Association. It was noted that Margaret Peden had also brought a large party. That Margaret Peden and her sister Barbara were well connected in Sydney society opened many doors.

Women had established their own cricket club at the University of Sydney in the late 1920s, with both Margaret and Barbara Peden playing for the side during their university days. To raise money for the forthcoming tour by the English women, the women graduates and undergraduates played against the university staff, including professors and administrators; notably the clerk of examinations; the registrar; the economists Hermann Black, John Crawford and Richard Mills; Professor of Medicine Harvey Sutton, and veterinary scientist Dr Ian Clunies Ross. The umpires were Test cricketer Charles Macartney (1907–26) and Dr Eric Barbour, who had co-authored the book *Anti Body-Line* with Alan Kippax in 1933. Playing for the women were Mollie Dive, sisters Margaret and Barbara Peden (daughters of Sir John Peden, Professor of Law at the university), and Kathleen Commins. *The Sydney Morning Herald* reported that:

> Great applause greeted the first hit of the Registrar, Mr W.A. Selle, which reached the boundary, but after executing several neat side steps from balls that caused the crowd to call 'body-line', he fell a victim to the wiles of Elizabeth Pope, who was immediately threatened with failure at the end of the year by umpire.

The staff won by 75 runs.

The Pedens held other matches to help raise funds for the English visitors, including a novel match that opened the women's cricket season at the Ku-ring-gai Club dubbed Ku-ring-gai versus 'Fathers and Friends', that included international cricketer Charlie Macartney, the Ku-ring-gai Deputy Mayor, the headmaster of Sydney Grammar School, and the trustees of Central Park.

Victorians Peggy Antonio and Nell McLarty recalled many matches played for charity against a variety of sides: 'We'd play against the radio stations, fire brigade, the air force, the navy, on Sunday picnic games.' The games were sociable with a picnic atmosphere but, importantly, in them the women perceived that they were taken seriously as cricketers and treated with respect. In an editorial in her English magazine *Women's Cricket*, Marjorie Pollard was able to write in 1933, 'As cricket players we are now being taken for granted. We are no longer a stunt – a novelty – or a spectacle. Surely, surely that is what we have been working for.' She published her popular book *Cricket for Women and Girls* in 1934. But not all remembered it as so clear cut. Nance Clements recalled: 'I don't think too many men thought we were really serious, except that going back to club cricket we used to play the fire brigade. We used to give them a bit of a shock, I think, you know, men's fire brigade team, and it was good fun in those days.'

Journalists, often at a loss to explain the standard of cricket played by women, or in the case of women sports journalists to draw attention to their high standard, invited comparison with exemplary male cricketers by giving women common epithets. 'Hilda Hills of Preston is a real "Duckworth" behind the wickets,' wrote Pat Jarrett in the *Sporting Globe*. Englishwoman Mabel Bryant, who played in England in 1903 when she scored 224 not out and took all wickets on debut, was described as the 'Grace of women's cricket'. Ruth Preddey in *The Australian Women's Weekly* wrote that 'Alice Wegemund, the Bertie Oldfield of Australian women's cricket, is also a forceful bat'. Thousands more instances of these comparisons are littered throughout the newspaper and magazine articles of the 1930s. Inevitably, the personal connections between cricketers were strong as well. Lorna Kettels played in her Clarendon team in Melbourne with Vi Darling, sister of former Test left-hander Len Darling. The English player Carol Valentine was sister of Bryan Valentine, the Kent captain.

When Betty Archdale arrived in Australia, the forthright English captain and daughter of a suffragette, threw down the gauntlet to the waiting press on her opinion of the bodyline controversies: 'The trouble with the men is that they take their cricket too seriously. The terrible controversies that turned the rest of the cricket world upside down left the women cricketers quite unperturbed.'

'Even bodyline?' she was asked.

'You never hear of leg theory or bodyline in women's cricket,' she replied. 'Sportswomen and sportsmen had to have a sense of humour if they were to get the best out of their games. All the big Test match troubles that had convulsed England and Australia in the last two big tours would have seemed very small and very easily settled if the contestants and their supporters had seen the funny side of it. Hang it all, it's only a game, after all,' said Miss Archdale. 'It is ludicrous to take it so seriously as to get wild and call each other nasty names.'

After Archdale's comments to the press and Margaret Peden's sporting declaration at the end of the England versus New South Wales game when she asked the visitors to score 57 in thirty minutes, a feat they easily achieved, some men began to question and re-evaluate their attitude to cricket. Their reactions ranged from unsettled to defensive. In direct response to Archdale's taunt, Journalist J. Mathers wrote a piece in the *Daily Telegraph* in Sydney in which he asked, 'Do We Take Our Cricket Too Seriously?' Although he noted the crowd at the game in question had left 'light of heart', he found a critic of Peden's sporting declaration in Robert Oxlade, chairman of the Australian Board of Control, whom he said had recently dealt with the big controversies to which Archdale referred:

> What right had the captain to present something to the opponents which they had not earned? ... Why should a team, which has fought hard to save the game, be penalised by its captain's action in closing the innings in disastrous circumstances? It is deliberately sacrificing the game.

Oxlade, he said, also disagreed with Archdale: 'Directly you eliminate the serious side of the game it ceases to be a game of any character.'

Harold Heydon secretary of the NSW Cricket Association added his own somewhat patronising comments:

> Women's cricket is still in its infancy, although, like the growing youngster it is making great strides toward the local ice cream shop. It is not yet old enough, however, to enter upon terrible controversies, but it will be decidedly interesting to note developments, in view of Miss Archdale's laudable statement. One wonders whether Jack Fingleton, who returned to his dressing-room with colorful bruises from neck to knee during a certain match on Sydney Cricket Ground, saw what Miss Archdale would ask him to see – the humour of it!

The journalist Mathers continued: 'Miss Archdale specifies that "Australian crowds have a great sense of humour, but one must possess humour to appreciate their barracking sometimes." Here Miss Archdale wins hands down. Everybody, with the possible exception of D.R. Jardine, will agree with her.'

Bodyline continued to bubble along; if only because it attained the status somewhat akin to word of the year, or word of the decade. Like the attractiveness of the phrase to the newspaper journalists, bodyline proved a popular reference in speeches and banter in other arenas of contest – especially in federal and state parliaments where it entered the everyday language. It was particularly apposite during discussions regarding tariff and protectionism within the British Empire and to unemployment issues.

With so few women elected to parliaments across Australia by the mid 1930s, they of course had no opportunity to indulge in parliamentary banter about bodyline. Outside parliament, in 1937, 'a prominent South Australian public woman', welfare worker and president of the Proportional Representation Group, Jeanne Young, declared herself wholeheartedly in support of women independent candidates standing for seats in the forthcoming state election. She gave a public speech at the Georgian Club on 'Bodyline bowling in politics', 'for she is interested, she says, in cricket, and she can see bodyline tactics slipping into other walks of life'.

Come mid 1935, Betty Archdale was back home in London unpacking her souvenirs from her trip. The tour had increased the interest of women and girls in cricket across Australia, especially in those areas visited by the English team in person. The momentum gained from the trip for cricket played by women in Australia was spreading to every corner. In South Australia, the Waratah Women's Cricket Club travelled their cricket team out to play against the four teams of the Broken Hill Women's Cricket Association in 1935. The association president remarked: 'We were not sure that the game would take with the public, but the attendance throughout the season has convinced us that the game is popular.' With the long-promised return trip to England by the Australian women's cricket team imminent, the *Melbourne Herald* photographed well-known Australian and Victorian medium-pace bowler Morris Sievers requesting the autographs of Elsie Deane, Peggy Antonio, Nance Clements and Winnie George at a fundraising event at Port Melbourne Town Hall. The tables were beginning to turn.

The Australian team relaxing on board the ship Jervis Bay *en route
to England in 1937. Front row (left to right): Hazel Pritchard, Peggy
Antonio, Alice Wegemund and Winnie George. Middle row: Kath
Smith, Sue Summers, captain Margaret Peden sporting a pith helmet,
Mollie Flaherty and Nell McLarty. Back row: Alicia Walsh, Amy
Hudson, Marie Jegust, Nance Clements, Elsie Deane and Patricia
Holmes. Missing from the voyage was the sixteenth player Barbara
Peden who was already working in London as an architect. Two others
on the trip were manager Olive Peatfield and journalist Pat Jarrett.*

Chapter 9

Rites of Passage

*'Can you imagine a man's team holding an
entertainment at night to raise funds for the
Australians to come over and play them?'*
— *Daily Express*, 1935

When the Australian men's cricket team embarked on their 1934 tour to England in the year following the bodyline series, the cricket writer for *The Referee*, John Corbett Davis, expounded in his column on 'The Wonders of a Cricket Tour'. He captured the excitement of such an adventure for young men, especially the long-standing traditions that the players could look forward to being inducted into, and the close bonds of empire that existed through cricket:

> London welcomes them as heroes, with crowds lined up in the streets cheering as they drive to their hotel. The enthusiasm and friendliness of the people astonish our youngsters. They get an idea for the first time of the character of older players, they never knew, who made the fame of Australia on the cricket fields of England. It shows them, too, how deep down in the heart of the Englishman is the love for cricket. Next day, with the other members of the team, they visit Lord's and look round the hallowed spot of cricket. 'Not as good as the Sydney Ground,' a Sydney youth thinks. 'Not, so good

as Melbourne,' thinks a young Victorian. And it isn't, but inside the pavilion they look shyly at the pictures and the relics of the game as played centuries back, and feel that they have come at last, to the place where cricket's spirit reposes. There it is protected from the fiery blasts of body-line, or anything else that might be inimical to its health ... While practising at Lord's, they meet, or see, great cricketers they have read about, or perhaps heard their fathers talk about – batsmen, bowlers, fieldsmen, wicketkeepers, captains, and, above all, great sportsmen. They discover that the Australians are welcomed at every theatre and music hall in the Great Metropolis. They meet many of the finest men and women in England ... They have long since discovered that membership of the Australian Eleven is an open sesame to the institutions and people that rank among the great in England ... These are photographed into the brain and there they will burn softly for the rest of life ... It is worth-while. All expenses have been paid, and, with it, at the end, comes a handsome cheque for £600, to give each young cricketer a start in life.

Such palpable history and traditions were not lost on the Australian women making their own grand journey across the world to play cricket – all that was missing from their rite of passage perhaps was the £600 cheque. Even before the English women had left Australia in 1935, talk had begun, and arrangements made for a return visit in two years.

But the obsession with bodyline and its ongoing link to women playing cricket would not die. In the lead-up to the return tour of Australian women to England in 1937, it was the English women's turn to fundraise and assist the tour. At the annual Women's Cricket Week, held in 1935 at Colwall, Herefordshire, 110 women participated in the cricket festival, among them Betty Archdale, Betty Snowball and

Myrtle Maclagan. Australian newspapers reported: 'Believe it or not, cricket is being played in England at present in which there is no bodyline, no recrimination, no inquests, and no spluttering indignant letters to the newspapers. Their motto seems to be "cricket for the fun of the game".' The *Daily Express* asked: 'Can you imagine a man's team holding an entertainment at night to raise funds for the Australians to come over and play them?'

Prior to the tour in 1937, the Duke of Gloucester spoke at the Marylebone Cricket Club's 150th anniversary dinner. The Duke had visited Australia in 1934, immediately after the bodyline tour and royal protocol had forbidden journalists to address questions to the royal party about the controversy. Three years later, at the MCC event the Duke stated:

> In spite of the convulsions that had shaken the outside world in the last 150 years, the cricket ground has remained a peaceful spot, and a haven of rest from the din and turmoil of modern life. The game today casts the same spell as during the time of George III, during whose reign the club was founded. That monarch would certainly have been startled if it had been suggested that the time was coming when a team of women from the antipodes would be playing cricket in England.

Startled indeed. Many at the dinner must also have gasped at the reference to the 'haven of rest'.

In a speech in reply, the Australian High Commissioner, Stanley Melbourne Bruce, raised a toast to the MCC and addressed the elephant in the room when he said 'that the club's authority and prestige were unchallenged. It had a difficult role in the body-line controversy, but that unfortunate episode was settled by the happy British instinct for compromise.'

Not the only ones with a happy instinct for compromise, on its 150th anniversary the *Times* newspaper published its 'MCC Supplement' and devoted a full page to the history of cricket played by women. It referred to the principles of the Women's Cricket Association established in England in 1926 in a piece likely penned by Marjorie Pollard: 'Women's cricket is now an established thing. We have kept to certain simple principles, such as no cricket either with or against men, no competitive matches, and the determination that the game shall always be played in strict order and decorum.'

On the Australian end, preparations were underway for the forthcoming journey. In November 1936 the Aberdeen and Commonwealth Line entertained members and officials from the New South Wales and Queensland teams at an afternoon tea on board the *Jervis Bay*, the ship on which the Australian team would travel to England in May 1937. The *Telegraph* reported: 'An interesting tour of the ship was made enabling the girls to view the cabins which will be available to members of the team. Even the chef at work came in for his share of examination.'

As with any selection of national cricketers, the team chosen to travel to England and Holland in 1937 was not without controversy. At least two years had passed, and it was no done deal that the players from 1934 would be considered favourably by the selectors. In addition, it had been decided that although the team would be selected on merit, that a representative from each state (with the exception of Tasmania, again) should be included in the touring party to further the game in their state on their return. A team of sixteen players with a manager would make the trip. Each would contribute £75 and provide their own equipment but, as mentioned, the English side would raise money to entertain and host the visiting cricketers – a reversal of positions from the tour of Australia. Both tasks were met with the usual enthusiasm and players were invited to put their names down if they wished to be considered for the tour.

Adding to the controversies, an initial squad of thirteen members was announced on 16 December 1936 with Barbara Peden, now an architect and working in England, to be included as an additional member of Australia's team, subject to England's approval. Two more names would be added after further trials late in December. When finalised, half the team of sixteen players were from New South Wales. Four of them had played in the 1934–35 series, including Margaret Peden (captain), Barbara Peden, Amy Hudson and Hazel Pritchard, and four were newcomers – Patricia Holmes, Mollie Flaherty, Alicia Walsh and Alice Wegemund. Five Victorians were selected – Peggy Antonio, Nell McLarty and Nance Clements, along with newcomers Elsie Deane and Winnie George. Kath Smith was the only Queenslander and she had also played in 1934–35. One player was selected from South Australia – Sue Summers – and one from Western Australia, Marie Jegust. No age limit was imposed on their selection, whereas the English team to Australia in 1934 had to be twenty-one or over.

Newcomer Patricia Holmes (born 1917) had learnt her cricket at Frensham School in Mittagong, New South Wales, and as games captain had led her team in a match against the University of Sydney. Margaret Peden was impressed with Patricia and rang the school to invite her to join the Ku-ring-gai Club. Patricia, an opening bat and useful slow-medium spin bowler, left school, joined Ku-ring-gai and began studying photography with Harold Cazneaux, also obtaining employment through his Sydney studio. Like many New South Wales players, Patricia was coached by Fred Griffiths. She recalled: 'Well, he got me going, and I always remember what he said: "You haven't played a good innings if you haven't scored off every ball you possibly can." And I think that is why some of our New South Wales people did well.'

The parochial press speculated on selection, with some names confirmed before others. Holmes recalled her telephone rang one evening after midnight: 'It was Margaret Peden ringing up to tell me I had been picked for the Australian women's team. And they'd had a conversation, a hook-up, all round the states to decide who was going to be picked in the [last] two places and Margaret had quite an argument to get me in.' Patricia's mother's

uncle offered to help her finance the trip: 'The family seemed
to rustle it up.' Patricia took the option of extending her ticket:
'The boat we went on had this all-round ticket – you could go
away for two years – and I said to my mother that we could
apply to stay over if we wanted to. And I said, well I'm going
to ... get a job in London because I mightn't ever get over there
again for a long time. I did that.'

Mollie Flaherty (born 1914) had played against the English
team for New South Wales in 1934. A tall right-arm fast bowler,
she was nicknamed 'the Demon'. A baseballer (she was the
Australian pitcher) as well as cricketer, she possessed a strong
throwing arm, easily returning the ball over the stumps from
the boundary. By 1936 she was lauded as 'Australia's greatest fast
bowler' and captured fifty-four wickets in the grade season. She
played for the Cheerio Club and destroyed many batting sides in
grade cricket. *Truth* newspaper dubbed her 'Mollie the Mangler'.

Flaherty was a dedicated true sports fan. She spent hours of
her time clipping newspapers and magazines to fill her scrapbook.
In an act of Depression-era make-do, she re-purposed a used
large ledger over which she pasted cut-out photographs of
thousands of sportspeople between 1932 and 1935. She clipped
images rather than text, but her catholic taste extended equally
to women's and men's sports. She included champion racehorses
(Phar Lap, Valicare and Windbag), newspaper photographs of
polo, swimming, the Olympic Games of 1932, the bodyline
series of 1932–33, the men's cricket series in England in 1934, the
women's cricket series in 1934–35, baseball, vigoro and rugby
union. She collected cigarette cards and signatures and pasted
them in her scrapbook. And while the dominant theme of her
scrapbook was cricket – the front cover featured Stan McCabe
and the back cover Bill O'Reilly – in between she created a truly
integrated assemblage – pages and pages of the interconnections
between women's and men's sport in the 1930s.

Alicia Walsh and Alice Wegemund were the other New
South Wales players added to the tour. Alicia Walsh (born 1911)

also played for the Ku-ring-gai Club with Margaret Peden. She was an all-round sportswoman who played hockey, tennis and golf. The 1934 tour by the English team piqued her interest in cricket and she set about serious training at the Fred Griffiths cricket school, with the intention of gaining selection in the 1937 touring team. She was a specialist slow off-spin bowler, tall and slim, and described as having a spider-like action – all limbs. A 'bright bat', she made several centuries for Ku-ring-gai. She worked as the Director of the Free Kindergarten in Balmain.

Alice Wegemund (born 1908) grew up in the inner Sydney suburb of Woolloomooloo. Her father was a German immigrant who worked as a wharf labourer. She had kept wicket for New South Wales against the visiting English team in 1934 and was inevitably described as the 'Bert Oldfield' of the team. She also played hockey, tennis and vigoro and was a champion swimmer, with experience travelling interstate to heats. Wegemund worked as a machinist and supervisor at a boot factory. After her selection, the Paddington City Council supported her as the only Eastern Suburbs representative in the team, organising fundraisers through dances in the Town Hall. The citizens of Paddington also presented her with an inscribed travelling bag; the Mayor of Paddington thought she would return from her tour of England, 'a better Australian than ever'.

The Victorian wicketkeeper and batswoman Winnie George (born 1914) was also selected on the tour. A player at the Raymond Club, she also worked as a machinist. She regularly topped Victoria's batting averages with many centuries.

Also included on the tour was Victorian state captain Elsie Deane (born 1909), who had played against the English in 1934 and who was appointed vice-captain on the tour. Deane, like Patricia Holmes, was a late inclusion in the team, confirmed through a telephone hook-up between the selectors. Born in Brighton, Victoria, she captained and coached the Semco Art Needlework Factory team at Black Rock, where she worked as a supervisor and for whom her two sisters, Violet and Mollie, also played cricket. She was a medium-pace bowler and a strong outfielder. The factory and associated people in Sandringham undertook fundraising for her tour and presented her with a cheque and speeches on her farewell; management remarked that the team would go as 'ambassadors as well as cricketers to show the type of womanhood developed in Australia from British stock', and added 'the team would do good work on behalf of Australia and the Empire'.

The two state representatives deliberately added to the team from the outset were Sue Summers from South Australia and Marie Jegust from Western Australia. Sue Summers (born 1917) from Adelaide was the captain of her club YWCA as well as captain of the South Australian team. She was a good batswoman and left-arm slow bowler. Summers worked as a domestic companion. She was a member of the South Australian Women's Electric Cricket Association, a small group of about half a dozen teams who played under lights in Adelaide in 1937. To raise money for her trip, a match was played between her South Australian team and a team of ex-international male cricketers, including Arthur Mailey, Charlie Macartney and George Duckworth. The match attracted over 2500 spectators at the Unley Oval, Adelaide, and easily raised the required funds. *The Advertiser* described her as a popular player who 'practises bowling each morning for about a quarter of an hour, and ends with skipping exercises'.

Marie Jegust (born 1911) had played against England in the state match in 1934. She was secretary of the Western Australian Women's Cricket Association, captained her local club YWCA, and was appointed as a selector on the tour. Described as a 'steady batswoman and break bowler', significant fundraising through dances, concerts and donations was instigated to send her to England. Jegust was born in Bromley, Kent, and emigrated with her family to Perth in 1925 after she sustained an injury to her right arm during an air raid in London during the war. A cure in Perth was effected and she immediately took up cricket to exercise the injured limb – 'It is now this arm that proves so damaging to the wickets of opposing teams,' the press surmised.

Other newcomers to the touring party were the manager, Olive Peatfield, and journalist Pat Jarrett. Mrs Olive Peatfield, originally a clothing designer, was considerably older than Betty Green, who had been England's player–manager on the 1934 tour. She was regarded as one of the most distinguished sports administrators in New South Wales, was vice-president of the NSW Women's Amateur Sports Council and sports secretary of the YWCA. She had managed the New South Wales cricket team as well as positions in baseball, rowing, basketball and hockey. Peatfield had won the role from Dorothy Waldron of Brisbane by one vote. She acted as a more traditional chaperone to the team, which unlike the English tour, contained several players under twenty-one years of age.

With the tour to England imminent, journalist Pat Jarrett approached her boss Keith Murdoch at the *Melbourne Herald* directly, and suggested she be sent with the team to cover the series in England and Holland.

'What do you think?' she asked him.

'I think it's marvellous,' he replied.

Pat recalled that there was indeed some incredulity at Murdoch's decision by one of her female colleagues at the *Herald*, who remarked, 'Good heavens, imagine the *Herald* sending a woman to England to cover a cricket match!' Described as 'a sturdy, young blonde woman with an Eton crop and a brilliant smile', she would later have a near-lifelong affair with Maie Casey, wife of Australian diplomat in Washington Richard Casey, when Murdoch 'loaned' her to the Caseys to help them with their media engagements in the United States. Whether she was romantically involved with any of the women on the Australian team, or indeed English women cricketers, remains a mystery. But she was certainly good fun, always pictured laughing and smoking, and sending back a stream of stories to the Australian papers.

Jarrett travelled on the same 'slow boat' with the cricketers and was with them all the time. Not only did she travel with them, she also stayed with them in the same hotels and even played in one of the friendly matches on tour. Jarrett's inclusion on the tour would have a profound effect on cricket played by women and prove a watershed moment in the coverage of the sport by the press.

Of the returning players from the 1934–35 tour, Margaret Peden was now sometimes referred to in the press by her married name as Mrs Ranald Peden. Her husband, Ranald Emanuel, had changed his name to Peden by deed poll three days before their wedding in 1935, thus the Peden name lived on in New South Wales through the elder daughter. Margaret was the only married woman on the tour. Not everyone was comfortable with the absent Barbara Peden's selection. The feeling may have been that the Peden family seemingly made its own rules. Quizzed on the controversy, Victorians Nell McLarty and Peggy Antonio acknowledged it but were tight-lipped. Peggy was reticent to discuss it even fifty years later – 'I think that is past history, shall we say.' When pressed over whether there was some controversy she simply replied, 'Mmm.' Betty Archdale remembered it with a chuckle: 'There was a bit of hoo-ha about it, whether she should play ... always trouble about something.'

As far as their own selection, 24-year-old Nell McLarty remembered that you had to submit your name but she was reluctant to do so. 'I didn't think I was good enough so I didn't put my name in, somebody else put it in for me, not that I didn't want to go but I thought I wasn't good enough.' When she was selected her training partners approved: 'Some of the boys that I played with, they grew up to be in the sides like Victoria and they weren't a bit surprised when I was picked in the team to go to England because they said I could always beat them.'

Nineteen-year-old Peggy recalled, 'When I knew that there was going to be a trip to England I thought, Oh, yes, that would be all right. I didn't feel it had to be the be-all end-all of everything. If it happened well and good, if it didn't happen, bad luck.'

In Annandale in Sydney, Amy Hudson had the same modest reaction: 'I didn't think about it. It was a complete surprise to me to be chosen in that team.'

Nance Clements, who had been regularly saving money for the tour, experienced both the disappointment and delight of selection in one memorable day:

> When it was announced my name was deleted in the *Herald* and I said to mum, 'Well, that's that. I've got money in the bank I wouldn't have had.' And then about an hour later some friends rattled on the door and it was a dear friend down in Ludbrook Avenue and his two brothers, and they hugged and they kissed me and everything. I said, 'What's this all about?' And he said, 'You're going to England.' I said, 'No, I'm not! I've got the paper and my name's deleted.' And he said, 'Well, it's not in the one I've got.' So I tore down to the corner shop and bought another *Herald*, and there it was ... it was just that the edition that I'd got earlier was different to a couple of hours later, they forgot about poor old me!

But, of course, there was real disappointment at the hands of the selectors for many women who had played in the 1934–35 series. Ruby Monaghan, who had been described in the mid 1930s as 'one of the most brilliant all-rounders playing in grade games this season' was disappointed with the selection committee. Based in Wollongong, Ruby always had trouble catching the selectors' eye and regularly travelled to Sydney for cricket. She recalled: 'Well, with me playing in Sydney, I think they used to have the different ones going around watching who could play and who were the best and you'd get picked from there.' Her community again backed her, knowing that if she was selected her working-class family would struggle to raise the funds:

> If I'd have got picked for that they would have definitely
> raised money for it, in fact they did raise money for that
> trip – they thought that I'd be picked. And they put it
> into the Wollongong Hospital … it was presented, the
> bed to the hospital, the money that they'd raised for me
> to go to England, and when I didn't get picked, so that's
> what we done with it.

Fifty years later the emotion was still raw, and it had changed
her attitude to the sport. 'I stopped playing cricket after the team
went to England … I didn't seem to play after that … I took on
other sports you know, vigoro and softball and tennis.'

Ruby wasn't the only one. She thought the Shevill and Blade
sisters were equally disappointed: 'They were good players and
they weren't picked either. They were good players, they just
weren't lucky enough to get picked.' Perhaps if they'd all played
for the Peden-controlled, North Shore-based Ku-ring-gai Club
things might have been different. Lorna Kettels in Victoria also
wanted to go to England but was more resigned to her fate at the
hands of the selectors: 'I don't think I was disappointed. What's
to be will be, type of thing. If you are not good enough, you're
not good enough, that's all there is to it.' She, too, had given up
cricket by 1939.

Spin bowler Anne Palmer from Victoria, who had achieved
impressive bowling figures against the English in 1934–35, was
selected to go to England but had to turn down her selection due
to finances when she learnt that each player must contribute £75
plus spending money and their own equipment. 'I remember
the family discussing it and my father was not working then
and there was no way we could have raised it. The club were
raising a certain amount, but you still had to find some money
and I just couldn't.'

Joyce Brewer in Brisbane also submitted her name for the
1937 tour. She was among five Queensland applicants but was
unable to take leave from her business to attend the trials,

which the selectors held on a working day – Tuesday – on South Brisbane Cricket Ground.

The resources available to many women were always stretched during the Depression era and cricket put extra strain on family finances through travel to interstate carnivals and other cricket events. The pressure was daunting, and many women would have to rely on private sponsors, public fundraising and frugal savings if they were to make the six-month journey. Amy Hudson, in working-class Sydney, recalled:

> The people round Annandale and the *Westgate Weekly*, a local Annandale and Leichhardt paper, started a bob-in fund ... and it was in the Depression time when most people were out of work and on the dole. And then my players that played in the team with me they went round, I wasn't game to go round myself, they went round from door to door and collected. And even if people only gave threepence and sixpence it was a help, and so that's how the team was financed. And the man who owned the theatre up in Johnston Street, the Annandale Royal, he gave quite a good donation – he was very pleased about it. So that was the only way; otherwise, I would have never got to England – [it was] only for the local people from Annandale, Leichhardt, Forest Lodge and Glebe.

When Brisbane-based Kath Smith was selected, the only Queenslander on the trip, her association began an appeal to help her raise the money required. By early February 1937 the appeal funds stood at only £17, well short of the target, despite fundraising dances and personal donations from cricket and hockey followers. She requested an extension of time to raise the money. No help seemed to be forthcoming from the men's cricket association, but fortunately Mr T.M. Ahern, the President of the Brisbane Amateur Turf Club, stepped in to guarantee the full amount. Peggy Antonio, whose father had died, was helped by her father's former employer at the Victorian Stevedoring Company. Elsie Deane's team and workmates at Semco factory organised money-raising events. Winnie George, who worked at softgoods firm D.J. Taylor, was the beneficiary of dances organised by her workmates. Nell McLarty's employers at Henry Bucks contributed money and her Collingwood club held a fundraising dance.

Nance Clements in Melbourne was a frugal but determined saver:

> The time when there was a possibility, and I stress that, of being in the first Australian side to go to England, and for two years I saved 5 shillings a week in case I was picked. So, my father got wind of this and he said, 'Well, I'll add 5 shillings a week but break down one week and that's the finish.' So, for two years I saved 5 shillings plus Dad's 5 shillings, so if I was chosen I'd have money for pocket money to go to England.

Sometimes she used to put in 7 shilling 6 pence instead of 5 shillings. But, of course, the tour had implications for the women's work and future finances as well as current ones.

Amy Hudson, working at McKenzie's in Sydney, had her job held open for her 'so they were pretty generous'. Nance Clements, who worked at the Australian Paper Company, knew that she would not be so lucky:

> When the team was picked, jokingly I said to my boss ... 'Now, if I get chosen in this Australian side you know it means my job,' and he said, 'Yes, that's right it means your job. How long are you going to be away, you said six months?' And I said, 'Yes six months.' And he said, 'Well, it will mean your job.' But I said, 'I don't mind that at all, I'll get another job.' So, he agreed and we got another lady in to show her the ropes and I left ... In my

book it was more important to play for Australia than
to be a typist and have all the worry of the office for six
months. I got another job.

Betty Archdale provided a preview of the likely Australian
players to the English readers of *Women's Cricket*. She thought
new vice-captain Elsie Deane was a good all-round player, but as
a hitter 'she is too easily tempted'. Peggy Antonio she considered
a certainty, and would rather meet her again in person than on
the cricket field: 'I do not think we have any bowler as good in
England.' Peggy could make the ball break several inches in any
direction, and when batting she hit the ball 'good and hard'. Betty
described Nell McLarty as 'tall, thin and very shy', 'the whirling
arms bring the chief terror'. She admired her brilliant close-in
fielding. Hazel Pritchard's batting she thought was 'graceful
and stylish'; Kath Smith was 'thick-set and sturdy' and 'a strong
bat' and her fast bowling 'very nasty indeed'. Interestingly, she
thought Ruby Monaghan would tour with her 'cheeky' batting,
and of the invaluable Anne Palmer she said, 'When we thought
all the good bats were back in the pavilion Anne Palmer would
come in and wag the tail merrily.'

Before their departure, each Australian player was required
to sign a long contract agreeing to the many terms of the tour,
which had arrived in the mail in 'interesting looking bulky
envelopes'. The voyage would take just over five weeks. The
women's luggage was 'limited' to two large suitcases, one hat
box, hand luggage and a cricket case, which all together needed
to accommodate over sixty items. The luggage was to be painted
with a two-inch green and gold stripe round its width for easy
identification. The signed contract with each of the players
explicitly outlined both their cricket uniforms and suggested
clothing. For cricket, each woman was to have three divided
skirts, six shirts, an Australian blazer, a long-sleeved and a
sleeveless sweater, six pairs of stockings, two pairs of boots – one

spiked and one rubber soled – one bat, one pair of batting gloves, one white hat with green lining, one skipping rope and one training tunic and shirt. Other clothing requirements were quite specific and took in all eventualities: a travelling rug, hot water bottle, raincoat, warm topcoat, light summer coat, strong walking shoes, evening dress and shoes, evening wrap, two dinner dresses, reception dress, two afternoon dresses, one coat and skirt, warm frock, thick scarf and gloves, small felt hat, play suit for boat, six pairs of tennis socks and a bathing suit and towel. The organisation seemingly left little to chance. All the women also needed to obtain both medical and dental clearances to travel, and were drip-fed weekly allowances from their £75 contributions by the appointed treasurer, Nance Clements.

The Australians selected were scheduled to depart from Sydney and pick up players in Melbourne, Adelaide and Fremantle, with practice games scheduled at each stop. When the team reached Fremantle, Nell McLarty and Nance Clements sat out the match against Western Australia as they were reportedly 'recovering from the effects of vaccination'. Nell McLarty, the daughter of well-known Western Australian horse trainer J.W. McLarty, was met at the dock by her father who she had not seen for several years. Between Melbourne and Adelaide many were affected by sea sickness; touring manager Olive Peatfield's cure was early morning exercise, deck sports and restful hours in the sun.

Like the English players before them, the women immediately began collecting souvenirs of the voyage, regarded as perhaps a once in a lifetime opportunity. Elsie Deane, the team's vice-captain, kept a diary of her adventure, recording the ship's stopovers in the exotic ports of Colombo and Port Said. Leaving the boat for half a day in Colombo, still a British colony and part of the British Empire, the women travelled by cars through the streets to the house of Sir Solomon Dias Bandaranaike, the aide-de-camp to the British Governor of Ceylon, where they were entertained and then driven to a 'nondescript' cricket ground for practice, which had to be abandoned due to rain. Deane was overwhelmed by the different customs, smells, food and sights they encountered in this corner of the Empire and commented that she had expected to see more white people: 'I did not think that everybody would be coloured,' she wrote in her diary.

Nance Clements, Hazel Pritchard and a few others got off the boat at Suez and went across the desert to Cairo to visit the Pyramids, something of a 'bucket-list' item for 1930s Australian travellers. Britain had continued its occupation of Egypt long after their independence in 1922, especially in having troops stationed to defend the Suez Canal. The ship picked the women up again at Port Said with the next stop being the British colony of Malta. Elsie Deane wrote in her diary that Malta 'was lovely and clean and quite different after Port Said … some of the shops are as good as you could see in Collins Street'. To avoid extra expense, the Australian Women's Cricket Council had rejected an invitation from South Africa to stop over and play in that country. Instead, they had added Holland as a short cricket destination from England.

Writing from Colombo, Pat Jarrett filed a long article with the Melbourne *Herald* on the hopes and aspirations of the Australian players outside cricket, which provides a window not only to the women's interests, but also to how class differences dictated those interests:

> Operas, the Coronation procession, old village inns, stamp collections, London's traffic and how it is controlled, bright green fields and primroses, and Holland with its bicycles and wooden shoes.
>
> These are a few of the things that Australia's girl cricketers told me they want to see on their tour besides the thrill they will get from the Test matches against England.
>
> Margaret Peden, the captain, is interested in names 'I will be very excited just at the sight of "The Strand" on a sign post,' she told me.

Fascinating names like St. Martin's-in-the Fields are making her very impatient to arrive in England, but the greatest treat for the Australian leader will be to sit with members of the Women's Cricket Association of England and talk cricket! Yet the interests of these Australian girls are varied.

If Mrs Peden has time, for instance, she will see some of the settlements connected with English Universities, and will also make contact with Girl Guide activities in England. For she is a Guide Commissioner (University Settlement) in New South Wales.

Stamp collecting, again, is a hobby with Nancy Clements, the treasurer of the team, and she will make the most of her trip abroad to add to her collection.

If Amy Hudson only sees the Coronation procession she will be satisfied – but she has an introduction to a professor at Oxford University and plans to spend some time there looking over the historical buildings and grounds.

Alicia Walsh, on the other hand, confesses that she has a greater interest in people. So she wants to live with an English country family for a few weeks and to experience everything typical of their daily life. Alicia at home is the director of a Free Kindergarten in Sydney, and she will remain in England after the tour to visit clinics and to study her work.

In her usual happy-go-lucky style, Pat Holmes, one of the best all-rounders in the team, told me that she will absorb all she can with an open mind! Her business in Australia is commercial photography, and she hopes to get some first-class pictures on the tour. Pat will also remain in England to study.

According to Peggy Antonio, pretty things can be bought on postcards – so she wants to visit some of the poorer districts of England.

'I want to see everything without its polish,' she told me, 'and I would like to do everything that is not possible at home, like motor racing at Brooklands, and an aeroplane ride at Croydon'.

Marie Jegust wants to climb a tree and pick a chestnut. The Western Australian was born at Beckenham within sound of Bow Bells. She came to Australia when she was 13. On this tour she wants to walk again through the woods—just to smell the violets and primroses.

Operas and concerts will be sought out by Sue Summers, who appreciates music. Nell McLarty wants to see how London's traffic is controlled, and to ride on top of a bus. If there is time, she will make a special trip to Scotland to see the sun rise and set over the heather.

Elsie Deane says that she will be interested to see the working conditions of girls employed in factories, and she will make a big effort to get a glimpse of the liner *Queen Mary*.

Birds and gardens interest Mollie Flaherty. This fair Eton-cropped young bowler has hundreds of love birds, finches and canaries in the garden of her home in Sydney, but she wants to hear an English thrush, to see fields covered with primroses and to ride a horse down a country lane. And so, you see, each has her own lively interests, outside the cricket-field.

Lively interests with many reflecting the strong connections to Empire, and the eagerness to experience the sights, sounds and smells of Britain.

Players ranged in age from Margaret Peden, who was thirty-two, to Peggy Antonio, who was nineteen, with ten of the sixteen women under twenty-four. In this era, individual sportswomen and women in teams were usually accompanied interstate and internationally by a chaperone. This had been the case in Australia since the Olympic Games in 1912. It was the practice to appoint a woman, usually married, who was an administrator in sport played by women. They performed the role of manager, but there was also a strong moral element in their appointment, and they were seen to be protecting the morals of the young women in their charge. In reality, it was often not the young women who were a moral danger to themselves, but rather the threat of other male passengers and the ships' crew.

It was also the manager's job to ensure that the women undertook sufficient daily exercise on the ship to keep their fitness up. Not all enjoyed the exercises, often performed in public view. Amy Hudson recalled, 'We played deck tennis and we had to do these stupid exercises right up on the front of the ship, where the captain and whoever steers the boat, in front of them! Gee, talk about feel terrible.'

The fact that it was a one-class ship appealed to many of the women. Amy said: 'We went over on the *Jervis Bay* and they were only one-class ships, the Aberdeen and Commonwealth, but I loved the sea trip. There were only two of us never got sea sick and I was one of the lucky ones.'

Peggy Antonio thought the trip was 'Marvellous ... it was lovely.' Nell McLarty thought it was 'Wonderful ... we never stopped.' They remembered dancing and deck games and daily practice with a rope ball. Peggy stated the other passengers 'thought it was marvellous, too. It was just a small boat and everybody seemed to get on very well with everybody else ... everybody was equal.'

Unlike the Test in 1934–35, when the Australian women had little time to meet and get to know players from other states, Nell thought she got to know the whole team and 'it turned out very good'. Nance Clements recalled, 'Practice every morning, very early in the morning, we used to get into our tunics, practice.' The age-old rivalry between New South Wales and Victoria began to slowly break down. Nance thought, 'Oh, yes, there was a little rivalry there ... we Victorians were all right, I had to really get to know the New South Wales girls. I got close to Mollie Flaherty. We were all fair mates but, as a friend, Mollie was a friend I would say more than any of the others.'

The Australian Women's Cricket Council had sent each player a long list of rules and regulations (which Pat Jarrett cheekily referred to as the 110 Commandments) that covered their behaviour on the ship and on tour in England. These included limitations on drinking, smoking and gambling; that none could be accompanied by husband, relation or friend; restrictions on areas of the ship they could visit after dinner; bed by 10 pm and exercises at 7.15 am every day except Sunday, and participation every afternoon in deck games. The press, especially the cartoonists, had a field day mocking the regulations.

It was Olive Peatfield's job to enforce this code of conduct, but in reality she helped many of the young inexperienced women prepare themselves for what would be required of them in England. Nell McLarty thought some of the rules 'were pretty hard, but on the whole I think we needed help. I know I did. I didn't even hold my fork the right way ... we had a lot of the social niceties or whatever you call it to learn, and I think it was up to us to try to learn them.' Amy Hudson added, 'Mrs Peatfield was a good manager. I think she was under a lot of stress, too, seeing that we were the first Australian team that went to England. I mean, she had to make sure that we all behaved ourselves and we were there to represent our country and not to make fools of ourself once we got to England.'

Patricia Holmes recalled that the rules 'didn't seem to be too stringent. We were all sort of young and not very sophisticated ... I didn't find the discipline terribly hard. Sometimes Mrs Peatfield got a little worried, but I don't think there was any trouble. I wasn't aware of it anyway, I wasn't that sort of type of person ... Although I was twenty-two, you know, I was unsophisticated and I didn't drink and so it didn't worry me.' Nance Clements remembered signing the rules which didn't worry her because she only drank grapefruit juice. Amy Hudson also only drank lemon squash or orange as did a few others in the team, but she told a story about the stress Mrs Peatfield was under:

> ... I think, she was a good manager. Well, she was kind to me any rate and one time there, I don't know whether I am allowed to tell you this incident, she was trying to make sure we were doing the right thing and weren't disturbing anybody on the ship, which we weren't cause we played deck tennis and went and had a look at movies and went to the library and read. But she was in my cabin and she came down one day to me and she said to me, 'Amy, I'm losing my hair.' I said, 'Are you? What are you worrying about?' She said, 'Oh, this is a bit of a trauma,' more or less. And I said, 'You don't want to worry about it, Mrs Peat.'
>
> Any rate, about a week or a month after, she come back to me and she said, 'I think my hair is starting to grow again, what do you think?' And her hair was cut short, and I looked at it, she put her head down. and I said to her, 'Oh, yes, I can see one hair growing there.' She said, 'Oh, you're good for my morale, aren't you!' because I just didn't think ... but see it was [because of] the worrying about us making a good impression when we got overseas and behaving ourselves on the ship, which we did.

Pat Jarrett reported that Mrs Peatfield 'has a big responsibility. She is a strong personality and is extremely popular with the team.'

The Australian team had nearly six weeks together to think about their opponents and to strategise around the forthcoming return Test series. It had only been two years since they played the English and many expected to see quite a few of the same players facing them in the Tests. While the Australians were travelling, news came that England had appointed a new captain for the Test series: Molly Hide. Sports journalist Pat Hansen wrote that the decision 'was not unexpected, though many hoped that the honor would be given to Miss Betty Archdale'. The English selectors had not chosen Archdale, but Hansen had seen Hide in Australia and remembered her as:

> ... a very tall, well-built and sunburnt girl, a student at Reading University, where she is taking a course in agriculture, captain of Reading University women's cricket club and a representative of Surrey. She proved one of the finest all-rounders seen in women's cricket in Australia. Her batting, like her personality, was vivid and forceful. She was a master of stroke play and had the big match temperament – calm, yet keen – and remarkable powers of anticipation. Her fielding was something to be marvelled at.

She also remembered that Hide had shown weakness against Australia's slow bowlers, especially Peggy Antonio and Anne Palmer. Old rivalries were set to be retested with English bowler Myrtle Maclagan also selected. She had been the touted-batswoman Hazel Pritchard's undoing. Hansen wrote that:

> England's slow bowler will find her opponent a different proposition during the Australians' tour of England. Miss Pritchard learned many of her weaknesses in 1934–35 and took steps to remedy them. For many months she has been coached by Mr. Griffiths at the New South Wales Cricket Coaching School, and her play now is of a very high standard. Never before has she so deserved the nickname, the 'Don Bradman of Women's Cricket,' and almost her last words before the *Jervis Bay* sailed for England were, 'I am just longing to get to the wickets and face the bowling of Maclagan'.

Wicketkeeper Betty Snowball was another inclusion in the English team – 'Petite, dainty, quick on her feet and extremely graceful, Miss Snowball was one of the most popular of the visitors with the Australian public,' Hansen wrote. 'Her wicketkeeping astounded even international men cricketers and won for her much publicity. Her batting was as attractive as her wicketkeeping.'

The Australians arrived in England early. The forthcoming coronation of George VI had caused their travel plans to be brought forward to ensure both sufficient berths on the ship and accommodation while in England. The authorities had anticipated a sudden upsurge in bookings due to the impending coronation. There were some misunderstandings about accommodation. On the boat journey to England, Jarrett recalled in a 1984 interview, that many of the women had become quite tanned from the time spent in the sun, causing some frightful interactions when they arrived in England:

> There is a place not very far from the Oval where the Australians had been booked in, and only a few months ago Betty Archdale was reminding me of this dreadful day, she came along with the captain of the team, the late Margaret Peden and me, and the woman said, when she looked at Margaret Peden and then she looked at me and then she looked at Betty Archdale, whose face was as white as this piece of paper, because we'd been on a ship for six weeks, she said, 'I thought you understood, Miss Archdale, that we don't take Australian Aboriginal people here.'

Pat Jarrett recalled that 'we got that ironed out and stayed at that place – it was walking distance to the Oval'. Interestingly, the encounter echoes back to the Australian men's tour of England in 1877 when some of the English were surprised the touring cricketers were white.

A more hospitable welcome was awaiting the Australian women, as expressed by Marjorie Pollard in her editorial of the May edition of *Women's Cricket*:

> Welcome to Australia, we assure them that we players in England have looked forward to their visit with the utmost impatience; we have dreamed and thought of little else and we hope that every moment of their stay will be happy and full of interest. History is indeed in the making, and we are so proud to be able to take part in this first visit of the Australian Women's Cricket team to England. Enterprise, initiative and determination were ever part of the character of team games and this visit certainly bears out the statement and shows that women's cricket now takes its place with the other great team games and does not suffer by comparison. To Mrs Margaret Peden and her players from across the world we say Welcome. We are grateful to them for coming and we hope before the end of the summer that many friendships will have been made and that women's cricket will have the means of cementing still further, in this coronation year, the good feeling that exists between the two countries.

*Members of the Australian team farewelling family and friends as they depart
Australia for England in 1937. Left to right: Peggy Antonio, Amy Hudson,
Alice Wegemund, Hazel Pritchard, Nance Clements and Elsie Deane.*

Chapter 10
Colonials Abroad

*'When Captain Cook planted the British flag on Australian soil
he must have planted a willow-tree, too ...
the same has got into the blood of the women.'*
— *The Referee*, 25 March 1937

The cricketers from Australia arrived in England on 4 May 1937, long before they were due to play any official matches. Two events were scheduled before the main tour itself got underway. The first was the Coronation of George VI on 12 May, surely the pinnacle of Empire expression and bonding, and the second was a short tour to Holland to play two games against Dutch teams from 21 to 24 May. In the intervening period, the women were billeted within a 100-kilometre radius of London. Nance Clements remarked: 'Most of the girls were billeted more or less with blue bloods – I'll put it that way – educated people.' John Corbett Davis had written that male cricketers on tour in 1934 would 'meet many of the finest men and women in England, to find them the most genial and modest of mortals'. Had manager Olive Peatfield imparted the right information for such settings by polishing some of the women players' manners and conveying the right etiquette tips on the voyage over?

The English Women's Cricket Association was in charge of the practical arrangements for billeting the players. The Australian team was met on their arrival in Southampton by some of the people who were to act as hosts for the first month of the tour.

The players would stay week about with different families: 'By moving on they will be enabled to see different parts of England at their leisure that they would otherwise miss.' In each district the women would join the local club for cricket matches – 'so great is the interest in the tourists, that the English association has been inundated with requests to billet players'. Of course, as the Australian players in 1934 had noted, many of the English women cricketers who travelled to Australia had been 'real class'.

Journalist Pat Jarrett sent reports back to Australia of the team's arrival at Southampton and the enthusiastic and spontaneous welcome they received. She said they were met at the wharf by English cricketers Betty Archdale and Carol Valentine, and by Barbara Peden. The Australians coo-eed and blew kisses to their friends and were all 'deeply sun-tanned and looking exuberantly healthy'. Jarrett wrote:

> Conversation on the subsequent journey to Waterloo Station consisted of a long series of 'Oh's' and 'Ah's' as we got our first glimpse of the English countryside and the quaint old villages gaily decorated for the Coronation. Indeed, the long carriage was in complete disorder as excited cricketers fell over each other in their eagerness to get from one window to another to absorb the beauty which was unfolded like a picture book.

Waiting at the station were English cricketers Mary Taylor, Grace Morgan and Mollie Child, together with the Women's Cricket Association Secretary Miss Vera Cox. After the Australians had been in such close quarters on the *Jervis Bay* for over five weeks, the English Association separated the team for practice and match competition. Hazel Pritchard and Patricia Holmes stayed with Archdeacon Edward Hardcastle and Alice Hardcastle at Canterbury, about 100 kilometres from London. The following week they moved to Kent to practise with the Comp Club. Margaret Peden stayed with her sister, Barbara, in London and practised with both the Gunnersbury and Comp clubs. Nance Clements and Sue Summers were billeted together in London and practised with Gunnersbury. Kath Smith and Marie Jegust stayed with Marjorie Pollard at Stevenage, 50 kilometres north of London. Peggy Antonio and Amy Hudson were billeted together and practised with the Cuckoos team at Cobham, Surrey, 25 kilometres from London. Carol Valentine hosted Mollie Flaherty and Alicia Walsh in Essex with the Ilford Wanderers Club. Winnie George stayed with Grace Morgan and practised with the Civil Service Cricket Club. Nell McLarty and Alice Wegemund were also at Stevenage, but would later transfer to the Cuckoos Club. Elsie Deane was at Wallington, 25 kilometres away in Surrey. Although apart, the women had a set of exercises to perform each day and were expected to retire to bed by 10 pm each night. The hospitality and billets were overwhelming to many of the Australians. Amy Hudson remembered:

> Oh, it was devastating, I thought, if that's the right word, because the houses were, well to put it in Australian, they were posh as far as I was concerned. When you come down to breakfast there were all these containers on the sideboard and you'd have to go over there and pick your own food, and there were all butlers and things like that. And I was with Peggy Antonio a good few of the times – Peggy might have been better off than me, but one thing was, when I was on the ship Mrs Peatfield, that's why I liked her so much, she taught me a lot of things you know about use this from [that], to do the right things. Mrs Peatfield was good like that and that was why I was glad that she was in my cabin. But Peggy, I don't know whether Peggy remembers or if Peggy said anything, but we used to look at one another, you know, with all these things, but we'd be billeted into all these different places, but oh they were posh.

Amy Hudson even perceived the class differences within the Australian team: 'I wouldn't want to go and intrude on, say, Margaret Peden, Alicia Walsh or Pat Holmes, that came from a better class than me. I wouldn't like to go and intrude into their company because I would feel like a fish out of water, and so I just kept to my own side of the fence.' Nance Clements and Sue Summers were billeted at first with the head of the Underground Railways in London, and later moved with Peggy Antonio and manager Olive Peatfield to the estate of Lady Dorothy Cantelupe and Sir George Jeffreys in Hampshire. When I spoke to Nance in 1990 about the cricket tour she showed great recall and provided extraordinary detail of her experiences with billets:

> We had a maid or she came to my room anyway to unpack and undress you and dress you in the mornings, so I had to kindly put her off. I said, 'No, I don't need your help and thanked her for it', and we were just normal as we would be in our own home ... but the meals! We sat at a ... very long, big dining room table, it was a mansion – I don't know the acreage but they had their own hunting grounds and all that, horses and everything else – and I can see her right now, she reminded me of the old Queen mother, very erect, pearls, this is at breakfast, pearls and pearls [indicating earrings and necklace]. He sat down the other end of the table with his cravat, riding boot gear on ... the Australian girls and Sir George and Lady Cantelupe and son Sir Charles and his wife Lady Rosemary at breakfast... And the butler would come along in the house gear ... Gee, it was funny to think that, you know, if you didn't wish to have that dish he passed on to the next person and another butler – well you had to have something the second time wouldn't you?

The chauffeur drove the women to the local pictures and on other evenings they played music with the family. Nance remembered, 'It just had to be our luck that we had to have the manageress with us ... At 10.30 pm, Mrs Peatfield said we had to retire, that was when Lady Cantelupe spoke. She said, "Oh, I think the girls are having a nice time." She said, "I don't think it's time to go to bed yet." We were there until after one in the morning.'

Kath Smith wrote letters home about being billeted with Marie Jegust, as guests of Marjorie Pollard. They travelled to Marjorie's weekend hut on the River Ouse and visited a local picturesque mill – 'probably the oldest in England' – and Kath and Marie 'tried their hands at rowing but after about two miles both suffered with sore hands'. Kath Smith had more luck playing golf with Marjorie Pollard at the Knebworth links.

Not only were the women hosted in fine English homes but they were invited to 10 Downing Street to meet British Prime Minister Stanley Baldwin's wife. Dame Lucy Baldwin, a former member of the White Heather Cricket Club 'is a keen sport [and] is taking much interest in the Australian girl cricketers' visit'. The Australian team were surprised when the British Prime Minister himself attended the afternoon tea. It was to be the start of a long list of social functions and receptions that would fill their days in the lead-up to the matches. A lunch at the British Sportsmen's Club, entertained by the Earl of Lonsdale, featured, as was the custom, toasts to the King and a menu in French. Fortunately, the women were not required to order their dishes. They were served Délice de Sole Sylvia (a folded fillet of sole) and Parfait aux Fraises (strawberry parfait), but there might have been some behind-the-hand whispering as to what was actually on their plate. Amy Hudson was a bit overwhelmed. She recalled:

> Gosh, yes, it was totally different to what I was used to. We were just homely people. Some of the dignitaries were very nice, you know, but when they would, a couple of people would talk to you, and when they'd ask you where you worked – I've got to be honest

about this – asked you what type of work did you do,
and I said I only worked in a factory, I just come from
the working-class side of Sydney. Mainly being men,
a man of some type, and he'd say, 'Ooh' – and that
would be that.

To many of the women on the tour, details of being at the
coronation event on 12 May proved a memorable highlight
of their trip, and many kept their coronation ticket, booklet,
program and instructions as life-long valued souvenirs. The
event followed the 1936 constitutional crisis when Edward VIII,
who had only assumed the throne in January 1936, proposed
to marry his consort Wallis Simpson, a divorced American. As
head of the Church of England, an institution that did not permit
remarriage after divorce, Edward chose to abdicate in favour of
his brother Albert in December 1936. The coronation of Albert,
who became George VI, took place in London at Westminster
Abbey on 12 May 1937. The public spectacle was attended by
massive crowds who lined the streets of the procession from
Buckingham Palace to Westminster Abbey.

Patricia Holmes remembered the generosity of the English
Women's Cricket Association, which secured their coronation
tickets:

> Because it was [going to be] the most marvellous pageant,
> I didn't want to go really. I was rather stuffy about crowds
> and I thought it was going to be ghastly, but I was so
> glad I had to because once I got there it was absolutely
> wonderful ... we saw the whole procession going down
> to take part and then we got it all over again.

The women obtained excellent seats on Constitution Hill from
where they could see the processions. Patricia wrote the details
of the coronation in her diary and described the pageant as it
unfolded:

Before your eyes, these troops from the last of the Empire pageants and they came from everywhere – India, anywhere there were British colonies – and spit and polish, heads high, horses ... bands, I had tears streaming down my face when the Black Watch went by with the pipes furling, and then finally when the royal coach came by.

Finally, when it was finished, we went down in front of the Palace and started yelling, I think it was Barbara Peden's lot started it, I wasn't with her, but they were 'we want our King', you know, so everybody started chanting this.

Nance Clements remembered getting to the coronation at a quarter past three in the morning to get their seat: 'You had a long wait. You could leave your seat and walk into the park or just walk around in the vicinity.' Nell McLarty marvelled at the arrangements: 'They had these toilets set up, they were made of hessian, something like that. And of course that astounded us, too.' Nell continued, 'Oh, it was wonderful ... it was organised beyond our idea of anything we'd ever seen.'

Peggy Antonio had a different take: 'I just thought it was marvellous to be able to go to the coronation as a historical event, but I think there must be something wrong with me, I'm immune to a lot of those things.'

Kath Smith wrote in her letters home that the coronation procession was 'her great thrill ... especially when the King and Queen passed in the gold coach. When [Australian Prime Minister] Mr and Mrs Lyons passed by the girls cheered and cried, "Good old Australia" ... during the Coronation ceremony we heard every word by means of loudspeakers.'

When the Australian team assembled their scrapbooks after the tour many of them used the commercially available Coronation Scrapbook, featuring an image of the new King and Queen on the cover, to preserve their cricket memories. Pat Jarrett also covered the coronation for the Melbourne *Herald*: 'I watched, [I] was in the streets of London when the present Queen's father went by, the Coronation, after Edward had abdicated. Very exciting day, but I just happened to be there with the cricketers.' Jarrett reflected in the *Herald* on the highly emotional day for the group of women: 'The Australians were too moved by the pageantry and colour of the procession at their first glimpse of the Royal Family to give a coherent impression of all they saw, but they were unanimous that this was the most thrilling experience of their visit.' In the evening the women gathered at Crosby Hall, the headquarters of the International Federation of University Women, to listen together to the broadcast of the King's speech.

The English women's team had already travelled to Holland (now Netherlands) to encourage and stimulate cricket in that country, part of the move to spread the game not only throughout the British Empire but also further afield. The Dutch, in return, were keen to expand their connections with the British Empire, and sport, especially cricket, provided one of the means to cement closer ties. Betty Archdale with her team Comp from Kent had travelled for a weekend to Holland in 1936 to play matches. Other teams from England had also made the journey. As Barbara Peden, now working in England as an architect, also played for Comp she had travelled with Archdale's team alongside her sister, Margaret, who visited England in 1936. Comp played the Dutch women's team at Overveen, beating them by 129 runs. Margaret Peden made top score, retiring on 77. Knowledge of Dutch cricket travelled through the Pedens and through Archdale's other connections to Australia. It was most likely during the tour by Comp in June 1936 that the Dutch Association formulated an invitation to the Australian team, which was received in Australia in June 1936 and accepted for the following year.

Cricket in Holland was popular and recommended; Betty Archdale told the *Sun*, 'The women cricketers should have a most delightful time in Holland. Dutch cricket is not strong, but the players are very keen.' She told the newspaper: 'Women's cricket was started in Holland three years ago by a Lancashire professional, who was coaching men's clubs there.' The Dutch hospitality had become legendary among the English women's teams that visited in summer 1936, playing matches on Saturday and Sunday. 'They were royally entertained. On Saturday night they were guests at dinner. On Sunday they had a swim and attended a dinner dance at the KLM aerodrome as guests of men cricketers. On Monday they were given a full day's sightseeing including the showplaces, Marken and Volendam, on the Zuider Zee.'

A short three-day tour for the Australian team was suggested and promptly arranged. It followed the same schedule as the 1936 Comp tour and it would enable the Australian women to experience other cultures and customs on the Continent before the English matches started in earnest. The Melbourne *Herald* noted, 'Women's cricket is not yet extensively played by the Dutch, but the Dutch association is very enthusiastic, and hopes by the visit of the Australians to stimulate interest in the game. Good fielding is a feature of the Dutch girls' game. Their bowling and batting lack variety and the footwork is not fast enough.'

The Australians were to arrive in Rotterdam on Friday, play their first match at Nijmegen on Saturday and second at Haarlem on Sunday, returning to London Monday evening. It was the first time that the Australian team had been brought back together after staying in their private billets. Separate travel arrangements had been made for them, but when Alice Wegemund and Nell McLarty were unexpectedly caught in a traffic jam and missed their train in London, they caught a later boat to Rotterdam and only arrived on Saturday at 2 pm, after their Rotterdam taxi driver took them to the wrong train and they became 'hopelessly lost'. Their lack of language skills caused further complications, and they travelled in three Dutch trains and arrived 'foodless since the previous day'.

The majority of the Australian team was met at Rotterdam by the president of the Dutch Cricket Association, Mrs N. Sabelson-Nieuwenhuys. They walked through picturesque gardens beside the harbour in Rotterdam and were shown places of interest in the city before leaving on a special bus for Delft, and then on to Scheveningen and the Hague to Haarlem. They had their first glimpse of Holland's windmills, canals, barges and tulip fields. They saw special concrete tracks for the thousands of bicycles along tree-lined roads, and walked the canals and quaint shops of Delft. At Scheveningen they visited the famous panorama by seascape painter Hendrik Willem Mesdag. They lunched at the Hague and visited the Palace of Peace and Princess Juliana's Palace, buying souvenirs in the courtyard. They had afternoon tea at an old Dutch farmhouse beside a canal. They were then billeted with Dutch families in Haarlem.

Hospitality was showered on the Australian team, with many taking up the opportunity for cycling. Margaret Peden cycled from where she was staying in Heemstede, a suburb of Haarlem, to meet other members of the team. Nance Clements remembered that, 'in those days, too, the streets were all cobblestone and there was a bike outside a lolly shop and Georgie [Winnie George] was with me at the time and I said, "I'm dying to have a ride on that bike and try these cobblestones." Well, it was the most dreadful experience.' She thought, 'It was ... a very, very clean country. Couldn't get over the cleanliness of it, windows sparkled, footpaths were scrubbed – I actually saw that.' Nance was determined to tick a few other items off her bucket list:

> We travelled by coach all the time ... I wanted a photo
> of a windmill and I said to Georgie, see if you can get
> the driver to, or ask somebody to ask Mrs Peatfield to
> stop the bus – I wanted a photo of that windmill. Well,
> it looked pretty close, you know. We got through the

fence, well we only got halfway, and we were in mud up
to our hocks, but I got a photo of the windmill. It was
very wet, you know, mushy.

Patricia Holmes remembered, 'We had nothing but friendliness
and we were billeted with the Voss family in Amsterdam.' She
stayed with Hazel Pritchard and succumbed to that other feature
of Holland – the steep internal house stairs:

> We had a dinner, they entertained us with a big dinner,
> and we came home, Hazel Pritchard and I, and you
> know these big high houses, we had to climb. We were
> up at the top and we got the giggles on the way up ...
> I don't know what the Voss parents thought of us. We
> absolutely collapsed halfway up.

The first things the Australian cricketers noted in Holland were
that the teams played in cream flannel trousers, and that all the
pitches were matting. The cricket matches were no contest,
but they did enable the Australian team to have some practice
and sort out batting and bowling line-ups, even if the Dutch
had requested that they not play their strongest team. Margaret
Peden won the toss and chose to bat first in both matches. Pat
Jarrett wrote, 'The sun was strong like a summer day at home.'
In the first match played on Saturday at Nijmegen, on a wicket
of cinders completely covered in matting with holes cut out
for stumps, the Australians 'overwhelmed' the Dutch, closing
their innings at 6 for 195 (Peggy Antonio 42, Winnie George
31, Kath Smith 30, Barbara Peden and Nell McLarty 24) and
dismissed Holland for 20 (Kath Smith 2–2, Sue Summers 2–1,
Nance Clements 2–1) and again 7 for 43 at stumps. A match
report read: 'The Holland team was inexperienced and had no
fast bowlers, but they were alert in the field.'

In the second match on Sunday, played at Overveen near
Haarlem, Australia scored 212 runs in 179 minutes declaring at

9 wickets (Patricia Holmes 44 (ret.), Hazel Pritchard 42 (ret.), Mollie Flaherty 25) and dismissed Holland for 36 (Marie Jegust 3–3, Nell McLarty 2–5, Mollie Flaherty 3–18) and 27 (Elsie Deane 3–3, Amy Hudson 2–4). Peggy Antonio and Winnie George stood as umpires. The Dutch were soundly defeated but they had spirit. Pat Jarrett wrote:

> The Australians were impressed with the splendid athletic physique and stamina of the Dutch players, who were particularly good fielders. Molly Haalmeyer, the fastest of the Dutch bowlers, gave a particularly fine display, bowling over 32 overs, eight of which were maidens, for two wickets and 72 runs. I have never seen a girl work so hard on a cricket pitch.

The Dutch captain, Dein Roos, also a Dutch international hockey player, 'showed good knowledge of stroke-making, but generally the Dutch players want plenty of coaching in batting and bowling. Their fielding was keen, and at times brilliant when several smart returns from the outfield broke the wicket.' With their limited English the Dutch had adopted an appeal that sounded more like 'Ow Izzie?' than 'Ow's Zat?'

After the match at Nijmegen, the players were entertained at a dinner and dance at a 'Continental' open-air restaurant. Pat Jarrett noted the clubhouses in the town and the Kennemer Lyceum ground at Overveen also had a 'Continental atmosphere that was greatly enjoyed'. Brightly coloured tables and chairs were set out-of-doors on spacious, tiled verandahs under big sun umbrellas: 'We all wished for something similar at cricket matches in Australia.' The team was entertained at a farewell dinner dance in Haarlem, and each of the players received a silver spoon from Netherlands Dames Cricket Board. Pat Jarrett noted that the Dutch women were eager to learn more of 'our language', but they were outclassed by the diplomatic efforts of captain Margaret Peden, who had prepared and practised her pronunciation for two days to deliver her farewell dinner speech in Dutch. Jarrett noted, 'The Australians did not understand a word, but the gesture was appreciated by her team and Dutch officials and players.'

Nance Clements and Sue Summers both kept their souvenir menus from the two restaurants they visited – the Metropole Café at Nijmegen and the Lido in Amsterdam – signed by Australian and Dutch players. Kath Smith wrote home that the team visited a restaurant 'at the Hicks Hotel where everything is eaten on bread'. They then spent Monday in a whirl of sightseeing and souvenir hunting in Volendam and on the Island of Marken, before shopping in Amsterdam. Back on Rotterdam wharf, 'The Australians said good-bye to their new Dutch friends and struggled up the gangway with parcels and wooden shoes – a lasting reminder of a hospitable country and of keen cricket enjoyed there in the sunshine.'

Fast-forward nearly fifty years to May 1983, and one of the Dutch players from this team in 1937, Sophie Broekmans, visited Australia keen to renew her acquaintances. She was reunited in Sydney with Patricia Holmes and the two women were interviewed together by cricket stalwart Ann Mitchell. Sophie was twenty-two in 1937 and she had played cricket in Holland for about five years but 'didn't know how the girls of Australia played cricket … We thought we are playing cricket but our results were so bad that we thought afterwards we are thinking what are we going to play.' She found the Australian girls more independent than the Dutch girls: 'They wore beautiful clothes, wearing green jackets and they are wearing a hat, a very good team.' Patricia Holmes remembered them as 'a tremendously friendly team, tremendously'. Sophie spoke about the ease of travel for the Dutch women playing cricket, due to the size of Holland: 'There was only one hour by train, or one and a half hour by train.' After their matches it was not uncommon for them 'to dance and to have fun with each other and then we are coming home at 12 o'clock in the evening or one in the next day … so when I started from home on Sunday my parents asked me at what time are you going back. I said, "Oh, I don't know, it may be tomorrow morning".' World War II halted the good times for Dutch women cricketers.

As usual, the hospitality and connections forged between the women from different cultures were almost as important as the cricket. Holland was keen to be included in the formation of an international women's cricket association – previously only thought of as an Empire Women's Cricket Federation with members Australia, England, New Zealand, South Africa and India. With Holland entering the field, the probability of forming an International Federation was mooted. Organised dinners, dancing and sightseeing paved the way for Holland's inclusion, despite their lack of cricketing experience. It was international diplomacy through hospitality, goodwill and friendliness, and the Dutch women had it in spades.

It would be another sixteen years before an Australian men's cricket team played in Holland, and twenty-seven years before a second men's team, featuring Bill Lawry, Graham McKenzie and Wally Grout, fresh from an Ashes win in England, lost to the Dutch men in August 1964 by three wickets. It was described by English sportswriter Jim Manning as the most staggering sporting message he had had to handle, with the exception of America's one–nil defeat of England at soccer in 1950.

During their nineteen-match tour of England from June to July 1937 the Australian players participated in a whirlwind of functions, dinners and events outside cricket and were presented to many dignitaries and officials at their games. Cricketers Marie Jegust, Nell McLarty, Peggy Antonio and Nance Clements meet the Mayor of Liverpool, Lord Derby (top hat).

Chapter 11

Summer Tests, England, 1937

> *'There can be no summer in this land without*
> *cricket ... these Australians ... have given us*
> *cricket such as we have never seen before.'*
> — Marjorie Pollard, 1937

From the first day of June 1937, the Australian newspapers proclaimed that the 'holiday period for the Australian women cricketers is over. Tomorrow the tour begins in earnest when they play their first match in England against Kent.' On the day before their first match the president of the All England Women's Cricket Association, Frances Heron-Maxwell, entertained the players at lunch at her home at Great Comp, Kent. 'Afterwards,' the media reported, 'the team will practise on her private oval at Great Comp, one of the loveliest grounds on which the women will play. This oval should remind the Australians of the traditions of English cricket, which had its beginnings on the village greens and on the ovals of private landowners.' Access to grounds for women in England, like in Australia, was an ongoing contentious issue. It was noted:

> Interest in women's cricket has grown since the inauguration of the Women's Cricket Association in England in 1926, as is evident from the action of the cricket clubs of England in granting the use of many of their most famous grounds for the women's matches

211

during this tour of the Australians. The only world-renowned ground on which the girls will not play is Lord's, but the MCC has by no means overlooked the visit of the Australians. It recently gave £25 to the women's association of England for its hospitality fund (the women have raised £1300), and has also invited the Australians to have lunch at Lord's as the guests of the MCC during the Gentlemen v Players match in July.

In fact, the English women had been lobbying to be part of the cricket on that day, a request refused by the Marylebone Cricket Club on the grounds that the program was already set. The sum of £25, while welcome, did little to allay their disappointment at such a snub.

The cricket program included three three-day Test matches versus England, ten one-day matches versus Counties and the Civil Service, and six two-day matches versus Districts and the 1934 Touring Team. In all, nineteen matches were to be played. The English Women's Association provided special buses for the Australian women to travel on during their fifty-six-day tour. 'This mode of travel as well as being more comfortable and less tiring than train travelling will give the Australians a great opportunity of seeing the English countryside.'

Pat Jarrett, meanwhile, would be travelling in a 'tiny car, with Monica Morris, the official scorer'. Jarrett set the scene for the next two months:

> Hop-pickers will be busy in Kent when the Australians turn out for their first official practice on June 1. From then the itinerary will take the team to Chelmsford near the east coast, Birmingham, Northampton, Leicester and Leeds. At Northampton the Australians will meet England in the first match of the Test rubber. A match at Old Trafford, one of England's most historic grounds, is also included in the itinerary before the second Test

at Blackpool, which will be played during the English summer holiday time. Moving south, the team will play at Cheltenham, in one of the prettiest districts of England. Then on to Basingstoke, then Winchester, and its cathedral, to The Oval, another famous old ground, for the third and deciding match of the rubber against England. The remaining matches will be played in the south district, Chiswick, Hove, Stevenage, Turnham Green and Maidstone. So we look forward to rural and industrial England at its best – in long summer twilight and Coronation time.

Noticeably absent from Pat Jarrett's reports are two of the issues that dominated coverage of the cricket matches in Australia in the summer of 1934–35. The first, of course, was the obsequious repetition of the 'came to mock, stayed to praise' mantra that so annoyed the women from that earlier tour. The second was the constant reference to the bodyline incidents. Had cricket matured enough to leave these two issues behind? Had the women finally overcome these controversies, and could they now play cricket in their own right?

Granted, the English press was much less likely than the Australian press to raise the spectre of bodyline. But, in reality, by Murdoch's agreement to send journalist Jarrett to cover the tour, the women had achieved what can only be dreamed of in sport played by women: control over the message. Peggy Antonio remembered, 'Pat had an open go and she used it.' Nell McLarty added, 'They'd have a whole page sent back from England to the local *Herald* in Victoria.'

Absent from the media, sadly, were articles by Ruth Preddey in *The Australian Women's Weekly*. Its editor, George Warnecke, had decided in July 1936 to replace the regular pages on sport with a gardening column. Thereafter the readers of the *Weekly* missed out on the drama of the sporting pages and the achievements of Australian sportswomen. In particular, they missed the knowledgeable and instructive articles by Preddey, whose publicity had aided recruitment to team sports, such as cricket, as well as interest in individual championship sports, such as tennis and golf. However, without the pressmen of the mainstream media controlling the tone and content, this cricket tour was presented differently.

Gone was the patronising style of language of fair maidens traipsing over the fields in flowing frocks, gone were the petty and belittling swipes and jibes by male cartoonists, gone were the editorials comparing their skills with men, gone were the comments of washed-up cricketers, gone were the recalcitrant letters to the newspapers by those bemoaning the incursion of women onto cricket fields. Well, of course, not completely gone. But for the first time the reporting by Jarrett, Pat Hansen and other women in the sports media was centre-stage and it effectively drowned out, if only for a brief time, the reporting that had gone before. It was fresh, it was lively, and it struck a balance between reporting the exciting cricket contests and introducing the women on the tour to the audience. It built their profile and created interest in their games, without the silliness demonstrated by many of the Australian pressmen just two years earlier. The women's bodies and bodyline were simultaneously liberated from the conversation. Everything was in place. Out came a new black *Empire Cumulative Cricket Scoring Book* to record every match on tour.

In the 1934–35 series Betty Archdale had claimed that not much separated the two sides. She considered England had won because of the advantage the touring team gained in travelling and living together, while the Australian team had only played together as opponents. In 1937 the positions were reversed. Australia won its first five matches on the trot, including the first Test played at Northampton. In all, Australia won 11 of its 19 matches, drew 7 and lost only one – the second Test at Blackpool. Eyewitness to the games, English cricketer Nancy Joy, later wrote:

What a change in two short years! How the Aussies improved! ... The standard was reflected in the results ... And all the time the Australians played some glorious cricket. The batting of Hazel Pritchard – graceful, fluent, flashing, was a revelation: so were Antonio's leg-breaks, and her cheeky 80s and 90s: the pace of Smith and Flaherty: McLarty's suicidal infielding: Pat Holmes's 200 at Basingstoke, the steady run-getting of the middle batsmen and the skill and study behind Margaret Peden's captaincy. All these, matched against England's pick in the three Tests, produced contests so closely fought that the issue of each of them remained in doubt until the closing overs.

Matches against Kent (2 June), East (4–5 June), Midlands (7–8 June), and Warwickshire (10 June) 1937

The standard of cricket was very high throughout the tour and individual women gave some memorable performances on the field. Against Kent, Hazel Pritchard scored 74 not out and Kath Smith 68 not out; bowler Mollie Flaherty took 7 for 33. Against East, Winnie George made 68. Against Midlands, Pritchard scored 96 and Kath Smith took 5 for 54. In the match against Warwickshire, Winnie George scored 69 not out.

After the match against Midlands in Birmingham, the third match of the series, Marjorie Pollard, who had been a participant, captaining Midlands and top scoring in the match, realised that the tide was turning. She wrote:

> I remove my hat and keep it removed to Mrs Peden for the wonderful way in which she captained a team of players, all of whom have character, ability, determination and views of their own. She kept a fresh bowler always at hand, and never once could a batsman relax. I was at the wickets, I suppose, for about three and a half hours

during the two days and I can truthfully say that always
I was conscious of the complete Australian team. I felt
them full of purpose and determination. I never had one
over in which I could relax and think, 'Well the next
ball won't matter much'. Also – never before have I, as
a captain, found so great a difficulty in setting a field to
cope with such versatile batting. We may have been able
to teach the Australians something in 1934 – they are
now repaying us, plus a thumping interest.

First Test against England, Northampton, 12, 14, 15 June 1937

The Australian women had renewed purpose and, in the
lead-up to the first Test, Pat Jarrett reported they had eschewed
sightseeing in Warwickshire in favour of practice at the small
Dorridge ground close to the village where they were staying.
There was still some respite, however. Elsie Deane wrote in her
tour diary about the time spent in Birmingham and her visits
to 'the most glorious garden anyone would wish to see'. The
team lunched at Bournville and were presented with a box of
chocolates before being driven to Kettering for practice, dinner
at 8.30 pm then an early night: 'We all went to bed to get ready
for the big day, our first Test match in England.'

After the first day of the first Test match between England
and Australia on English soil on 12 June 1937 at Northampton,
Pollard, who commentated the game live on radio, wrote:

> This has been a day I shall remember all my life. I have
> seen 5000 people watching a women's cricket match at
> Northampton. I have talked with Mr Levenson Gower
> and more 'MCC Ties' than I have ever seen gathered
> together before. I have seen Australia make 300 runs,
> I have been thoroughly nervous over giving a running
> commentary on the game.

Elsie Deane wrote in her diary, that the weather wasn't kind: 'The light was very dull when [Margaret] Peden and Antonio went out to open Australia's innings in the first Test in England between women cricketers.' Australia won the toss and batted. It was a strong team with seven recognised batters, including Hazel Pritchard at first drop. Winnie George was preferred as wicketkeeper over Alice Wegemund to strengthen the batting. Pollard wrote, 'At the ground there was an air of something about to happen – there was excitement, and that peculiar tenseness that foretells events of moment.' Pritchard made 87, including 10 fours in an impressive display described by Pollard:

> She drove, cut and glanced and it is quite true to say that this small and rather fragile looking player has set a new standard for us in batting. We have seen nothing like it before for sheer fluency of style and for ease of execution. For one so small it is amazing how she hits the ball so hard and yet keeps her poise and balance.

Kath Smith batted at six, and accumulated 88 runs to take the Australian score to 300. In reply England made 204 runs with Myrtle Maclagan top scorer on 89 and Peggy Antonio taking 6 for 51. Runs were not as easy in Australia's second innings with Nell McLarty top scoring with 23 from a total of 103. Needing 200 to win, a tense run chase ensued with English openers Maclagan and Betty Snowball scoring 58 before the loss of their first wicket. At one stage Margaret Peden sportingly recalled Mary Taylor after she had been given run out, believing the wickets had been broken early by the wicketkeeper. The drama continued. Jarrett wrote: 'The whole Australian team ran up to embrace Nell McLarty when she rolled headlong for a brilliant catch. Australians rushed the ground to hug Peggy Antonio when she bowled the last English batswoman.' Australia's first Test victory against England made both the front and the back page of the Melbourne *Herald*.

Matches against Yorkshire (17 June), North (19, 21 June), and Lancashire (23 June) 1937

The Australians continued their success. In the next match against Yorkshire, Peggy Antonio was left stranded on 99 not out. Pat Jarrett described her as unlucky, 'Going in early in the innings, Antonio drove and hooked in fine style and showed her best cricket in a chanceless innings. Summers, the last to bat was run out when going for a second run, which would have given Antonio a century.' Against North, Pritchard was 144 not out and George 87 not out; against Lancashire both Antonio and Patricia Holmes were 103 not out and Mollie Flaherty 5 for 40.

Second Test against England, Blackpool, 26, 28, 29 June 1937

After England's loss in the first Test, Pollard contemplated that perhaps the English attitude of 'it's only a game' was working against them. Before the start of the crucial second Test she wrote: 'There is a feeling going about, and it is not altogether being whispered, that we do not take cricket so seriously as the Australians; that they are making of these games, matters of utmost importance, and because of that they are winning.' Hard to think you would save and sacrifice for two years, like Nance Clements, just to treat it as 'only a game'.

For the second Test at Blackpool, in line with England's policy to have the Test matches umpired by women, Phyllis Bryant and F. Hardcastle (whose parents were billet hosts) were appointed. Bryant was a noted hockey player and had toured Australia in 1927 with the English hockey team – staying in Australia to take up a position for three years as sports mistress at Frensham School in Mittagong. Her reconnection with the Australians, including Patricia Holmes, who had attended Frensham as a student at the same time, led to Bryant accepting a position as its headmistress later in September 1937, a position she held for nearly thirty years. Such were the ongoing connections between sport and empire.

The second Test match began on 26 June 1937 with England batting first and Myrtle Maclagan – despite being described by Pat Jarrett as 'not a stylist, but she built up 115 with delightful freedom' – the top scorer in a total of 222. In reply, Hazel Pritchard 'the girl McCabe of the Australian team', scored 67, while Kath Smith scored 63 and Winnie George 62 in a 302 total, despite Jarrett hoping for a score near 400. Jarrett described the scene: 'Icy winds blew across the ground all day. Boards and windows rattled in the pavilion and numbers were blown off the scoreboard. The huge tower of Blackpool disappeared behind a screen of rain and mist. The crowds went to the pictures, but the cricketers remained to shiver. Several delays were caused by the rain.'

In their second innings England made 231 with Peggy Antonio taking 5 for 31. In another tense finish Patricia Holmes, Hazel Pritchard and Winnie George were the only batswomen to make double figures, 'the wind veered and played tricks with the bowling' and Australia collapsed to be all out for 126, only 25 runs shy of a second victory. A remarkably impartial Jarrett declared to her readers: 'There was no excuse for the Australians.'

Matches against Gloucester (1 July), West (3, 5 July) and Hampshire (7 July) 1937

Against Gloucester, Pritchard scored 53; against West, Antonio took 5 for 16 and Patricia Holmes made a double century. Twenty-one-year-old Patricia, a late inclusion in the Australian side due to Margaret Peden's intervention, had a great tour. 'I think we did pretty well,' she recalled. Her double century against West District at Basingstoke in the two-day first-class game was not without drama. The game started on Saturday and Holmes had scored 125 not out at stumps. Sunday was a rest day and the women returned to their billets. However, on Sunday morning Pat woke with 'a frightful gastric. So, at eight o'clock I was in the loo wishing I was home with my mother, not knowing what I was going to do. So, they asked me if I was going to church and I didn't tell them about it. I said, "No, thank you."'

Despite the gastric, rather than Sunday church she played a set of tennis with a male guest, 'because I knew if I had to make a rush I could get to the necessary apartments to cope with it'. Both she and Alicia Walsh were sick after tucking into steak and kidney pie: 'We leapt onto it because mostly what we got for lunch was salmon, and it was a great delicacy, but we were so sick of it.' Returning to the cricket field on Monday, Patricia remembered: 'I was terrified they'd all get out because I really wanted to get it, and I went in on the Monday with 70 to make 75, and I did, and it was a world record.' Once her double century was achieved, captain Margaret Peden sent out a message that she was 'wanted on the phone', a singular yet charming way to retire the batter. Patricia was personally 'tickled pink' with the double century: 'I really felt very pleased that I had done it because it meant that she [Peden] was right in her choice. I was glad they couldn't knock her for it.' Against Hampshire, all-rounder Kath Smith took 5 for 10.

Third Test against England, at the Oval, 10, 12, 13 July 1937

With the Test matches levelled at 1-all, the English selectors recalled Betty Archdale for the third and final Test at the Oval. From the outset Betty had been an integral part of the tour, its planning and coordination, travelling to all the grounds and even umpiring some of the matches. She played against Australia in the matches for Kent and East, but she had yet to play in another Test:

> I was very angry … I was upset at not being selected, fair
> enough, and very pleased when they decided … I think
> the people who were a little bit annoyed when I was sent
> as captain in 1934, I think they thought Molly Hide, who
> would have been a marvellous captain should have got

the job. She was a much better cricketer than I was and I think they were sort of 'getting back'. I may be quite wrong and it must have been a natural reaction. I can remember being very annoyed and very hurt, too, and very glad when I played. Yes, I played at the Oval, and I made – not terrific – but I made quite a reasonable score.

The importance of the occasion was emphasised by Marjorie Pollard: 'For months now we have been saying to each other, "See you at the Oval".' She noted that 6123 people, including groups of schoolgirls, had paid to see the match on the first day. Holmes continued her form into the third and final Test at the Oval, which began on 10 July 1937. By this stage, newspapers around Australia carried the results and descriptions of the match as reported by Jarrett. Australia won the toss, in what was described as 'unsettled weather'. A heavy downpour flooded the ground before Holmes opened the batting with Margaret Peden and made 70 in Australia's score of 9 declared for 207.

Patricia Holmes remembered the sky was dark and there had been some rain. Scoring was slow: 'I was finding it very difficult to see properly because it was so black, and out of the crowd came almost like an Aussie voice, it might have been, roaring I heard over the field "Come on Marie Stopes" ... Well, I thought that was hysterical. I've never forgotten it. It reminded you a bit of home and the Sydney hill.' Ann Mitchell explained the reference to Marie Stopes for the 'younger ones' listening to her interview with Patricia in 1983: 'She was the woman that had something to do with introducing contraception.'

In a rain-interrupted second day attended by the Duchess of Gloucester, Nell McLarty took 3 for 29, including the wicket of Archdale on 29. Betty Snowball was run out for 99 in a total of 9 declared for 308. In Australia's second innings Pritchard top-scored with 66 in a total of 224. Set 123 runs to get in 15 minutes, England lost 3 wickets for 9 before the match was drawn in front of eight thousand spectators who 'mobbed the players as they left the field, patting them on the backs'. The three Test series was levelled at 1–all.

Matches against Civil Service (15 July), South (17, 19 July), Herts (21 July), Middlesex (22 July), 1934 Touring Team (24, 26 July) and Surrey (28 July) 1937

In the remaining matches of the tour, against the Civil Service, Amy Hudson made 47 and Flaherty took 3 for 27. Wegemund took four catches and made two stumpings. Against South, George made 60 and Antonio took 7 for 102. Against Herts, Margaret Peden made 44. Against Middlesex, Antonio made 96 and Amy Hudson 74. Against the 1934 English touring team, Antonio made 70 and Nell McLarty took 6 for 21. Against Surrey, Patricia Holmes made 55 and Mollie Flaherty took 5 for 31.

There were impressive batting performances from the touring team, with three Australians averaging over 50. Winnie George topped the batting averages at 58.63, followed by Peggy Antonio on 51.92 and Hazel Pritchard on 51.53. Antonio topped the bowling figures with 50 wickets at 11.94, Mollie Flaherty took 41 wickets at 11.44 and Nell McLarty 33 wickets at 16. Close-in 'suicide' fielder Nell McLarty, with the 'go-gadget' arms, snared 20 catches in the series, ten more than the wicketkeeper Alice Wegemund. Pollard described the tactic employed against the East of England match on 4 June 1937: 'Flaherty runs about fifteen yards, bowls at or just outside the leg stump. The ball swings and sometimes kicks. Batsmen attempt a half cock – purely self-defensive stroke – and give McLarty, standing at silly short leg, the present she has been waiting for.' Two years earlier this comment could not have been made without reference to the infamous bodyline tactics.

McLarty's superb reflexes didn't go unnoticed. When Nell was in England she received a letter from her employer at the exclusive firm Henry Bucks, who had proudly framed a photo of one of her most spectacular catches on tour. 'They wrote and told me they had this photo in the window and the men would be standing looking in the window at my legs,' she said. Still some traces of bodyline, then! She claimed to have never seen the photo, and it was still on display in Henry Bucks' Collins Street, Melbourne, store in 1990.

Nance Clements played solidly in many of the tour matches, but missed selection in any of the three Tests – 'That's what I can't understand,' she said. Her averages as an all-rounder she thought were as good as other players: 'I never made a Test which I was disappointed about, but never showed it. I suppose it's up to them [the selectors] and you can't query it.' She attended all the matches 'except one day when I nicked off to buy some fruit – I was dying for fruit, I love my fruit. So, I went up the street and when I saw the price of one apple and a bunch of grapes I nearly died. I came back with nothing. It was very expensive.' Like Betty Archdale for England, Amy Hudson was recalled to the Australian Test side for the third Test at the Oval. Marjorie Pollard singled out Hudson's fielding; she described her throw as 'wonderful-effortless and accurate'.

The recollections of the women cricketers – from Peggy Antonio, Nell McLarty, Amy Hudson, Nance Clements and Patricia Holmes, together with opposition player Betty Archdale – and their contemporary accounts, including a comprehensive forty-four-page tour diary published by Marjorie Pollard drawn from articles published in *Women's Cricket*, as well as Elsie Deane's diary, all provide a personal snapshot and impression of singular events on the long and exciting tour.

Peggy Antonio and Nell McLarty both had memorable tours. Peggy thought it was 'Marvellous. We all travelled around in the bus with the one driver, and he was very good, and it was just a novelty seeing so much of the country. I personally hadn't travelled, only in the interstate games here in Victoria, so it was just strange and new.' In the countryside Nell recalled, 'they'd have signs and hoardings up saying that we were coming'. She remembered many school children at the matches, 'Some of the girls in the English side, they were teachers, and they'd be playing and the children would be barracking for "Miss Snowball". Then they'd want our autographs – that was really something we hadn't been used to.' Marie Jegust told the children, 'We're going to be famous one day – you better keep that autograph.'

Like on any long tour, the women were selected or rested in each match to even out the workload, but many still came to watch every match with days in between spent on travelling further afield. Nell recalled, 'We did have free days now and again and perhaps the English people would take us somewhere. I know I went to Boonah Beaches near the end of the trip with one of the English girls and that was lovely.' Kath Smith described the grounds she had played on:

> The county grounds had beautiful settings, and I shall never forget the lovely chestnuts at Chelmsford where we played the East, the avenues of limes round the Basingstoke ground where we played the West of England, and the Green Jackets Ground at Winchester where we played Hampshire alongside the spire of St Cross. The historic grounds Old Trafford and Kensington Oval where we played, and Trent Bridge and Lord's, which we visited, were all that has been written about them.

Publicity around the tour was well organised and varied. By the end of the two-month-long tour reportedly over one hundred thousand people had witnessed the cricket first-hand. Many more had listened to Marjorie Pollard's live broadcasts of the Tests and summaries on BBC radio, and the series later rated a mention in *Wisden*. Kath Smith thought, 'The English crowds were always very appreciative of good cricket on both sides and the attendances were good.' At the last match at Mitcham Green in Surrey, fifteen thousand watched the game. Marjorie Pollard wrote the crowd contained 'more prams, dogs, small children, ice-cream men and bikes than I have ever seen before anywhere!'

At the conclusion of the final game, which Australia won, the crowd surged everywhere. Marjorie Pollard wrote, 'I felt that as wonderful a summer as any I have ever experienced had come to an end. There can be no summer in this land without cricket ... these Australians ... have given us cricket such as we have never seen before.' Betty Archdale thought the press coverage in England was good:

> I think most of the papers reported the game. I don't think any paper was rude, you know. They may not have given it the coverage they would have given a men's team, but I don't think any of them said well women shouldn't play cricket, you know. No I think we got pretty good coverage. There was no TV then.

Many barriers had been broken, although it took until 1976 for the MCC to relent and allow women to play at Lord's.

Scrapbooks and Souvenirs

On the return journey by sea, the luggage of the Australian women bulged with souvenirs of their trip. In recognition of her contribution, bowler Mollie Flaherty had been presented with cricket balls from both the first and second Tests. She brought home as many of Marjorie Pollard's magazine *Women's Cricket* that she could fit in her suitcase, together with cuttings, photographs and programs to add to her scrapbooks at home. Amy Hudson later assembled her photographs into an album. She kept her coronation ticket and all the menu cards from the many functions the women attended – House of Commons, British Sportsmen's Club, Overseas League, among others – and shipboard memorabilia. Her loose newspaper cuttings would also later be assembled into a scrapbook.

Nance Clements, the great collector, brought home everything that wasn't tied down – photographs, news clippings, invitation cards, membership cards, coronation ticket, baggage tickets, multiple signed menus from Holland and England, theatre tickets, cricket programs, the printed private business papers from her trip to the House of Commons, a gum leaf made of willow from her visit to bat manufacturers Gunn & Moore, and soap received as a present from her billet. Her collecting continued on the boat home, where she souvenired her members ticket from the Ceylon Turf Club and, cheekily, a sailor's cap ribbon from the *Largs Bay*. In her cricket bag she stowed away the bat she used in 1934 and on the 1937 tour – now with an impressive set of signatures from Australian and English women and men cricketers, and a similarly signed stump souvenired from the first Test match at Northampton. Marjorie Pollard noted in her tour diary that at the end of the match, 'There was a scramble for the ball, the stumps, and the bails.' Nance was perhaps on as a substitute fielder for the injured Flaherty and grabbed her prized trophy.

Sue Summers kept newspaper cuttings, coronation souvenirs, cricket scorecards, dinner menus, invitations, letters and programs to later compile into a scrapbook. Alicia Walsh kept programs, copies of *Women's Cricket*, and newspaper cuttings to assemble into a scrapbook. Elsie Deane brought home the scorecards from each match, pamphlets and seating plans from luncheons, invitation cards, entrance tickets, and enough photographs to fill an album. Alice Wegemund also filled a scrapbook with newspaper cuttings, as well as a separate photograph album. And what did Nell McLarty keep? Ironically, all that was left in her possession in 1990 was a pair of the hated white lisle stockings.

All these items were not just the contents of their return journey suitcases, they were items that were treasured for over fifty years. Nearly all the women kept articles of clothing and cricket items from their kit from this era – from the hats on their heads to the boots and sprigs on their feet, and everything in between. This alone speaks to the importance of the tour to the women and the importance of cricket in the full context of their lives. Even Betty Archdale, when she later packed up all her possessions and emigrated to Australia in 1946, brought on that trip her official blazers from the tours, photograph albums and even a poster advertising the England versus Australia match at the Oval in July 1937.

How do we decide what to keep and what to throw away, and who is to say what items are worthy of travelling with us across to the other side of the world?

English middle order batter Joy Partridge, one of the seven sports or games mistresses in the team, adds her signature to Nance Clements' bat. Clements assembled an impressive range of memorabilia and souvenirs throughout her career, many illuminating the close relationship between women's and men's cricket in the 1930s.

Chapter 12
Fixed It

*'Women's cricket has reached such a stage
that it needs no defence.'*
— Australian Women's Cricket Council, 11 September 1937

What an extraordinary period in the long history of Anglo–Australian cricket matches the five years between 1932 and 1937 turned out to be. The world of cricket was almost turned upside down from the drama and bitterness of the men's bodyline series but was lifted with the spirit of the women's 1934–35 and 1937 tours. By 1937, through the efforts of a determined group of women who were passionate about cricket and flourishing in the opportunity to play the sport at the highest level, their cricket had helped weld shattered Empire relations. Australian women had even become ambassadors of the Empire game with their short tour to the Netherlands, sixteen years before the men's cricket team played on the Continent in 1953.

Of course, men's cricket had not stopped, stood still or been abandoned over the friction of bodyline in this five-year period, with the Australian men's team having returned to England in 1934 for a somewhat fractious tour where some bitterness lingered. The English men's team had toured Australia in the summer of 1936–37. The Australian men would return again to England under the captaincy of Bradman in 1938 in a team that retained the Ashes won in 1934.

In this era the intermingling of women and men cricketers

from Australia and England in coaching schools, at training, in fundraising games, created, for Nance Clements at least, a unique collection of cricket memorabilia featuring the signatures of the game's finest players from the 1930s. The symbolism of the signatures preserved on her bat and stump, speaks to an era of cooperation and support between players, of mutual respect, and enjoyment of cricket returned to its ideal and purest form. Indeed, such understanding between members of the British Empire, it could be argued, was essential as the possibility of a world war drew ever nearer. It would be a war where the lessons learnt on the cricket field would be even more relevant to the sacrifices required and the character that needed to be shown by men and women across the Empire.

Five Australian women from the tour in 1937 took the opportunity to extend their stay in England for a brief period. Patricia Holmes and Alicia Walsh stayed on for another six months to further their careers and shared a flat in London with a school friend of Patricia's. Marie Jegust and Peggy Antonio also stayed on – Peggy to visit friends in the north – and both played in Cricket Week at Colwall, Worcestershire, with Barbara Peden. They visited Paris before returning to Australia. Peggy Antonio also stayed with Molly Hide, the English captain, at Molly's farm in Hazelmere, Surrey, where they enjoyed fishing and shooting.

Missing the last half-dozen or so games of the 1937 tour, Queenslander Kath Smith was struck down by appendicitis while in England. Surgeons removed her appendix on 19 July 1937, but the operation so close to the team's departure date put in doubt her ability to travel home. Pat Jarrett reported that if she was deemed unfit to travel 'arrangements have been made for her convalescence in England under very pleasant conditions. Many owners of beautiful country houses have sent invitations to her to accept their hospitality.' In the end those offers were not required and Kath was carried aboard the *Largs Bay* on a stretcher, and completed her convalescence at sea. On her arrival back in Brisbane she was greeted at the dock by her worried and anxious mother who had 'counted the days and hours' to see her again. Before her mother spotted her on deck prior to her disembarkation, her mother had told the waiting press, 'Look for the left-handed wave.'

On the return of the women's team in 1937, a reception was held at the Sydney Town Hall by the Lady Mayoress, Dorothy Parkes, who stated, 'How well you upheld Australia on the other side of the world.' Gone was the overt rhetoric of mending bodyline or playing cricket as it was meant to be played. There was work to do. Margaret Peden noted there were two hundred teams in England and seventy in Australia from which to draw players in 1937. She returned to Australia with a passion and two clear objectives – to introduce cricket to girls' schools and for women to acquire their own grounds. So serious was she in the pursuit of these aims that, to achieve them, she devoted herself full-time to the administration of cricket, deciding to step down, for a season, from grade and state cricket. The Melbourne *Herald* supported her drive to get cricket into girls' schools: 'Everything you learn at school regarding good sportsmanship, fairness, your readiness or promptitude to concede a point where it is due and your ability to make correct decisions rapidly, is tested in cricket, as well as your ability to play the game.' Peden also floated the idea that a magazine similar to *Women's Cricket* should be published in Australia.

While the controversies of the bodyline series and the fractured relationship between Australia and England remained beneath the surface, much of the newspaper hysteria had dissipated by 1937. The Australian women had imbibed the Empire on their cricket tour, reinforcing friendships new and old, visiting relatives and playing cricket in venues from village greens to ovals steeped in decades of cricket tradition. The tickets to the coronation, the trip to Holland as ambassadors of the spread of cricket outside the Empire, afternoon tea at 10 Downing Street, the lived experience of 'posh' English life with billets, the boat stopovers in British outposts, all contributed to a strengthening of personal ties to that Empire. That they were capable of playing the game to such a high standard, losing only one match on the two-month-long tour, solidified their place in it, and underlined that they were worthy colonials to portray the very best of the ideals of cricket. And it should be remembered that just like my own grandmother, who had been born in Sydney in 1894 but nevertheless always considered England as 'home', despite her own grandparents residing in Australia, the crimson threads of kinship held Australia tight to the Empire in many households across Australia.

I remember meeting with a landowner outside Launceston, Tasmania, who, despite being born and bred in Australia, stated he was conflicted when it came to supporting a team in cricket, and did indeed support England. Similar personal stories were present in every family and in every community in Australia well into the late twentieth century. While cricket had the ability to polarise opinion, it could also reinforce and sustain attachment to Empire. That attachment was not something that could be legislated or enforced from above – not from politicians, not from the law or the courts. It came from the hearts and minds of individuals. The cricket played by Australian and English women in the 1930s did much to repair the equilibrium of that attachment.

The English women were scheduled to arrive in Australia in the summer of 1939 to continue the Anglo–Australian contests, and Betty Archdale had again been selected as the touring captain. Tour arrangements had been finalised; the touring uniform of the English, including white blazers with their emblem on the pockets, had been manufactured, fitted and distributed; billets and hospitality were arranged and grounds secured, but the war intervened and the tour was abruptly cancelled. Betty Archdale had won the position of captain from Molly Hide in a close vote. Archdale thought that Hide was a better player but not as good a captain, a weakness that had been demonstrated in the

1937 series. Archdale recalled, 'I think she was oddly sort of socially conservative ... she was terrific but she did have rather firm ideas about things.'

With the tour abandoned and England at war, Archdale joined the Women's Royal Naval Service (WRENS). Always a leader and a rebel, she went to the officers' training course at Greenwich Naval College, after which the forthright Archdale was sent home for three weeks' reprimand when she gave her candid opinion on what she had learnt on the course: 'I was honest enough to say I hadn't learnt a thing!' She was sent to Great Yarmouth in Norfolk as a cipher officer. When an Admiralty Fleet Order was issued saying WRENS were wanted overseas, she volunteered and was sent to Singapore. When Japan entered the war, she was shuffled to Colombo and then to Kenya. After the war ended in 1945, instead of returning to the bar, Archdale applied for and was offered a position in Australia as principal of Women's College at the University of Sydney – the Pedens still had strong connections to the university, although Sir John died the following year. In 1958, despite overtures for her return to St Andrews in Scotland, she accepted the position of headmistress at Abbotsleigh School in Sydney – the school the Peden sisters had attended. Cricket had changed the course of her life: 'If I hadn't played cricket, and if I hadn't come out in that team, I would never have been principal of Women's College, I would never have been headmistress of Abbotsleigh.'

Archdale was known at the university and school as a cricketer but her ability to promote the sport to women was limited. However, over the years she maintained a regular and brusque correspondence with the editor of *The Sydney Morning Herald* concerning his paper's woeful coverage of cricket and other sports played by women. Archdale named Marjorie Pollard as the most outstanding cricketer she played with, and the first match England played in Perth on the 1934 tour on Australian soil as her most memorable: 'There was a terrific thrill.' Her cricketing years she named as the most important in her life.

On their return to Australian shores, Margaret Peden led the praise for the English tour: 'This first tour of ours has been a great adventure. We knew, from our meeting with the English women players in Australia, that we would be well received, but we had no idea how gracious and how kindly that welcome would be.' The long arm of Peden and the Australian Women's Cricket Council (AWCC) had accompanied the 1937 players home and sought to control the messages. The Brisbane *Telegraph* had trouble understanding why players were being 'gagged', as the newspaper looked forward to 'an interesting budget of gossip'. In hindsight the motives of the AWCC in controlling the messages from the tour seem understandable in light of some of the press coverage from the previous tour. Kath Smith outlined the gag to the waiting media:

> 'I'm sorry, I can't say anything to you about the things you would really like to talk on. I have been told by Mrs Margaret Peden, the captain, that I was not to say anything to any newspaper representative unless she had previously approved it. Here' – handing the interviewer the written statement published below – 'is something I have prepared for you. Mrs Peden has read it.'

In her statement, Smith wrote about the development of cricket, her commitment to helping that development and the plan to extend cricket in the schools, all objectives of the tour. She described the tour as 'satisfactory'.

Kath Smith didn't immediately resume her cricket playing, preferring to coach cricket for a season, go back to hockey playing, and take up competitive golf. Nevertheless, she was still an active cricketer, described proudly by the Brisbane *Telegraph* in 1941 as the 'Bradman of women's cricket'. In 1942 she joined the air force as 'a mess woman' and served in the WAAAF throughout the war, developing her golf among other things.

For the Australians who returned home after the tour, many of them felt a real obligation to honour their signed ten-page contract, especially the final clause 38, which stated: 'Players will be expected on their return to take an active part in furthering Women's Cricket in Australia.' Amy Hudson fulfilled both her contract and honoured her mother's efforts in establishing a cricket team:

> We had some sort of a contract, you know, and I sort of kept to it, but I think it was because of my mother – she'd done so much to start that Annandale team. Like, to do that – she loved me playing and my sisters were playing and they were both state players and I just kept on playing. I think it would have taken something out of her life if I didn't keep on playing because she had a lot of confidence, more confidence in me than I had myself, and only for her I wouldn't have gone to half of those [places] – and that was the reason why I kept on playing on account of my mum.

Amy had run out of funds on the voyage home and wrote to her mother from Ceylon to ask her to send money, which was waiting for her when she arrived in Western Australia. 'I don't know where Mum got the £10 from but it was waiting for me in Perth when I got home. My tax had come in and she done my tax and I got £10 back, so Mum got her £10 that way.' Amy settled back into her home, cricket and work routine: 'I just went back into it.' She played club cricket during World War II: 'I didn't go interstate or anything like that because I couldn't get time off being under the manpower. Well, I wouldn't even ask any rate, I was all for the war effort, let's put it that way.' She continued playing international cricket and was selected for the 1951 tour to England, the only player from 1937 to make the return tour. 'I was always called evergreen, you know. When you start off at fourteen and you play through to the age I played to – thirty-four going on thirty-five – people think that you are old, you know, that you're about 108!'

She knew the moment to retire had come when, at a cricket match, 'they got Mollie Dive out [Dive had captained Australia to its first ever Ashes win over England in 1949], and they made a great big fuss about getting Mollie Dive out. And I thought, Amy it is time to get out while you are on top.' She retired from cricket in 1952 and such was her importance to the team that the Annandale club only lasted one more season:

> It just fell down and went boom. But we left all our cricket mats and whatever we had at Tasker Park ... there's no good bringing them home to rot. And we gave whatever we had there, and I gave the rest of the gear away to people that could ill afford to buy them, like my own gear too. It's no good hanging on to them, let somebody use them. That's the way I felt any rate.

On reflection, Amy knew that cricket gave her opportunities she might otherwise never have had: 'I would never have got out of Sydney! Let alone to go all round Australia and go to England and go to New Zealand.' Asked to judge the importance of her cricketing career, she stated: 'They were the most important days of my life, I would say.' Her cricketing highlight was her very first Test wicket – 'I always remember getting the wicket of Myrtle Maclagan. That was my first Test wicket that I ever got.' When Amy Hudson played in the 1949 Test series, opening the batting against England in Australia, her old opponent Englishwoman Myrtle Maclagan was also in the opposition, both still a thorn in the other's side after fifteen years.

Of her teammates, Amy Hudson considered that 'Hazel Pritchard was one of the prettiest bats that we had'. Hazel Pritchard, whose stylish batting had impressed so many spectators, teammates, opponents and pundits, continued with her cricket after her marriage in 1938, even interrupting her honeymoon plans to play cricket. She moved to Mount Isa, Queensland, with her husband, and continued playing in Mount Isa men's teams. Revered English cricket writer Neville Cardus, said of her talent in the 1937 Tests:

> Pritchard alone made us wonder why, indeed, that England could ever win. All the time she was at the wickets it appeared that her side would win comfortably. It is impossible to describe her innings without becoming tiresome in superlatives. Cut, drive, hook, forcing back-shot with all the same pretty dancing – full of youth – and sunshine.

Pritchard also turned to coaching cricket, coaching boys in Kyogle, New South Wales, through the 1940s. She died in 1967, aged fifty-three years.

On her return from England fellow New South Wales player Alice Wegemund ran coaching classes in wicketkeeping at the Sydney School of Cricket. Alicia Walsh continued playing for the Ku-ring-gai team and New South Wales, playing against New Zealand. Her daughter played cricket for the University of Sydney in the 1960s. Walsh died in 1984 and Wegemund in 1979.

In Victoria, Nance Clements, who had been forced by her employer to resign from her work at the Australian Paper Company, found it more difficult to settle back into her routine. She intended to stay home for a while with her mother and father but 'got itchy feet' and applied for a local job as an assistant at a newsagency at Middle Brighton. When World War II broke out she enlisted, despite her boss at the newsagency withholding his support. She continued playing cricket in the WAAAF, captained their softball team and played hockey and table tennis in the services. She continued playing cricket even after she had two children:

> My husband looked after Wayne and I took Nanette to cricket and the rest of the team looked after Nanette

because ... we had a ground in Caulfield where there
were ... voltage from a railway building and she only
had to get through the fence, so the girls just looked after
her while I was batting or fielding.

Nance continued watching women playing cricket over the
years and was adamant that the standard of cricket in the 1930s
had been superior to that of later years. She put that down to
practice: 'As far as I was concerned, I put a lot of hard work into
it in the backyard here and I think a lot of the girls practised
a lot.' She pointed to the skills of Peggy Antonio and Nell
McLarty and, despite the long hours of practice, called them
both 'naturals'. She singled out the latter's bravery: 'There's been
no one to field where Nell McLarty fielded in women's cricket.'
In later years, Nance channelled her sporting talent and drive
into lawn bowls: 'The only thing I haven't done is row a boat
and kick a football.' Today, the Collingwood AFLW Club may
well have come calling.

When the tour of England ended, Marjorie Pollard described
Peggy Antonio and Nell McLarty 'as a pair of great bowlers.
We shall miss them very much. Would that we could produce
such a pair!' Peggy Antonio stayed an extra month or so in
England to see friends in Scotland, play in Cricket Week and
sightsee in Paris. On her return to Australia 'you just had to
down tools and pick up other tools which paid money', she
said. There was little reception from the press or crowds of
autograph hunters, but she began to feel pressure of another
kind. Marjorie Pollard had remarked that Peggy was 'without a
mannerism, an affectation, or seemingly a temperament of any
kind, just went on bowling'. Twelve months after returning to
Australia at the age of twenty-one it was all over:

Well, just simply the pressure. I'd go in and I'd be
expected to make a hundred and I was told all of these
things and take ten wickets and, quite frankly, I hated

the publicity and so on. And I thought 'that's it' and I gave it away ... We were at a match one day and the usual pressures came up sort of thing, and I said, 'Right, I'm finished. That's it. Put the twelfth girl in.' And that was the end of everything.

On reflection Peggy expounded on how cricket had affected her life:

It helped me to mature. The trip to England, nothing that I learnt here ... it was just mixing with the upper class in England that I feel helped me to mature. And, because you'd have to go back to the type of environment that both Nell and I were involved in – it was just working class and in those days it was just a question of surviving – it was really that. Whereas over there, that environment was gone temporarily and, well, one started to think, I know I did, and realise it was a big world and there were lots of things to think about. I think that's the only reason it changed me.

Later, married and with four children, Peggy claimed of her two daughters and two sons: 'I don't think any of them would know what a cricket bat was ... well, see I have got a husband who wouldn't know the difference between a cricket bat or a football, and it was a subject that was never pushed.'

Although held at bay over many years, cricket was still in her blood. In 1990 she expressed regret: 'Actually, I feel more like it now. I'd like to have a hit and a bowl because once I said no that was it.'

Although it skipped a generation, she found that her granddaughter and grandson both had a great interest in cricket. Peggy Antonio died in 2002 aged eighty-four.

Nell McLarty, on the other hand, eschewed marriage and children, and devoted the rest of her life to cricket: 'We came back and played cricket straight away.' But other problems emerged for Nell:

> After the English tour, I think I played for a season but I was getting back trouble. And then it got to the stage where, one day I was playing and all of a sudden, it was a very extremely hot day and it changed, you know the rapid changes we can get [in Melbourne], and it got freezingly cold and I never felt the cold. Oh, I got so cold and I started to shiver and I started to go blue and I had to stop playing and I never ran again after that. It turned out that I had this spinal complaint, which we didn't know about for years after. It was an unusual complaint and then they discovered what it was and I had to go into extensive treatment for that.

Nell turned to coaching cricket: 'I was asked to coach by a lass named Lil Noble and I thought I'd never be able to coach – I'd have to do the physical side – but she persuaded me to go to their club and talk to them, and that's why I started to coach and get involved in cricket again.' Her reputation spread: 'When I began to coach, people would say would I coach so and so and that's the way that would build up.' At seventy-eight years of age in 1990, she was still coaching cricket:

> I'd coach the mother and then I'd get their daughter or their son. At one stage I was coaching the boys and men and I thought, I'll never be able to coach men. I said no, no, and then the girls would bring their brothers along and it worked out quite well. They really took orders from me, which was amazing, you know. I wasn't a boss, but we all enjoyed it so much.

As a factory worker, Nell remembered the privilege of spending six months playing cricket outside:

I love nature and just getting across to England and seeing all the different trees and the natural things I always appreciated it ... it was so enlightening. I just love living, even though I could be dying I would still want to live. I just love every minute of living and that's what it was. You had six months – six months, mind you, of being inside. I didn't like being inside a factory. I'd be looking out the window to see what sort of day it was and wishing I was out there. I just loved being outside and, this was the thing, it opened up a new world.

Nell put the same intensive effort into her coaching as she had into her playing career:

I tried to do it properly, and I read and I watched, I never missed, it didn't matter who was playing, I would go and watch them play. And I got this all into my mind and then I sorted it all out what I thought is what I would want a coach to coach, and that is the way I coached. And then I didn't know if I was on the right track but there was a lass named Jeannie Carroll and her father [Hughie Carroll] was a good coach – he coached [Keith] Miller and [Lindsay] Hassett and a lot of those Australian players – and one day, unbeknown to me, he came down and watched me coach. And he told his daughter that I was on the right track so that gave me a bit of confidence ... I really feel, now that I'm old, that I can coach. I've learnt so much myself.

Nell's coaching career included the outstanding Australian player from the 1940s and 1950s era, Betty Wilson (born 1921). According to Nell:

She retired and she wanted to make a comeback and she came to me and said, what about it? And she'd put on a lot of weight and I said, 'Well, first of all, I was still coaching, [and] if you want to make a comeback you'll have to get rid of that weight.' And, yes, she'd do that, and I coached all day Sunday at a turf wicket down at Murrumbeena. So she came back and we worked very hard and we got her back to the standard that I thought that she was all right. Then she made a comeback and I think she made a century and got a hat trick ... But, of course, actually, she denies that I ever coached her now, but there's plenty of people that could tell you that that's true.

Nell recalled that among her peers, Hazel Pritchard 'was absolutely spot on with her technique', and Patricia Holmes 'had a very good technique'. Peggy Antonio 'was the best spin bowler I saw, then and now'. She admired fast bowlers Mollie Flaherty and Kath Smith for their all-round game. Of the English players both Nell and Peggy named Molly Hide among the top: 'Molly stood out like a beacon.' Nell envied the social side of the modern game: 'They have after-match drinks and we never had any of that. I do think maybe they do spend a lot more time together that way. We just went home, we didn't have any money for drinks.' Peggy thought, 'Getting into the car when it suits you – we had to run for a train', was something she would have liked.

When the English women toured Australia again in 1949, Peggy Antonio and many of her 1937 teammates, including Margaret Peden, Winnie George, Mollie Flaherty, Nance Clements, Kath Smith, Amy Hudson, Elsie Deane and Sue Summers, together with Betty Archdale, agreed to come out of retirement and play in a special Nell McLarty Testimonial Match held to aid McLarty, whose back complaint had become debilitating and costly. The testimonial fund was closed when it reached £500, and was described as 'by far the biggest testimonial ever given to an amateur sportswoman in Australia and reflected clearly her popularity'. Nell McLarty continued coaching at the Richmond Cricket Ground nets. She died in 1998 aged eighty-six.

Patricia Holmes was another of the players who had chosen to extend their stay in England by six months while she worked in London: 'I might never get there again – opportunities! One of my best pals from school was over there so we shared a flat together.' On her return to Australia she continued to play for her club at Ku-ring-gai and for the New South Wales state side, but then 'I sort of fizzled out'. She expressed the view that she had 'blotted her copybook' with Margaret Peden:

> I came back and my first match was in the middle of Randwick Racecourse ... Well I said it to a friend, and it got back to Margaret Peden, I said, 'I can't wait till I get back to England to play on those lovely fields.' And I got a telephone call to say that she was dropping me from the state side because I wasn't keen, so I finished that summer's cricket and I retired ... I probably could have talked my way out of it if I'd been a bit older but I was so stunned I just thought, 'Oh, well.' ... I don't mean to be unkind about that but, really, I didn't think that remark meant that I hated playing cricket and pulling my weight.

The journalist Pat Jarrett on her return to Australia, after a long career covering sports, was ambitious and decided, 'There's got to be more in life for me in journalism than just sports writing.' She was getting older:

> I'd been at the *Herald* long enough to see the other opportunities that were there for special writing and reporting, magazine writing and reporting, and it wasn't hard for me because I was encouraged by Frank Murphy, the chief of staff ... and Keith Murdoch ... to bring in stories that were different, so I gradually got myself weaned off the sports side.

She spent the war years as a special war correspondent, before her life and career became enmeshed with Maie and Richard Casey in the 1940s. She covered the Helsinki Olympic Games in 1952 for the *Herald*, and was later woman's editor for the *Sun* newspaper. She died in 1990 aged seventy-nine.

The women who had missed selection for the 1937 tour had signed no contract and made no commitment to promote the game. Anne Palmer, who had to turn down her selection due to finances, had good qualifications but had found difficulty finding a regular job during the Depression. She put her name down on a waiting list with a bank, 'and lots of other places', but it was not until war broke out in 1939, as some men left the workforce, that her career in the bank got a chance. Her years in cricket she described as 'a pleasant memory'. She played cricket for twelve years in total and recalled two outstanding aspects from her career:

> The 7 for 18 in that first Test in Brisbane [in 1934] against the English women would be an outstanding thing. I've still got the ball. They mounted the ball and gave it to me and, possibly because of that, that brings it back to my mind more than lots of other things. But then another thrill was that partnership with Peggy Antonio in the third Test here on the MCG [in 1935], and we went in at ninth and tenth, I think. They didn't consider that we were worthy of going any higher and yet we batted at that particular time better than the regular batsmen ...
> I really had some very good interstate games, too.

The highlight of her cricket career was 'my participation in the sport at state and international level, it was a most enjoyable experience'. She considered the value in cricket and sport generally was that:

> It tends to guide you towards fair play and sportsmanship, and in the overall pattern I think it helps a person's

character as they go through life. You see, playing sport
you learn that you lose more than you win, and the
interpretation of the sport really is, 'How do you lose?'
It's easy to win and smile – how do you lose – and that
to me is a true sportswoman or man.

Anne Palmer later joined the police force, becoming Victoria's
first uniformed policewoman, was involved in the Girl Guide
Movement, and played competition badminton, squash and
lawn bowls. She died in 2006, aged ninety-one.

Ruby Monaghan in Wollongong retired from cricket after
the disappointment of her non-selection for the 1937 tour: 'I
think there was no interest in cricket down there after I gave
cricket away. It seemed to all fall through or something.' She
acknowledged that cricket had given her opportunities: 'I
travelled where I would never have travelled. You know, things
were bad, times were bad then, and I think travelling to Brisbane
and Melbourne and travelling back and forwards to Sydney to
play was quite enjoyable.' When questioned on the importance
of cricket in her life, she stated emphatically, 'My cricket was
very important.' Instead of cricket she took up softball and
vigoro: 'I love sport. See, I carried on sport after I got married. I
still played softball and tennis and that.'

Ruby married in 1940 and while her children were not
interested in cricket, her granddaughter was. Ruby was proud to
have ironed out a few issues with her granddaughter's bowling:
'The ball was going over to the wides and I told her she had to
bring her arm back over and nearly brush her ear. So, she went
down and the next day – even in that little bit of tuition – they
said, "Who's teaching you, Liza?" "Nanna" ... She thinks I'm
wonderful.'

She nominated her opening batting partner Hazel Pritchard
as 'one of the best cricketers'. Ruby kept the pocket from her
Australian blazer and years later proudly sewed it back on to a
green blazer when invited to attend an Illawarra sports function

for local Australian representatives. She died in 2012 at the age of ninety-six.

Lorna Kettels, the Victorian player who also missed selection in 1937, kept the blazer pocket, but donated the blazer to a neighbour who was sending clothing parcels to England during the war. She noted with irony, 'I had no use for the blazer, so I gave it to them and they sent it. It finished up over in England.' She continued to play cricket with Kensington and the state team and became close friends with Vi Darling, the sister of Australian cricketer Len Darling. She progressed at work from sales assistant to bookkeeper with help from her cricket coach. She retired from cricket with the Kensington club in 1939 when she married and then joined a mixed social club that went away on picnics: 'The men would play cricket and football in the winter and the women would take the lunches.' Although she was an international cricketer she just sat and watched the game – 'I did not like playing against men.' On reflection, she stated, 'Cricket was important to me. Otherwise, it was a very monotonous life ... there was no other interest at all.'

Lorna considered the highlight of her cricketing career was scoring 94 against England and hitting a six. She died in 1997 aged eighty-five.

Joyce Brewer, the second Queenslander in the 1934–35 team whose work schedule prevented her from attending the trials for selection in 1937, continued playing cricket in Brisbane. With her sister Dulcie she began playing cricket after the war with the Redland Bay team. Joyce again gained selection for Queensland to play against the visiting English team in 1948 as opening bat. She married in 1941 and, while in Sydney for her honeymoon, she sent for her running spikes and entered the 880-yard event at Rushcutters Bay in a championship athletics meeting, having previously finished second to Thelma Peake (gold medallist from the 1938 Sydney Empire Games) in the Queensland championships. By 1953 she was involved in athletics administration in Queensland as state secretary, and state athletics selector. Joyce was awarded an Australian Sports Medal in 2000 and died in 2011.

At the beginning of World War II the close ties that bound cricket, particularly in New South Wales and particularly involving the Pedens, were again utilised to raise money. In October 1939, the women's NSW state side played against a NSW men's side of international cricketers at North Sydney Oval, 'for the first time in history', in aid of the Lord Mayor's Patriotic Fund. Women players included Margaret Peden, Edna Ogden, Mollie Dive, Patricia Holmes, Alicia Walsh, and fast bowler Mollie Flaherty, described as 'the "Larwood" (not bodyline) of Australian women bowlers, being regarded as the fastest woman bowler in Australia'. Amy Hudson was selected but could not obtain leave from work on a Wednesday. Playing for the men's team were long-time supporters of cricket played by women: Charlie Macartney, Bill O'Reilly, Stan McCabe, Arthur Mailey and Alan Kippax.

The women were worried about the inclusion of the only male player who was neither a national nor international standard player – the cartoonist Jim Bancks, who drew the comic strip Ginger Meggs. Cartoonists had in the past demonstrated that they could not be trusted by women who played cricket, and anxiety lingered. *The Sydney Morning Herald* noted the women 'hope that he looks on the game with a friendly eye'.

Five hundred spectators turned up to watch the novelty fundraising match. This group of international male cricketing colleagues had a variety of reasons for supporting cricket played by women – they mixed socially with them at events, both inside and out of cricket; they shared a passion for the sport; they watched each other's games or followed them in newspaper reports and listened to radio coverage of their matches; they shared training spaces in indoor nets and cricket schools; and they understood its importance as a game that taught much about life. Mostly, though, it came down to the women's high level of skill and their obvious respect for the game itself.

At a reception at the Port Melbourne Town Hall to present a cheque to Peggy Antonio for her forthcoming tour to England in 1937, Australian Test cricketers Morris Sievers and Ross Gregory were photographed by the Melbourne *Herald* 'turning the tables' and becoming 'autograph hunters' when they sought the signatures of Peggy, Elsie Deane, Nance Clements and Winnie George. The spectators at women's matches had long outstripped just the family and friends of players, with thousands of men and boys paying to watch the game. Many of them could have seen women in the 1930s as equal partners in cricket, with a clear role to play in delegating the bodyline era to history.

The support of these male cricketers, many long-time champions of women playing cricket, had been publicly tested immediately after the 1937 tour when the chairman of the Australian Board of Control for Cricket, Allen Robertson, made some gratuitous and blokey remarks to those present at a Junior Cricket Union meeting. These remarks were inevitably widely reported across Australia and reached England:

> Robertson, referring to women's cricket, said that he did not, favor it. (Laughter.) It militated against the prestige of the game. He hoped that there would not be frequent visits of women's teams from England to Australia. If they did come, he hoped that they would have to call on the cricket authorities here to help them financially. That would make them hesitate about coming again. Women should be kept out of cricket.

He added that he doubted whether the standard of English men's Test cricket would ever again come up to the Australian standard. Once outside the room, both statements attracted loud and immediate universal condemnation.

Robertson, a medical doctor who had never enjoyed a cricket playing career of note, had also been on the Control Board during the bodyline tour of 1932–33, and responsible for the intemperate and ill-timed cable to the MCC, and the bungling of the response. He probably had never seen the Australian or English women play cricket. Far from women mitigating against the prestige of the game, in reality he had a lot to thank the women cricketers for.

The international cricketers and other men who had played, trained and socialised alongside the women over the decade immediately jumped to their defence. Charlie Macartney, described as 'the great Australian batsman of a few years ago', said that Robertson's remarks about the standard of English cricket and about the game played by women were 'ill-timed, inappropriate, and unfounded'. Because the standard of the game in England had been below par for some time, there was no reason to assert that it could not improve. He stated that Robertson's remarks might upset the present harmonious relations. He concluded that there was a hint of jealousy in Robertson's view about women's cricket, seeing that the organisation of the women's executive was so efficient that, at their first attempt, they were able to get a visit by an English team and return the visit shortly afterwards. He added, 'Women were fully entitled to play cricket, especially as they played it well and attractively.' Macartney concluded, 'To say the least of it, Dr Robertson's remarks are not cricket.'

Men piled on their criticism of Robertson. Victor Richardson, 'who has played in many Tests, and captained the Australian team to South Africa', said 'cricket officials and supporters all hastened to dissociate themselves from the sentiments reported to have been expressed by Dr. Robertson'. Joe Darling, a specialist batsman who had captained Australia in twenty-one of his thirty-four Tests between 1894 and 1905 and, by 1937, was a member of the Tasmanian Legislative Council, claimed, 'The Board of Control consists largely of money grabbers and notoriety seekers, who do not understand the game, and never played it ... women's cricket,' he considered, 'was a fine thing. It was an advertisement to Australia and helped to keep the Empire together.' Harry Brereton, the secretary of the Victorian

Cricket Association, expressed the view that 'women's cricket was a great fillip to the game. Their fixtures do not clash with the Sheffield Shield or international matches and you will always find women cricketers at these matches with their men friends. In no way whatsoever shall the V.C.A. ever discourage interest in cricket shown by women.' Even a fellow member of the Board, Reginald Morton, criticised Robertson: 'Women's cricket is a good thing for the game,' he said. 'It is a good thing that cricket should be held in such high esteem by both sexes.'

Speaking for the South Australian delegates to the Board, Henry Hodgetts was sorry to learn that Robertson 'held personal views with which they entirely disagreed'. Former Test cricketer and the Queensland delegate to the Board, Roger Hartigan, warned, 'Anyone who starts an argument with women is asking for trouble.' Cricketers Woodfull and Bradman chose only to respond to Robertson's remarks about the standard of English cricket, and made no remarks either for or against women. Former Australian cricket captain Bill Woodfull said he 'did not think recent events bore out Dr. Robertson in his opinion of English cricket, and he did not think future events would, either. The Englishmen were within an ace of victory in the rubber here last season.' The current men's captain, Don Bradman, echoed those words: he 'was considerably surprised that the Chairman of the Board should say that English cricket would not again come up to the Australian standard. He certainly did not endorse such an opinion. England had many youthful players of promise who would delight Australian crowds in the future. England would win again.'

How did women respond to Robertson's comments on women mitigating against the prestige of the game? Elsie Feige, the president of the Queensland Women's Cricket Association, called his comments 'ridiculous':

> Dr. Robertson, she said, must admit that the financial
> success of the recent tour by Australian women cricketers

in England proved that the English public did not regard women players as a menace to the prestige of the game. That two more clubs would be in action in Brisbane in the coming season was an indication that women's cricket was taken seriously here, and its increased popularity throughout Australia was apparent, from the fact that the secretary of the Australian Women's Cricket Association, Mrs. R. Peden, who captained the recent touring team in England, had decided to devote herself to organising the game in the schools in the coming season and to coaching players.

The national body, the Australian Women's Cricket Council, refused to respond, taking the same line as the English WCA when faced with criticism: 'Women's cricket has reached such a stage that it needs no defence.'

To write about the 1930s and bodyline and not write about women playing the same game in the same era misses half the story, just as if you looked at the MCG banner with the name Larwood and failed to read the name Clements on its verso. The richness that the two interwoven stories create convey something of the complexity of reactions to the series, from both men and women, at a time of great national and international controversy, and questioning about the ties of empire. Women were tasked or tasked themselves with showing the world that cricket still had much to offer and that the old standards and judgements of 'it's just not cricket' were true and worth defending. Two later controversial cricket incidents have relevance here.

Women bore the fall-out and repercussions of the notorious cricket underarm bowling incident of 1981; so too were women looked to after the sandpaper ball tampering incident in 2018. In the first of these incidents, Trevor Chappell was instructed to bowl underarm to New Zealand batsman Brian McKechnie at the MCG on 1 February 1981 to prevent an opposition win, causing an international incident and a lasting bitter legacy between the two countries. Before the Australian men's team could tour New Zealand the following year, the Australian women, led by captain Sharon Tredrea, met the New Zealand women in the Women's World Cup in January 1982 in New Zealand, paving the way for harmonious relations between the two cricketing countries, but copping it from New Zealand crowds. Tredrea commented, 'We've been getting it rubbed in everywhere we've been.'

In the second incident, in March 2018 in the third Test match against South Africa, Australia's men were caught with sandpaper on the field with the intention of roughing up the ball. Player sanctions, announced on 28 March 2018, generated a review of culture and conduct, as the men's team rapidly lost popularity as well as respect. This incident was followed less than nine months later by the Australian women's triumphant T20 World Cup win against India under captain Meg Lanning at the MCG before 86,174 spectators, which went a long way towards restoring national pride in Australian cricket. One journalist wrote, 'the success – and particularly the joyful nature – of the Australian women seems a wonderful counterpoint to the black clouds still hovering over their male counterparts after the sandpaper disgrace'. He continued, 'The Australian women's cricket team provides the good news story that we need. In this fraught cricketing summer, it is the way an Australian cricketer plays as much as the result itself that seems to matter most.'

After the bodyline summer of 1932–33, the cricket world had been tilted off its axis. Cricket was well and truly broken, and these teams of women were the good news story that fixed it.

Drinks break after fifty years. Members of the Australian cricket teams from the 1930s honoured at the jubilee dinner held at the Melbourne Cricket Ground on 30 January 1985. Standing (left to right) Winnie George, Anne Palmer and Peggy Antonio. Seated (left to right) Amy Hudson, Hilda Hills, Nance Clements and Nell McLarty.

Acknowledgements

The spark for this book was lit in 1989 when the editors of the *Australian Dictionary of Biography* commissioned me to write a short biographical piece on Margaret Peden, Australia's inaugural cricket captain from the 1934–35 Test series against the English team captained by Betty Archdale. At the time I was working in the Department of History, Research School of Social Sciences at the Australian National University (ANU). It was known in the Coombs building that I was a keen cricketer, captained the ANU team, had represented the ACT in the national championships, played intervarsity cricket, travelled to Sydney every weekend to also play for the University of Sydney on the 'Square', and had captained a team that toured the north and south islands of New Zealand. More importantly though, I was a keen participant in the annual cricket match between the history departments of the Faculties and the Research School on ANU's Village Green featuring staff and some PhD students including a young Frank Bongiorno. Although Margaret Peden had passed away in 1981, I discovered that some of her teammates were still alive, so myself and another keen cricketer, Mary Lou Johnston, set about tracking down the women and their stories from the 1930s on behalf of the National Museum. One of the women – Winnie George, who passed away in 1988 – was the mother of my teammate Lynne O'Meara alongside whom I played club and state cricket. Lynne O'Meara was the most stylish and elegant batter, and occasional wicketkeeper, I ever witnessed.

So that is how I came to meet and talk with a group of remarkable, unassuming and talented international cricketers from the 1930s whose lives and experiences form the body of this book. They include Nance Clements, Peggy Antonio, Nell McLarty, Amy Hudson, Lorna Kettels, Ruby Monaghan, Anne Palmer and Betty Archdale, together with journalist Kathleen Commins. I only wish I could have met all the others. Today, all the players and officials from these Test matches have passed away. Likely, few spectators or eye witnesses to the games remain alive.

I would like to acknowledge the work over many years of women involved in cricket who had an eye to history and the importance of preserving documentary and material evidence relating to women's lives. In this regard, Ann Mitchell OAM deserves to be singled out.

I am grateful for the generous enthusiasm for this book by the University of Queensland Press, especially publishing director Madonna Duffy and managing editor Jacqueline Blanchard. It was a pleasure to work with such a supportive and vibrant publishing house.

I thank Professor Frank Bongiorno and former Australian cricket captain Alex Blackwell for their backing and kind words. I thank Professor Celmara Pocock for her new-found interest in all things sport, this time cricket, and her unwavering support and love. I am grateful to Dr Jane Palmer who gifted me two invaluable cricket books written in 1893 and 1920 from her mother's estate. Heartfelt thanks to Heather Reid AM and Danielle Warby, both co-travellers in the quest to recognise and celebrate all things sport and women.

At the National Museum I thank Dr Sophie Jensen, together with the museum's copyright and photography team, and the National Library of Australia's photographic department.

And lastly, an ironic thank you to my alma mater Ravenswood School for Girls, Gordon, for not introducing cricket until I was in my final year of high school, when it was just too late to be distracted from the Higher School Certificate and my entry to university.

This book deliberately avoids using the term 'women's cricket'. There is no different game called women's cricket, it is the same game no matter the gender playing; it is called cricket.

Turner. Richards. Barbara Peden. Myrtle Gillham.
agan. Spear. Maclagan. Burletson.
Green.

During their 1934–35 tour of Australia the English players stayed in a
variety of accommodation, including hotels and private billets. Here they
arrive with their substantial luggage and trunks at Women's College,
University of Sydney, 1935. Left to right: Grace Morgan, Doris Turner,
Mary Richards, Mary Spear, manager Betty Green, Myrtle Maclagan,
Australian player Barbara Peden, Mary Burletson, and Myrtle Gillham
the liaison officer appointed to the team by the NSW WCA.

Notes

Introduction: Cars and Corsets

For car advertisements see *The Brisbane Courier*, 8 April 1920, p. 3; *The Call*, Perth, 28 December 1923, p. 5; *Truth*, Sydney, 5 September 1926, p. 11; *News*, Adelaide, 18 October 1927, p. 12; *The Argus*, Melbourne, 7 March 1929, p. 10. Cayce-Paul Motors is from *The Sun*, Sydney, 14 May 1921, p. 2. Women's fashions are from *Evening News*, Sydney, 29 November 1929, p. 14; *Sunday Times*, Perth, 8 April 1923, p. 12. The most coveted cricket trophy is from *Sunday Times*, Perth, 26 October 1930, p. 13. For Bradman and the Chevrolet model see *The Daily News*, Perth, 24 October 1930, p. 1; *The Australian Women's Weekly*, 21 July 1934, p. 18; *The Age*, Melbourne, 25 October 1930, p. 14; *The Sydney Morning Herald*, 4 November 1930, p. 6; *South Western Tribune*, Bunbury, 29 November 1930, p. 4; *Daily Mercury*, Mackay, 7 January 1931, p. 7; *The Daily News*, Perth, 12 November 1930, p. 4; *Midlands Advocate*, Perth, 27 November 1930, p. 2; *Sunday Times*, Perth, 26 October 1930, p. 13. Bradman's mother is from Jack Pollard, *Australian Cricket: The Game and the Players*, Angus & Robertson, North Ryde, 1988, p. 189; *The Southern Mail*, Bowral, 22 December 1944, pp. 1–2. Jessie Menzies is from *The Australian Women's Weekly*, 21 July 1934, p. 18; *Daily Mercury*, Mackay, 1 December 1932, p. 14; *The Port Macquarie News*, 16 April 1932, p. 5. For the formation of the English and Australian cricket associations see Rafaelle Nicholson, *Ladies and Lords: A History of Women's Cricket in Britain*, Peter Lang, Oxford, 2019, pp. 55–67; Marion Stell, *Half the Race: A History of Australian Women in Sport*, Angus & Robertson, North Ryde, 1991, pp. 14–16, 50–53. The Bradman song is from *The Queenslander*, Brisbane, 1 September 1932, p. 42.

Chapter 1: New Cricketers

Unless otherwise attributed, all direct quotations are transcriptions from interviews with the women, see the bibliography for details. For Eric Barbour see *The Sydney Morning Herald*, 17 September 1934, p. 13. Simpkins was appointed to umpire the Sydney Test in 1934; see also *The Referee*, Sydney, 20 May 1931, p. 23. Pritchard sisters are from *Sydney Mail*, 18 November 1931, p. 35; *The Referee*, Sydney, 18 March 1931, p. 11; *Daily Telegraph*, Sydney, 7 December 1933, p. 14. For Barbour on the Shevill family see *The Sydney Morning Herald*, 17 September 1934, p. 13. For Peggy Antonio and coaching see *The Herald*, Melbourne, 16 April 1936, p. 36. For women sports journalists see *The Sydney Morning Herald*, 22 September 1938, p. 26. For malthoid pitches see *Border Watch*, Mt Gambier, 25 July 1935, p. 2. Anne Palmer is from *Sunday Mail*, Brisbane, 30 December 1934, p. 2. The descriptions of Lorna Kettels are from *The Argus*, Melbourne, 7 November 1934, p. 18; *The Herald*, Melbourne, 25 October 1934, p. 20 and 12 November 1936, p. 39. Harry Youlden is from *Truth*, Sydney, 9 August 1931, p. 3; *The Age*, Melbourne, 22 February 1919, p. 7; *The Herald*, Melbourne, 9 May 1935, p. 20. For Ernie Spencer see *Sporting Globe*, Melbourne, 20 March 1926, p. 6. For Brisbane teams see *Truth*, Brisbane, 15 November 1931, p. 5. For the Brewer sisters see *Truth*, Brisbane, 28 January 1934, p. 7.

Chapter 2: The Bodyline Series

In this era, the Marylebone Cricket Club (MCC) organised international tours on behalf of the England cricket team for playing Test matches. For Plum Warner see *The Australasian*, Melbourne, 12 November 1932, p. 8. For cricket books see Anthony Bateman, *Cricket, Literature and Culture: Symbolising the Nation, Destabilising Empire*, Ashgate Publishing Company, Farnham, 2009; K.S. Ranjitsinhji, *The Jubilee Book of Cricket*, William Blackwood and Sons, Edinburgh, 1897, pp. 448, 465; Richard Daft, *Kings of Cricket: Reminiscences and Anecdotes*, Arrowsmith, Bristol, 1893, preface; Lord Harris and F.S. Ashley-Cooper, *Lord's and the MCC: A Cricket Chronicle of 137 Years*, Herbert Jenkins, London, 1920, p. 211. For reactions to white cricketers see *Daily Examiner*, Grafton, 25 April 1935, p. 3. The Ashes were so named in 1882 and presented, according to legend, by Florence Morphy. For dinner at the Piccadilly Hotel see Jack Pollard, *Australian Cricket: The Game and the Players*, Angus & Robertson,

North Ryde, 1988, p. 147. For Larwood on the tactic see Harold Larwood, *Body-Line?*, Elkin Mathews and Marrot, London, 1933, serialised in Australian newspapers. For English managers see *Smith's Weekly*, Sydney, 4 February 1933, p. 4. Condemnation of crowd behaviour and Hugh Buggy are from *News*, Adelaide, 5 November 1932, p. 3. Shock bowling attack and newspaper headlines are from *The Herald*, Melbourne, 28 November 1932, p. 3; *News*, Adelaide, 11 November 1932, pp. 1, 7. For tour match at MCG see Pollard, *Australian Cricket*, p. 148; *News*, Adelaide, 19 November 1932, p. 4; *Daily Telegraph*, Sydney, 18 November 1932, p. 3. For Buggy's report see *The Herald*, Melbourne, 30 November 1932, p. 4; *News*, Adelaide, 19 November 1932, pp. 1, 3; Pollard, *Australian Cricket*, p. 150; *News*, Adelaide, 28 November 1932, p. 5; *The Herald*, Melbourne, 25 November 1932, p. 14. Arthur Mailey is from *The Advertiser*, Adelaide, 30 November 1932, p. 16. For the first Test see *The Herald*, Melbourne, 28 November 1932, p. 1; *The Examiner*, Launceston, 2 December 1932, p. 1; Pollard, *Australian Cricket*, p. 150. Reference to skittles in a poem published in *The Argus*, Melbourne, 10 December 1932, p. 9. For naming of bodyline see Pollard, *Australian Cricket*, p. 150. The cartoon is from *The Mail*, Adelaide, 3 December 1932, p. 4. The claim that bodyline was not a newspaper invention is from *Arrow*, Sydney, 13 January 1933, p. 2. The cartoon war is reported in *Daily Telegraph*, Sydney, 17 December 1932, p. 1; *The Sun*, Sydney, 27 November 1932, p. 1. For poets see *The Argus*, Melbourne, 10 December 1932, p. 9; *The Brisbane Courier*, 17 December 1932, p. 20. A sward is an expanse of green grass. Oriel was a collaboration between John Sandes, E.T. Fricker and D. Symmons. For speculation on abandoning the tactic see Pollard, *Australian Cricket*, pp. 151–52. Kelly's letter was quoted in Alan Kippax and Eric Barbour, *Anti Body-line*, Sydney and Melbourne Publishing, Sydney, 1933, p. 34. For third Test see Pollard, *Australian Cricket*, p. 152; *The Worker*, Brisbane, 25 January 1933, p. 16. For Oldfield and the cable see *Brisbane Telegraph*, 17 January 1933, p. 1. Speculation about public protest, and statements by James Byrne, Monty Noble and Arthur Mailey are from *The Worker*, Brisbane, 25 January 1933, p. 16. Barbour is from Kippax and Barbour, *Anti Body-line*, p. 39. The historian is Patrick McDevitt, 'Bodyline, Jardine and Masculinity' in Anthony Bateman and Jeffrey Hill (eds), *The Cambridge Companion to Cricket*, Cambridge University Press, Cambridge, 2011, p. 74. See *Arrow*, Sydney, 13 January 1933, p. 2. Letters to the editor see *The Advertiser*, Adelaide, 19 January 1933, p. 12. Squealing is from *The Worker*, Brisbane, 25 January 1933, p. 16; manliness is from *Arrow*, Sydney, 13 January 1933, p. 2. For Alan Kippax see Kippax and Barbour, *Anti Body-line*, p. 65. Lover of Good Sport is from *The Advertiser*, Adelaide, 21 January 1933, p. 22. Patricia is from *Shepparton Advertiser*, 1 January 1935, p. 3. For sportswomen's associations see Stell, *Half the Race: A History of Australian Women in Sport*, Angus & Robertson, North Ryde, 1991, pp. 48–79. For Pat Jarrett see *The Herald*, Melbourne, 26 January 1933, p. 22; *Sporting Globe*, Melbourne, 8 February 1933, p. 11.

Chapter 3: National Hysteria

For Eddie Gilbert see Raymond Evans, 'Eddie Gilbert', *Australian Dictionary of Biography*, 1983, <adb.anu.edu.au/biography/gilbert-edward-eddie-6379>; *The Mercury*, Hobart, 21 January 1933, p. 9. For MCC cable see *Chronicle*, Adelaide, 26 January 1933, p. 41. For the iron hand see *The Examiner*, Launceston, 26 January 1933, p. 7; and for elderly dukes see *Smith's Weekly*, Sydney, 4 February 1933, p. 4. Hobbs spoke to the *Star,* quoted in *News*, Adelaide, 15 May 1933, p. 1. For the Board of Control cable see *Smith's Weekly*, Sydney, 4 February 1933, p. 4; Jack Pollard, *Australian Cricket: The Game and the Players*, Angus & Robertson, North Ryde, 1988, p. 155. For the sorry business see *Smith's Weekly*, Sydney, 4 February 1933, p. 4. The Dee brothers were quoted in *Nelson Evening Mail*, New Zealand, 11 March 1933, p. 3. For the Waratah Girls Cricket Club controversy see *Sunday Times*, Perth, 29 January 1933, p. 11; *News*, Adelaide, 30 January 1933, p. 5, 1 February 1933, p. 5 and 15 May 1933, p. 1; *The Advertiser*, Adelaide, 2 February 1933, p. 10; Rafaelle Nicholson, *Ladies and Lords: A History of Women's Cricket in Britain*, Peter Lang, Oxford, 2019, pp. 38, 74, 82–3. Gilbert Mant is from *The Press*, Canterbury, 25 March 1933, p. 10. For spread of the term bodyline see *Shepparton Advertiser*, 27 March 1933, p. 4. Anzac Spirit is from *The Telegraph*, Brisbane, 9 May 1933, p. 10. For Larwood on protest see *The Herald*, Melbourne, 21 June 1933, p. 2. A.P.H. is quoted in *The Arrow*, Sydney, 10 March 1933, p. 10. For Warner see *The Worker*, Brisbane, 25 January 1933, p. 16. For Larwood's book see *News*, Adelaide, 15 May 1933, p. 1. Larrikinism is from *The Herald*, Melbourne, 9 May 1933, pp. 1, 7. For dirty linen see *Daily Telegraph*, Sydney, 12 May 1933, p. 8. Jardine's book is from *Daily Standard*, Brisbane, 10 July 1933, p. 2; *Sunday Times*,

Perth, 9 July 1933, p. 3; Alan Kippax and Eric Barbour, *Anti Body-Line*, Sydney and Melbourne Publishing, Sydney, 1933, preface. Bradman and bodyline is from *The Herald*, Melbourne, 22 July 1938, p. 2. For Warner see *The Sydney Morning Herald*, 5 June 1933, p. 1. Story by C.S. is from *The Sun*, Sydney, 5 February 1933, p. 6; *Smith's Weekly*, Sydney, 4 February 1933, p. 4. Bodyline in New Zealand is from *The Herald*, Melbourne, 10 March 1933, p. 13. For impact on juniors see Kippax and Barbour, *Anti Body-Line*, p. 19. Mabel Bryant is from *The Central Queensland Herald*, Rockhampton, 3 August 1933, p. 18. For Dot Debnam see *Sporting Globe*, Melbourne, 8 February 1933, p. 11; *Barrier Miner*, Broken Hill, 13 May 1933, p. 5. For Phyllis Greene see *The Telegraph*, Brisbane, 9 March 1933, p. 6. All-leg sleaze is from *Sunday Mail*, Brisbane, 12 March 1933, p. 2.

Chapter 4: The Great Leg Pull

Vera Cox and Elsie Bennett are from Rafaelle Nicholson, *Ladies and Lords: A History of Women's Cricket in Britain*, Peter Lang, Oxford, 2019, p. 62; *Daily Telegraph*, Sydney, 13 May 1933, p. 2; *The Australian Women's Weekly*, 1 July 1933, p. 42. For finance not bodyline see *Daily Telegraph*, Sydney, 13 May 1933, p. 2. For bodyline barred and the New Zealand tour see *The Australian Women's Weekly*, 1 July 1933, p. 42. For Marjorie Pollard see *Daily Telegraph*, Sydney, 13 May 1933, p. 2. Jean Sutton was reported in *Barrier Miner*, Broken Hill, 13 May 1933, p. 14. 'Mrs X' is from *The Newcastle Sun*, 16 August 1933, p. 6. The Leason cartoon is from *Table Talk*, Melbourne, 28 September 1933, p. 19 (disappointingly, many secondary sources on cricket have reproduced these cartoons from the 1930s without analysing or critiquing their content or intent). Refusing to accept ridicule is from Nicholson, *Ladies and Lords*, pp. 71–72. For Pollard's editorial see *Hockey Field and Lacrosse*, special issue, June 1929, pp. 2–3. For Ruth Preddey see Stell, *Half the Race: A History of Australian Women in Sport*, Angus & Robertson, North Ryde, 1991, pp. 229–35. Interview with Pat Jarrett by Mark Cranfield, National Library of Australia, 4 September 1984, transcribed by author. For Preddey and rules see *The Australian Women's Weekly*, 30 September 1933, p. 43. 'M.P.S.' is quoted in *The Telegraph*, Brisbane, 16 October 1933, p. 11. Tittle-tattle is from Nicholson, *Ladies and Lords*, p. 126. Myrtle Elvins and Jarrett's reporting is from *The Herald*, Melbourne, 7 November 1933, p. 7. The WCA comment is from *Toowoomba Chronicle and Darling Downs Gazette*, 28 October 1933,

p. 7. Mudgee is from *Mudgee Guardian and North-Western Representative*, 30 October 1933, p. 7. Adelaide is from *The Mail*, Adelaide, 4 November 1933, p. 2. For obstinate old woman see *The Referee*, Sydney, 23 November 1933, p. 13. Acceptance of invitation, expenses and no bodyline are from *The Telegraph*, Brisbane, 9 March 1934, p. 28. Muriel Segal's reporting is from *The Australian Women's Weekly*, 7 April 1934, p. 39. For W.G. Grace see his *WG's Little Book*, George Newnes, London, 1909, pp. 62, 63, 65. Arthur Mailey's opinion on demarcation is from *Daily Standard*, Brisbane, 20 June 1934, p. 4. Businessmen is from *The Telegraph*, Brisbane, 27 August 1934, p. 10. For the great leg-pull see *Daily Standard*, Brisbane, 15 December 1934, p. 4. Old theme is from *The National Advocate*, Bathurst NSW, 19 June 1934, p. 1. Bradman's remarks transcribed by author from 'Don Bradman talks about the 1934 Ashes Tour', YouTube, 2015, <https://www.youtube.com/watch?v=gX1AgWAzfZA>. For Jack Hobbs see *The Advocate*, Burnie, 20 December 1934, p. 4. Conspiracy theory is from *Labor Call*, Melbourne, 25 October 1934, p. 1. For the death of bodyline see *The Courier-Mail*, Brisbane, 23 November 1934, p. 14. For Pollard and bodyline, Archdale's reassurances and Muriel Segal see *The Australian Women's Weekly*, 1 September 1934, p. 39. Archdale and unpleasantness is from *Voice*, Hobart, 8 September 1934, p. 2. Other Archdale interviews were carried in many city and regional papers including *The Advocate*, Burnie, 20 October 1934, p. 9. For Brisbane and seriousness see *The Courier-Mail*, Brisbane, 20 October 1934, p. 15. The Molly Dutton controversy is from *News*, Adelaide, 17 December 1934, p. 5; *The Herald*, Melbourne, 18 December 1934, p. 3. For the *Yorkshire Observer* see *Women's Cricket*, vol. 4, no. 2, June 1933, p. 23. For Pollard writing on bodyline see *Women's Cricket*, vol. 4, no. 2, June 1933, p. 31; vol. 4, no. 3, July 1933, p. 46; vol. 4, no. 5, September 1933, p. 94; vol. 5, no. 3, July 1934, p. 1. Cementing empire is from *The Sydney Morning Herald*, 29 November 1934, p. 2.

Chapter 5: Old Rivalries

Ironmonger's lies are from Jack Pollard, *Australian Cricket: The Game and the Players*, Angus & Robertson, North Ryde, 1988, p. 588. For Australian selectors see *Daily Telegraph*, Sydney, 14 December 1934, p. 4; 20 December 1934, p. 13. For the origins of English players see *The Gisborne Times*, New Zealand, 23 September 1933, p. 11. Pollard's

profiles of English players are from *Women's Cricket*, vol. 5, no. 3, July
1934, p. 38. Green's profile of English players and the voyage report are
from *The Daily News*, Perth, 21 November 1934, p. 5. For Archdale's
1936 opinion of Peden see *Women's Cricket*, vol. 17, no. 2, June 1936,
p. 24. The scorebook is digitised at <womenscrickethistory.org/Scores/
England_in_Aus_NZ_Scorebook_1934-35/84/index.html#zoom=z>

Chapter 6: The Clothing Divide
For opinions on leg pads and gloves see Lord Harris and F.S. Ashley-
Cooper, *Lord's and the M.C.C*, Herbert Jenkins, London, 1920, p. 87.
For Ponsonby-Fane see 'Introduction' in Lord Harris and F.S. Ashley-
Cooper, *Lord's and the M.C.C*, p. xv; Mr Budd was Edward Hayward
Budd (1786–1875). W.G. Grace's comments on style are from his *WG's
Little Book*, London, George Newnes, 1909, pp. 93–94. The harlequin cap
is from *The Daily News*, Perth, 20 October 1932, p. 12. For the wearing
of neckerchiefs see photograph by Herbert Fishwick, Adelaide Oval
1933, National Library of Australia, PIC/15611. For Sea Island cotton
see *Morning Bulletin*, Rockhampton, 18 July 1933, p. 8. Woollen ties are
from Commonwealth of Australia, House of Representatives, *Hansard*, 27
April 1933, p. 1016; and woollen socks from *News*, Adelaide, 4 September
1937, p. 2. For facial hair see *The Referee*, Sydney, 23 December 1931, p.
15. For Selfixo trousers see *The Daily News*, Perth, 13 February 1934, p.
6; *South Western Times*, Bunbury, 14 February 1934, p. 2; *The Southern
Districts Advocate*, Katanning, 29 January 1934, p. 6. For Elasta-Strap
trousers see *The Queenslander*, Brisbane, 2 September 1937, p. 50. For
washing trousers see *The Don Dorrigo Gazette and Guy Fawkes Advocate*,
NSW, 31 January 1936, p. 2. For Queensland cricket costumes see *The
Telegraph*, Brisbane, 14 February 1934, p. 13. Learie Constantine also
coached English player Betty Snowball. For Hendren's comment see
Goulburn Evening Penny Post, 24 May 1933, p. 3. For Daft see Lord Harris
and F.S. Ashley-Cooper, *Lord's and the M.C.C.*, p. 170. Catching fire is
from *The Telegraph*, Brisbane, 10 August 1937, p. 3. David Wax's methods
are from *The Courier-Mail*, Brisbane, 26 April 1934, p. 15. For English
uniform see *Women's Cricket*, vol. 5, no. 4, August 1934, p. 76. For natty
appearance see *The Referee*, 2 August 1934, p. 14. For player's hostility to
stockings see *Albany Advertiser*, 9 August 1934, p. 4. Pollard's comment
on Flaherty is from Marjorie Pollard, *Australian Women's Cricket Team in*

England, 1937: A diary, p. 40. Burlesque and leg show is from *The Sun*, Sydney, 30 November 1932, p. 17. Constance D'Arcy was reported in *The Sydney Morning Herald*, 24 February 1934, p. 9. For Margaret Peden's new cricket costume see *The Herald*, Melbourne, 7 December 1934, p. 2; *The Argus*, Melbourne, 24 December 1934, p. 5. For Aertex fabric see 'The History of Aertex', *The Age*, Melbourne, 29 November 1939, p. 9; the factory was the Cellular Clothing Co. in West Melbourne. For Green's reflections on uniforms see *Women's Cricket*, vol. 6, no. 2, June 1935, p. 32. Pollard on stockings is from Marjorie Pollard, *Women's Cricket*, vol. 7, no. 4, September 1936, p. 66. For England's romper suit and ice-cream see *The Daily News*, Perth, 21 November 1934, pp. 1, 5. For Western Australian costume see *Mirror*, Perth, 10 November 1934, p. 16. For English team in Brisbane and Archdale's refusal to be drawn see *The Courier-Mail*, Brisbane, 21 December 1934, pp. 9, 12. Betty Green's reflections on variety of uniforms in Australia and New Zealand is from *Women's Cricket*, vol. 6, no. 2, June 1935, p. 32. For the novelty game in Sarina see *Daily Mercury*, Mackay, 30 October 1934, p. 9.

Chapter 7: Summer Tests, Australia, 1934–35
The Tasmanian Women's Cricket Association was not yet affiliated with the Australian Women's Cricket Council. For bodyline as a royal taboo, see *The Mail*, Adelaide, 9 March 1935, p. 3. For loyalty and devotion see *The Sydney Morning Herald*, 29 November 1934, p. 2. The Duke's song is from *Sunday Mail*, Brisbane, 2 December 1934, p. 3. The player–writer ban is from *The Herald*, Melbourne, 20 November 1934, p. 8. For tour rules see *Women's Cricket*, vol. 6, no. 2, June 1935, p. 33. Jarrett's journey and opinions are from NLA oral interview; *The Herald*, Melbourne, 20 November 1934, p. 8. No Ashes is from *The Courier-Mail*, Brisbane, 21 December 1934, p. 9. For shaping well, Jegust and Evans see *Mirror*, Perth, 10 November 1934, p. 16. Archdale's opinion of Western Australia is from *Women's Cricket*, vol. 6, no. 1, May 1935, p. 1. Ethel Joyner is from *The Daily News*, Perth, 23 November 1934, p. 13. For English team recreation see *Sunday Times*, Perth, 18 November 1934, p. 6. Archdale's revised opinion of Western Australia is from *Women's Cricket*, vol. 6, no. 4, August 1935, p. 68. Seething mass and royal treatment are from *The Australian Women's Weekly*, 8 December 1934, p. 59. For England match in Victoria see *Women's Cricket*, vol, 6, no. 4, August 1935, p. 68;

The Argus, Melbourne, 5 December 1934, p. 15; *The Age*, Melbourne, 7 December 1934, p. 13; *The National Advocate*, Bathurst, 8 December 1934, p. 4. For England in Deniliquin see *The Argus*, Melbourne, 7 September 1934, p. 12; *The Independent*, Deniliquin, 13 November 1934, p. 3; *The Independent*, Deniliquin, 14 December 1934, p. 2; *The Australian Women's Weekly*, 15 December 1934, p. 63. For England match against New South Wales see *Daily Telegraph*, Sydney, 12 December 1934, p. 2; *The Newcastle Sun*, 13 December 1934, p. 21; *Sydney Morning Herald*, 17 December 1934, p. 9; *Women's Cricket*, vol. 6, no. 1, May 1935, p. 1; *Newcastle Morning Herald and Miners' Advocate*, 20 December 1934, p. 8; Gwendolen Game, *Barging Days: A Farewell to New South Wales*, Angus & Robertson, Sydney, 1934, pp. 15, 24; *The Sydney Morning Herald*, 17 December 1934, p. 4; *Catholic Freeman's Journal*, Sydney, 27 December 1934, p. 11; *The Propeller*, Hurstville, 24 March 1938, p. 2; Peter Spearritt, 'Walder, Sir Samuel Robert', *Australian Dictionary of Biography*, 2006, <adb.anu.edu.au/biography/walder-sir-samuel-robert-1096>; *Daily Telegraph*, 11 December 1934, p. 14. For England match in Wollongong see *Daily Telegraph*, Sydney, 20 December 1934, p. 13. For England match in Newcastle see *Daily Telegraph*, Sydney, 14 December 1934, p. 15; *Newcastle Morning Herald and Miners' Advocate*, 19 December 1934, p. 8. For England in Queensland see *The Courier-Mail*, Brisbane, 21 December 1934, p. 9; Ricketts was presumably the same F. Ricketts, sports journalist, and strong swimmer who in his youth had rescued several children and adults from drowning, showing great bravery and courage each time, see *The Bendigo Independent*, 18 June 1913, p. 4; *Sunday Mail*, Brisbane, 23 December 1934, p. 3 (captions to images); *The Courier-Mail*, Brisbane, 22 December 1934, p. 8; *The Telegraph*, Brisbane, 27 December 1934, p. 7; *Daily Standard*, Brisbane, 19 December 1934, p. 6. For the First Test see *The Argus*, Melbourne, 20 December 1934, p. 7; *Women's Cricket*, vol. 6, no. 4, August 1935, p. 68; *The Courier-Mail*, Brisbane, 23 March 1929, p. 21; *The Courier-Mail*, Brisbane, 1 January 1935, p. 2; *Women's Cricket*, vol. 6 no. 2, June 1935, p. 26; *The Telegraph*, Brisbane, 28 December 1934, p. 18; *The Courier-Mail*, Brisbane, 28 December 1934, p. 10; *Daily Standard*, Brisbane, 31 December 1934, p. 6; *Morning Bulletin*, Rockhampton, 2 January 1935, p. 4; *The Courier-Mail*, Brisbane, 29 December 1934, p. 10; *The Sydney Morning Herald*, 29 December 1934, p. 15; *The Newcastle Sun*, 28 December 1934, p. 8; *Daily Standard*, Brisbane, 31 December

1934, p. 6; *The Telegraph*, Brisbane, 21 December 1934, p. 17. The actual quote from Henry V, Act 4 Scene 3, is: 'Then shall our names, Familiar as household words – Harry the King, Bedford and Exeter, Warwick and Talbot, Salisbury and Gloucester – Be in their flowing cups freshly rememb'red.' For the second Test see *Women's Cricket*, vol. 6, no. 2, June 1935, p. 33; *The Sun*, Sydney, 3 January 1935, p. 20; *Women's Cricket*, vol. 6, no. 2, June 1935, p. 28; *Sydney Sportsman*, 12 January 1935, p. 16; *The Courier-Mail*, Brisbane, 9 January 1935, p. 8; *Sydney Sportsman*, 12 January 1935, p. 16; *Women's Cricket*, vol. 6, no. 1, May 1935, p. 10; *Daily Telegraph*, Sydney, 8 January 1935, p. 14. For England match in Canberra see *The Courier-Mail*, Brisbane, 28 December 1934, p. 7; *Women's Cricket*, vol. 6, no. 2, June 1935, p. 28; *The Canberra Times*, 10 January 1935, p. 2, 28 December 1934, p. 2; *The Canberra Times*, 4 January 1935, p. 3. For England match in Goulburn see *Goulburn Evening Penny Post*, 11 January 1935, p. 3, 14 January 1935, p. 3, 7 June 1935, p. 4. For England match in Leeton see *Narrandera Argus and Riverina Advertiser*, 8 January 1935, p. 4, 22 January 1935, p. 2; *The Murrumbidgee Irrigator*, 15 January 1935, p. 2; *The Sydney Morning Herald*, 14 January 1935, p. 13. For England match in Junee see *Daily Advertiser*, Wagga Wagga, 16 January 1935, p. 6; *The Albury Banner and Wodonga Express*, 4 January 1935, p. 36; *The Australian Women's Weekly*, 15 December 1934, p. 63; *Daily Advertiser*, Wagga Wagga, 11 January 1935, p. 5, 15 January 1935, p. 6; *The Murrumbidgee Irrigator*, 18 January 1935, p. 1; *The Albury Banner and Wodonga Express*, 25 January 1935, p. 41; *Daily Advertiser*, Wagga Wagga, 17 January 1935, p. 3. The third Test is from *The Herald*, Melbourne, 15 January 1935, p. 18; *The Argus*, 17 January 1935, p. 12, 18 January 1935, p. 13; *The West Australian*, Perth, 19 January 1935, p. 9; *The Examiner*, Launceston, 21 January 1935, p. 8; *The Northern Star*, Lismore, 22 January 1935, p. 8; Betty Green, *Women's Cricket*, vol. 6, no. 1, May 1935, pp. 10–11; *The Northern Star*, Lismore, 1 February 1935, p. 4; *The Australian Women's Weekly*, 23 February 1935, p. 51; *The Age*, Melbourne, 23 January 1935, p. 12; *The Age*, Melbourne, 24 January 1935, p. 6; *The Courier-Mail*, Brisbane, 21 December 1934, p. 12; *The Sydney Morning Herald*, 26 January 1935, p. 17; *Women's Cricket*, vol. 6, no. 2, June 1935, p. 33; *Barrier Miner*, Broken Hill, 2 February 1935, p. 6. For England in New Zealand see Jack Pollard, *Australian Cricket: The Game and the Players*, Angus & Robertson, North Ryde, 1988, p. 789. Advertisement, *Goulburn Evening Penny Post*, 6 June

1933, p. 2; *The Hokitika Guardian*, 5 October 1933, p. 3; *The Waikato Times and Thames Valley Gazette*, 2 October 1935, p. 11; *The Auckland Star*, 28 September 1934, p. 13; *The Opunake Times*, 1 September 1933, p. 3; *Wairarapa Daily Times*, 17 November 1933, p. 6; *The Ashburton Guardian*, 30 January 1935, p. 2; *The Auckland Star*, 12 January 1935, p. 8; Nancy Joy, *Maiden Over: A Short History of Women's Cricket and a Diary of the 1948–49 Test Tour to Australia*, Sporting Handbooks, London, 1950, pp. 47–48; *The Franklin Times*, 13 March 1935, p. 8. For Archdale at home see *Tweed Daily*, Murwillumbah, 23 July 1935, p. 7.

Chapter 8: Larwood Lingers

Archdale's view on attending matches is from *Sporting Globe*, Melbourne, 1 December 1934, p. 5. Jarrett's comment on women cricketers is from *The Mercury*, Hobart, 21 November 1934, p. 7. For women as invaders see *The Daily News*, Perth, 10 October 1934, p. 6. The indoor practice school is from *The Sydney Morning Herald*, 17 September 1934, p. 13; *The Australian Women's Weekly*, 11 August 1934, p. 43. The Cricketers' Ball is from *The Sydney Morning Herald*, 30 June 1933, p. 4. The Sydney university game is from *The Sydney Morning Herald*, 4 October 1934, pp. 11, 17; fathers and friends from *The Australian Women's Weekly*, 15 September 1934, p. 39. Pollard's editorial is from *Women's Cricket*, vol. 4, no. 5, September 1933, p. 1. For epithets see *Sporting Globe*, Melbourne, 8 February 1933, p. 11; *The Central Queensland Herald*, Rockhampton, 3 August 1933, p. 18; *The Australian Women's Weekly*, 30 September 1933, p. 43. Archdale's comment on bodyline is from *The Courier-Mail*, Brisbane, 21 December 1934, p. 12. Mathers' response is from *Daily Telegraph*, Sydney, 5 January 1935, p. 6. For various parliamentary comments on bodyline see Commonwealth of Australia, House of Representatives, *Hansard*, 14 March 1933, p. 224; Commonwealth of Australia, Senate, *Hansard*, 7 June 1933, p. 2141, 27 June 1933, p. 2627, 11 July 1934, p. 386; *The Mercury*, Hobart, 16 August 1934, p. 3; *The Sydney Morning Herald* quoted in Commonwealth of Australia, House of Representatives, *Hansard*, 1 November 1934, p. 106; New South Wales Legislative Council, Sydney Corporation Amendment Bill, 26 June 1934, pp. 1236, 1238; Queensland Legislative Assembly, 17 August 1933, p. 53, 6 September 1934, p. 188; Western Australia Legislative Council, *Hansard*, 4 October 1933, p. 1213; Western Australia Legislative Assembly, *Hansard*, 1 October 1935, p. 943. Regarding the election of women parliamentarians: Edith Cowan was elected in Western Australia in 1921, Millicent Preston-Stanley in New South Wales in 1925, Irene Longman in Queensland in 1929 and Millie Peacock in Victoria in 1933. Women were not elected to the Australian House of Representatives or Senate until 1943 (Enid Lyons and Dorothy Tangney). For Young see *The Herald*, Melbourne, 2 July 1937, p. 13. For Broken Hill see *News*, Adelaide, 29 March 1935, p. 8. The photograph of Sievers is from *The Herald*, Melbourne, 18 March 1937, p. 46.

Chapter 9: Rites of Passage

For John Corbett Davis, who also wrote under the name of 'Not Out' for *The Referee*, see his obituary in *Sporting Globe*, Melbourne, 19 February 1941, p. 10; *The Referee*, Sydney, 12 April 1934, p. 23. Believe it or not and a man's team is from *The Herald*, Melbourne, 3 October 1935, p. 38 and among others, *Tweed Daily*, Murwillumbah, 21 October 1935, p. 5. Stanley Melbourne Bruce captained his school cricket team, was prime minister (1923–29), and had been Australia's negotiator at the Ottawa Conference in 1932, winning concession and quotas and renegotiating Australia's debt in London, see Heather Radi, 'Stanley Melbourne Bruce', *Australian Dictionary of Biography*, 2006, <adb.anu.edu.au/biography/ bruce-stanley-melbourne-5400>; *News*, Adelaide, 16 July 1937, p. 6. The MCC Supplement is from *The Australasian*, Melbourne, 24 July 1937, p. 26. For the *Jervis Bay* see *The Telegraph*, Brisbane, 23 November 1936, p. 16. Team selection is from *The Sun*, Sydney, 16 December 1936, p. 6. For Flaherty see *The Sun*, Sydney, 29 November 1936, p. 27; *Truth*, Sydney, 25 October 1936, p. 10. For Wegemund see *The Labor Daily*, Sydney, 8 March 1937, p. 9, 18 March 1937, p. 11. The Semco statement is from *The Age*, Melbourne, 20 March 1937, p. 31. Playing under lights is from *The Advertiser*, Adelaide, 29 January 1937, p. 14. Summers is from *The Advertiser*, Adelaide, 17 December 1936, p. 16. For Jegust see *The Sun*, Sydney, 16 December 1936, p. 16; *The West Australian*, Perth, 11 March 1937, p. 9. For chaperons see Marion Stell, 'Women with Altitude: Resisting the Role of the Australian "Chaperone" in Mexico 1968', *The International Journal of the History of Sport*, vol. 36, nos 9–10, 2019, pp. 779–95. For Jarrett see Pat Jarrett, National Library of Australia, Session 3, Tape 2, Side 1; Diane Langmore, *Glittering Surfaces: A Life of Maie Casey*, Allen & Unwin, Sydney, 1997, p. 64. For Peden see Marion Stell, 'Margaret

Elizabeth Maynard Peden', *Australian Dictionary of Biography*, 2006, <https://adb.anu.edu.au/biography/peden-margaret-elizabeth-8009>. Monaghan is from *The Sun*, Sydney, 7 February 1934, p. 3. Brewer is from *The Telegraph*, Brisbane, 23 October 1936, p. 31; *The Courier-Mail*, Brisbane, 25 November 1936, p. 11. For Smith see *The Courier-Mail*, Brisbane, 6 February 1937, p. 17. McLarty is from *The Evening News*, Rockhampton, 20 January 1937, p. 12. For Archdale's view of the Australian team see *Women's Cricket*, vol. 7, no. 1, May 1936, p. 4; *Women's Cricket*, vol. 7, no. 2, June 1936, pp. 24–25. The contract is from *The Argus*, Melbourne, 9 January 1937, p. 7. For vaccination effects and sea sickness see *The Daily News*, Perth, 3 April 1937, p. 6. Jarrett's team profile is from *The Herald*, Melbourne, 6 May 1937, p. 15. The 110 Commandments and Peatfield are from *The Advertiser*, Adelaide, 2 April 1937, p. 19. Hansen's opinions are from *The Sun*, Sydney, 9 May 1937, p. 30. Pollard's welcome is from *Women's Cricket*, vol. 8, no. 1, May 1937, p. 1.

Chapter 10: Colonials Abroad

John Corbett Davis is from *The Referee*, Sydney, 12 April 1934, p. 23. For billeting see *The Sydney Morning Herald*, 15 April 1937, p. 27. For Jarrett's reports see *The Courier-Mail*, Brisbane, 25 May 1937, p. 19. The host Edward Hardcastle was a keen sportsman and had played first-class cricket for Kent County. For Kath Smith's letters home see *The Telegraph*, Brisbane, 22 June 1937, p. 17. For Lucy Baldwin see *Bunyip*, Gawler, 12 March 1937, p. 9. Jarrett on emotional day is from *The Herald*, Melbourne, 3 June 1937, p. 14, 14 June 1937, p. 26. For cricket in Holland see *The Sun*, Sydney, 20 January 1937, p. 24; *The Herald*, Melbourne, 20 January 1937, p. 24; *The Advertiser*, Adelaide, 24 May 1937, p. 9; *The Sun*, Sydney, 24 May 1937, p. 2; *The Courier-Mail*, Brisbane, 25 May 1937, p. 14; *The Telegraph*, Brisbane, 22 June 1937, p. 17. Jim Manning is quoted by Jack Pollard, *Australian Cricket: The Game and the Players*, Angus & Robertson, North Ryde, 1988, p. 777.

Chapter 11: Summer Tests, England, 1937

For the holiday is over and Great Comp see *The Sydney Morning Herald*, 1 June 1937, p. 20. For Lord's see *The Australian Worker*, Sydney, 24 March 1937, p. 12. Special buses are from *The Sydney Morning Herald*, 1 June 1937, p. 20. Jarrett's transport and match preview are from *The*

Sun, Sydney, 29 May 1937, p. 7; *The Courier-Mail*, Brisbane, 7 April 1937, p. 25. The Australian improvement is from Nancy Joy, *Maiden Over: A Short History of Women's Cricket and a Diary of the 1948–49 Test Tour to Australia*, Sporting Handbooks, London, 1950, pp. 48–49. Pollard's report is from *Australian Women's Cricket Team in England, 1937: a diary*, pp. 8–9. Jarrett's report on Dorridge is from *The Herald*, Melbourne, 11 June 1937, p. 22. On Northampton match see *Australian Women's Cricket Team in England, 1937: a diary*, pp. 10, 11. Jarrett on McLarty is from *The Herald*, Melbourne, 16 June 1937, p. 1. For Yorkshire match see *The Sun*, Sydney, 18 June 1937, p. 2. For Australians taking cricket seriously see Pollard, p. 16. For the second Test see *The Herald*, Melbourne, 28 June 1937, p. 22, 29 June 1937, p. 30, 30 June 1937, p. 30. For the third Test at the Oval see Pollard, p. 29; *Queensland Times*, Ipswich, 12 July 1937, p. 8; Pat Jarrett, *Newcastle Morning Herald and Miners' Advocate*, 14 July 1937, p. 6. For East of England match see *Women's Cricket*, vol. 8, no. 2, June 1937, p. 30. For Hudson see Pollard, p. 26. Kath Smith's description of grounds and crowds is from *The Telegraph*, Brisbane, 13 September 1937, p. 2. For match at Mitcham Green see Pollard, p. 40. The scramble for the stumps at Northampton is from Pollard, p. 13.

Chapter 12: Fixed It

For those who extended their stay see *The West Australian*, Perth, 9 October 1937, p. 11; *The Age*, Melbourne, 16 October 1937, p. 19. For Kath Smith's illness see *The Courier-Mail*, Brisbane, 23 July 1937, p. 16; *The Telegraph*, Brisbane, 13 September 1937, p. 2. For receptions on return see *The Sydney Morning Herald*, 10 September 1937, pp. 5, 15. Peden's passion is reported in *The Herald*, Melbourne, 16 September 1937, p. 40. Peden's praise is reported in Marjorie Pollard, *Australian Women's Cricket Team in England, 1937: A diary*, foreword. The gag and Kath Smith are from *The Telegraph*, Brisbane, 13 September 1937, p. 2, 12 February 1941, p. 14. Neville Cardus on Pritchard is quoted in *The Kyogle Examiner*, 9 September 1949, p. 7. For Antonio and McLarty see Marjorie Pollard, *Australian Women's Cricket Team in England*, 1937, pp. 35–39. For McLarty's testimonial see *The Herald*, Melbourne, 24 September 1949, p. 20. For Joyce Brewer see *The Telegraph*, Brisbane, 10 February 1941, p. 10. The Lord Mayor's Patriotic Fund match is reported in *The Sun*, Sydney, 12 October 1939, p. 25; *The Sydney Morning Herald*, 2 November 1939, p. 16. Bancks collaborated with his first wife Jessie Tait on the J.C. Williamson production *Blue Mountain Melody* that the English women playing cricket in Australia had attended in 1934. For Morris Sievers see *The Herald*, Melbourne,18 March 1937, p. 46. The controversy created by Allen Robertson is reported in *The Age*, Melbourne, 10 September 1937, p. 18; *The West Australian*, Perth, 11 September 1937, p. 9; *The Courier-Mail*, Brisbane, 11 September 1937, p. 12; *The Advertiser*, Adelaide, 10 September 1937, p. 29. The AWCC response is from *The West Australian*, Perth, 11 September 1937, p. 9. Sharon Tredrea is from *The Canberra Times*, 30 January 1982, p. 41. See Richard Hinds, 'The Australian Women's Cricket Team Provides the Good News Story that We Need', *ABC News*, 2018, <abc.net.au/news/2018-11-23/richard-hinds-australia-womens-cricket-team/10547760>.

Wet weather in Australia interrupted or shortened several of the tour games in 1934–35. The English eleven pose over their reflections. Century-maker Molly Hide steps into the puddle watched by wicketkeeper Betty Snowball.

Bibliography

Anthony Bateman, *Cricket, Literature and Culture: Symbolising the Nation, Destabilising Empire*, Ashgate, Farnham, 2009.

Anthony Bateman and Jeffrey Hill (eds), *The Cambridge Companion to Cricket*, Cambridge University Press, Cambridge, 2011.

Richard Daft, *Kings of Cricket: Reminiscenses and Anecdotes*, Arrowsmith, Bristol, 1893.

Gwendolen Game, *Barging Days: A Farewell to New South Wales*, Angus & Robertson, Sydney, 1934.

W.G. Grace, *WG's Little Book*, George Newnes, London, 1909.

Lord Harris and F.S. Ashley-Cooper, *Lord's and the MCC: A Cricket Chronicle of 137 Years*, Herbert Jenkins, London, 1920.

Joan L. Hawes, *Women's Test Cricket: The Golden Triangle*, Book Guild, Lewes, 1987.

Nancy Joy, *Maiden Over: A Short History of Women's Cricket and a Diary of the 1948–49 Test Tour to Australia*, Sporting Handbooks, London, 1950.

Alan Kippax and Eric Barbour, *Anti Body-line*, Sydney and Melbourne Publishing, Sydney, 1933.

Diane Langmore, *Glittering Surfaces: A Life of Maie Casey*, Allen & Unwin, Sydney, 1997.

Deirdre Macpherson, *The Suffragette's Daughter: Betty Archdale: Her Life of Feminism, Cricket, War and Education*, Rosenberg, Dural, 2002.

Rafaelle Nicholson, *Ladies and Lords: A History of Women's Cricket in Britain*, Peter Lang, Oxford, 2019.

Jack Pollard, *Australian Cricket: The Game and the Players*, Angus & Robertson, North Ryde, 1988.

Marjorie Pollard, *Australian Women's Cricket Team in England, 1937: a diary*.

K.S. Ranjitsinhji, *The Jubilee Book of Cricket*, William Blackwood and Sons, Edinburgh, 1897.

Marion Stell, *Half the Race: A History of Australian Women in Sport*, Angus & Robertson, North Ryde, 1991.

Marion Stell, 'Margaret Peden', *Australian Dictionary of Biography*, vol xi, MUP, Melbourne,1989.

Oral Histories

Interviews by Marion Stell and Mary-Lou Johnston, transcribed by Marion Stell

Peggy Antonio and Nell McLarty, 1 July 1990

Betty Archdale, 27 July 1990

Nance Clements, 2 July 1990

Kathleen Commins, 27 July 1990

Amy Hudson, 28 July 1990

Lorna Kettels, 3 July 1990

Ruby Monaghan, 16 June 1990

Anne Palmer, 3 September 1990

Interview by Ann Mitchell, transcribed by Marion Stell

Pat Holmes and Sophie Broekmans, May 1983

Interview by Mark Cranfield, transcribed by Marion Stell

Pat Jarrett, 4 September 1984, National Library of Australia

Essie Shevill was one of three sisters – along with Rene and Fernie – who played for the Sans Souci Club and NSW team. Essie was described as the best batswoman in New South Wales, 'correct, steady and attractive to watch'. She played in all three Tests against the English team in Australia in 1934–35, top scoring with 63 not out.

The Australian players step out after the president of the Women's Cricket Association Frances Heron-Maxwell hosted them to a welcome lunch at her home Great Comp, Kent, after which the team practised on her private oval, June 1937. The media reported that Great Comp 'should remind the Australians of the traditions of English cricket, which had its beginnings on the village greens and on the ovals of private landowners'.

Index

numbers in italics are images